Care for Sale

....

ISSUES OF GLOBALIZATION

Case Studies in Contemporary Anthropology

Series Editors: Carla Freeman and Li Zhang

*Waste and Wealth: An Ethnography of Labor, Value, and
Morality in a Vietnamese Recycling Economy*
Minh T. N. Nguyen

*Haunted:
An Ethnography of the Hollywood and Hong Kong Media Industries*
Sylvia J. Martin

*The Native World-System:
An Ethnography of Bolivian Aymara Traders in the Global Economy*
Nico Tassi

*Sacred Rice:
An Ethnography of Identity, Environment, and Development
in Rural West Africa*
Joanna Davidson

*City of Flowers:
An Ethnography of Social and Economic Change in Costa
Rica's Central Valley*
Susan E. Mannon

*Labor and Legality:
An Ethnography of a Mexican Immigrant Network*
Ruth Gomberg-Muñoz

*Listen, Here Is a Story:
Ethnographic Life Narratives from Aka and Ngandu Women
of the Congo Basin*
Bonnie L. Hewlett

*Cuban Color in Tourism and La Lucha:
An Ethnography of Racial Meanings*
L. Kaifa Roland

*Gangsters without Borders:
An Ethnography of a Salvadoran Street Gang*
T. W. Ward

Care for Sale

An Ethnography of Latin American Domestic and Sex Workers in London

ANA P. GUTIÉRREZ GARZA

New York   Oxford

OXFORD UNIVERSITY PRESS

Oxford University Press is a department of the University of Oxford.
It furthers the University's objective of excellence in research, scholarship,
and education by publishing worldwide. Oxford is a registered trade mark
of Oxford University Press in the UK and certain other countries.

Published in the United States of America by Oxford University Press
198 Madison Avenue, New York, NY 10016, United States of America.

© 2019 by Oxford University Press

Library of Congress Cataloging-in-Publication Data

Names: Gutierrez Garza, Ana P., author.
Title: Care for sale : an ethnography of Latin American domestic and sex
  workers in London / Ana P. Gutierrez Garza.
Description: New York, NY : Oxford University Press, [2019] | Series: Issues
  of globalization : case studies in contemporary anthropology | Includes
  bibliographical references and index.
Identifiers: LCCN 2018036212 | ISBN 9780190840655 (pbk.)
Subjects: LCSH: Foreign workers, Latin American—England—London—Social
  conditions. | Women foreign workers—England—London—Social conditions. |
  Women household employees—England—London—Social conditions. |
  Prostitutes—England—London—Social conditions. | Latin
  Americans—England—London—Social conditions.
Classification: LCC HD8398.L38 G85 2019 | DDC 331.6/209421—dc23
LC record available at https://lccn.loc.gov/2018036212

9 8 7 6 5 4 3 2 1
Printed by Sheridan Books, Inc., United States of America

This book is dedicated to Sara,
a wonderful woman who left her children
in the care of others to love and care for me
when I was a child, and to the women
who compose the stories of this book, to the guerreras.

CONTENTS

ACKNOWLEDGMENTS

I am deeply thankful to my friends in London for inviting me into their lives, for their hospitality, for being willing to collaborate in this project, and for their friendship and wisdom. Thank you for opening the doors of your homes, of your employers' homes, and of the flats where you offered your caring work. Thank you for becoming my family in London and letting me share a little bit of Latin America with all of you. Thank you for allowing me to accompany you in daily life and for letting me understand the complexities and wonders of your lives. Your warmth, your wisdom, and the friendship you gave me pervade this book and without doubt made me a better person. I hope that this book evokes the dreams, efforts, and hopes all of you pursue on a daily basis. You are extraordinary women who I keep and will always keep close to my heart.

This ethnography grew from my PhD dissertation at the London School of Economics (LSE). I have been incredibly privileged to have studied anthropology in such a collegial and caring department and to find constant encouragement from great colleagues, friends, and academics who always made me feel inspired. I have been extremely lucky to have the support, expertise, care, and tireless commitment throughout my PhD and the development of this book from Deborah James, my PhD supervisor and my mentor. Her commitment to her students, to thinking, and to the world sustained me as a graduate student and as a postdoctoral researcher. Thank you *jefa*, I could not have no done it without you. I am also indebted to Catherine Allerton, who took me under her wing as my PhD supervisor. Thanks for contributing to the intellectual growth of both this book and myself. Both offered me guidance, support, and intellectual stimulation. I would also like to thank Nicholas De Genova who examined my thesis, provided me with great feedback and has supported my work throughout the years.

Along the way I have been academically and emotionally supported by a long list of people who I was lucky to meet at the LSE. I shared parts of this work over the past several years, including at LSE's Friday Seminar, the Latin American Seminar, and the Anthropology of Economy Seminar. My deep thanks go to Laura Bear, Charles Stafford, Harry Walker, Mitch Sedwick, and Natalia Buitron for reading my papers and providing me with wonderful insights and feedback. Thanks to Rita Astuti who has inspired me to become a better teacher, thank you for your unconditional friendship. I have been incredibly fortunate to be surrounded by brilliant colleagues in my department. Thanks to all of the people who participated in the writing-up seminar and commented on my work.

To my friends Ruben Anderson, Anna Tuckett, Matt Wilde, Insa Koch, and Mohammed Zaki, I am especially thankful for your advice and support throughout this process. Thank you for reading parts of this writing at early and late stages. I also benefited greatly from conversations with my dear friends Maxim Bolt, Hans Steinmuller, George St Clair, Elizabeth Frantz, Indira Aruguman, Alice Tilce, and Jessica Jacobson. Thank you for your friendship and support throughout the years. I am thankful to Gwendolyn Beetham and Joanna Hoare who always reminded me to keep my feminist heart and my mind in the right place. Special thanks go to those who we chose as family when we are far away from home, I would like to thank Melissa Fernandez, who not only had the patience to read my work and give me feedback but also provided words of comfort and wisdom throughout the years. Gracias *hermana*, your friendship is invaluable to me.

This book would not have been possible without the financial support from CONACYT in Mexico as well as the financial support that I received from the Anthropology Department at the LSE, the Central Research Fund from the University of London, and the Newby Trust Award. I would also like to thank the ESRC Grant ES/M003825/1 'An ethnography of advice: between market, society and the declining welfare state', because its funding made possible the writing of this book.

I thank Meredith Keffer of Oxford University Press for believing in this book and for her support, feedback, and enthusiasm, and the reviewers who provided incisive and helpful comments: Meryl Altman, DePauw University; Ari Ariyaratne, College of DuPage; Blenda Femenías, University of Maryland University College; Claudia Garcia-Des Lauriers, California State Polytechnic University Pomona; Heather Hindman, University of Texas at Austin; Peta Ann Katz, University of North Carolina at Charlotte; Mary Lorena Kenny, Eastern Connecticut State University; Heather Merrill, Hamilton College; Rhacel Salazar Parreñas, University of Southern California; Jack M. Schultz, Concordia University; Miriam Shakow, The College of New Jersey; and Livia K. Stone, Illinois State University.

This book would not have been possible without the support of my family. Thanks go to my parents, who have always been by my side, interested in my life project and believing in my dreams; to my brother Jose for being a solid rock in my life who, regardless of distance, is always close to me; to my sister-in-law Angelica, who has always been interested in and following my craziness, asking questions, and genuinely interested in my life; and to my sister Gabriela, my treasured soulmate, my best friend. You are my rock, the voice in the back of my head that always tells me what to do and where to go. Thanks for believing in me and walking with me, side by side, always.

LIST OF CHARACTERS

....

Sabrina (forty-three), single mother from Brazil. She migrated to London in 2007 with her son and worked in domestic work before moving into sex work. She went back to Brazil in 2011 and then returned to London with her son in 2012 by paying a Portuguese man for a partner visa. She still works in London as a sex worker.

Eva (forty-seven), single mother from Peru. She migrated in 1991 to Spain and embarked on a second migration to London in 2008. She worked in domestic work in both countries. She continues to work for a cleaning company and started selling beauty products in London.

Rosa (forty-seven), married from Peru. She migrated to Spain in 1997 with her husband. She embarked on a second migration to London in 2008 on her own. She worked and still works as a live-in domestic worker in London. In 2012 her husband joined her in London.

Cecilia (thirty-seven), from Bolivia. She migrated to London in 2005 on her own. She met her current partner, Antonio, in London and had a baby girl with him. She still does domestic work and is still waiting to sort out her documents in the United Kingdom.

Amanda (thirty-six), single mother from Brazil. She migrated to London in 2008 and did domestic work and then sex work until she married a British man in 2015. She no longer works as a sex worker.

Jovanna (thirty-eight), single mother from Bolivia. She migrated to London in 2002 on her own and brought her daughter and mother in 2007. She died of breast cancer in April, 2013. Her daughter and mother returned to Bolivia.

Juliana (fifty-one), married and mother of three adult sons, from Brazil. She migrated in 2006 to London on her own, worked as a domestic worker, and returned to Brazil in 2013.

Cristina (fifty-five, Spanish passport), divorced, mother of three, from Ecuador. She migrated to Madrid in 1994 and embarked on a second migration in 2008. She worked as a live-in domestic worker until 2011. She still does domestic work in London.

Angelica (thirty-two), single mother from Brazil. She migrated to Portugal in 2003 and was deported in 2005. She found her way back to the United Kingdom in 2005. She returned to Brazil in 2012.

Vanessa (twenty-seven), from Colombia. She migrated to London in 2008 and worked as a cleaner before moving into sex work. She continues to live in London and no longer does sex work, but maintains several "sugar daddies" to support her lifestyle.

Lourdes (forty-seven), mother of three, from Bolivia. She migrated to London in 2004 with her two sons and her husband, Pedro. She worked for a while in domestic work. Pedro works for a cleaning company and both currently work in a pyramid-scheme business in London.

Amelia (fifty-three), divorced, from Spain but grew up in Venezuela. She migrated to London in 2009 and was a live-in domestic worker until 2011. She went back to Venezuela for a while until 2013, when she returned to London for six months. She moved back to Spain, where she currently lives.

Mariana (thirty-eight), from Brazil. She migrated to Italy in 2006, where she married a Colombian man. She embarked on a second migration to London in 2008 and worked as a domestic worker/nanny until 2012. She returned to Brazil with her husband, had a baby, and got divorced. She still lives in Brazil as a single mother.

Felipa (forty-one), from Mexico. She migrated to London in 1989 to work as a live-in domestic worker for a Mexican family until 1994. She continued working as a live-in domestic worker until she became pregnant in 2000 with a baby girl. She is a single mother and continues working as a freelance domestic worker in London.

Sarita (forty-seven), married, mother of three, from Honduras. She migrated to Spain in 2005 on her own. By the end of 2005 she migrated to London to join her husband and daughter, where she works as a domestic worker.

Sonia (forty-six), divorced, mother of three, from Bolivia. She migrated to London in 2007 and worked as a cleaner and domestic worker until 2009, when she was hit by a taxi driver. After winning a lawsuit she returned to Bolivia in 2011.

Monica (thirty-six), from Brazil. She migrated to London in 2005 on her own. She initially did domestic work and later moved into sex work. She married a client back in 2013 and had a child. She is now separated, and as a single mother works sporadically in sex work.

Giselle (thirty-eight), from Brazil. She migrated to London in 2004 on her own. She initially worked as a cleaner before moving into sex work in 2006. She still works as sex worker in London with Sabrina.

Luciana (fifty-seven), from Brazil. She migrated to Italy in 1999 before moving to London in 2005. She works as a cleaner in London.

Sally (twenty-eight), from Colombia. She migrated to London in 2005 and worked as a nanny for one year before moving into sex work. She returned to Colombia in 2013.

Denise (thirty-five), from Brazil. She migrated to Portugal in 2002 and returned to Brazil in 2004. She migrated to London in 2006 and worked as a domestic worker for a year before getting into sex work. She is still in London working sporadically as a sex worker and selling beauty products.

Melissa (thirty-nine), from Brazil. She migrated to London in 2006 on her own. She worked as a nanny/domestic worker until 2009, when she moved into sex work. In 2011 she married a British man. She no longer works in sex work.

Carolina (thirty-three), from Brazil. She migrated to London in 2005 with her sister. She initially worked as strip dancer for four years until she started working in a private flat as a sex worker. She still works in several flats around London.

Barbara (forty-five), divorced with two children, from Colombia. She migrated to Spain in 1998, where she married a French man and had two children. In 2004 she came to London and worked as a cleaner until 2012, when she returned to Spain. She still lives in Spain.

Care for Sale

I arrive at Sabrina's flat in the new financial district of London; it is one of my regular visits, the place where she lives and works as a sex worker. She opens the door wearing a fluffy pink dressing gown that conceals her nudity. As usual, she receives me with a hug and a smile. Sabrina has a particular way of always making me feel welcome. I guess it is her quirky smile, sparkling eyes, and unaffected attitude toward me that makes me feel so close to her. She lives in a cozy two-bedroom flat with a living room featuring two big white sofas and a television. The flat, except for the bedroom that functions as her working space, is full of her things. Her laptop, which is always turned on in case her son is on Skype, is open on the table next to a pack of cigarettes, a bottle of water, and nail polish, while her sofas are strewn with sportswear. Although she complains about being tired, she likes to talk about her job to make some sense of "the craziness" she is going through. Talking to me about her life as a sex worker in London gives her some perspective and distance whenever she feels she cannot do it anymore.

"Sometimes I feel this is like a dream. When this is over in December, I will go back to my life and my son in Brazil. Everything will go back to normal; I will go back to who I really am," she tells me. She makes coffee for us and asks me if I want a cigarette. We then take our coffee to one of the windows that faces the street and light our cigarettes. As we look through the glass, Sabrina gestures toward a woman who is leaving the opposite building. "She is a working girl as well," she says. "There is another flat in that building but she does not stay overnight, she works only during the day." As the figure of the woman slowly disappears down the street in the drizzle, Sabrina continues her story. She tells me that she once bumped into some girls while coming back from the supermarket. She overheard an accent that sounded as though they were from northeastern Brazil. "There are so many of us here, all these Brazilians, all these migrants coming to London: the land of opportunities," she says with thick irony. She tells me that they all come with the expectation of making good money, for adventure, to learn English, or to support their families: "You name it, there are so many various reasons, but we keep on coming and we end up being maids or whores."

Sabrina is from Brazil. She migrated to London in 2007 with a suit-case and her eleven-year-old son, Alex. Like many other migrant women, she envisioned London as the place where her son could have a better life. Aspiring to an upper-middle-class lifestyle back in Brazil, she came to London prepared to be a domestic worker. But after two years of struggling to earn enough money to live on—let alone send remittances back to Brazil, learn English, or spend time with Alex—Sabrina decided to start working as a strip dancer in nightclubs. In just a few hours, she could earn at least twice as much as she earned in a week as a domestic worker. Working as a stripper led her into prostitution, which forced her to send Alex back to Brazil so she could have the time, space, and privacy she needed as a sex worker.

Eva, from Peru, has a similar story. She migrated to London in 2008 with her daughter after living in Madrid for seventeen years. Eager to secure a better future for her daughter, Eva started as a domestic worker and cleaner in the city. She wakes up every morning at three thirty to get to her first cleaning job at four o'clock; her day is filled with different jobs around London until ten o'clock at night. "*Esto no es vida,*" "this is no life," she tells me while we walk down the road toward the place where she lives with seven other people, all Brazilians. Once we are in the flat, we go straight to the room she shares with her daughter—her house, as she calls it. The room is full of things that Eva has accumulated since coming to London; she explained that these things will furnish and decorate her future home. She throws off her jacket with a sigh, telling me how tired she feels. "I do not know if I will be able to survive this work rhythm," she tells me. She is constantly sick and exhausted but must keep working to care for her daughter. While we are in the bedroom, Eva shares her migration journey with me, a journey that started before her seventeen-year-old daughter was born. Back in Peru, she decided to move to Spain after realizing that she was pregnant; she wanted to avoid the shame of single motherhood and being associated with the indigenous background of her daughter's father.[1] After working in Madrid as a domestic worker for seventeen years, Eva decided to migrate to London to find better job prospects and offer her daughter a better future. "I came to London for good—I do not want to go back to Spain or Peru, I want to construct a normal home for my daughter and myself in London. This is the place where I can actually achieve that dream," she says.

In homes and brothels around the world, migrant women are selling a unique commodity: care.[2] This book tells the stories of a group of middle-class women from various parts of Latin America who worked temporarily as domestic and sex workers in London. They came from Bolivia, Honduras, Brazil, Colombia, Peru, Venezuela, Ecuador, and Mexico and had been in London for a period of four to ten years when I met them. Illuminating the complexities of migration and care work, I offer an in-depth study of women's lives and the factors that affect their choices between these forms of work, including but not limited to their concerns about money and morality. Rather than concentrating only on the economic and political aspects of migration and labor, I focus on the creation and (re)creation of migrants' subjectivities—their sense of themselves—within precarious realities. The book's point of departure centers on the construction of a type of person, the middle-class migrant who is forced to become a care/intimate laborer as a result of her migration. For self-identified middle-class women from Latin America who have no English skills, no recognized educational qualifications, no relevant work experience in the United Kingdom, and—for some—no legal status, the opportunities are few and far between. As a result, they are "pulled" into occupations that they once considered menial or lowly. Domestic work and sex work represent sharp downward status mobility that produces significant fractures in women's sense of selves; class, racial, and social dislocation; and moral conundrums. I explore these ruptures, these dislocations, by considering the ways in which women migrants, as more than *economic* actors, are involved in the shaping of intimate relations within and outside the care work market and how in the process they find themselves ethical actors shaping new relationships and enacting new futures.

Why Do Dislocations Matter?

The term dislocation is both an analytical category and an *emic* one. On the one hand, I use the term as way to explain how structural economic conditions, class and racial identifications, insecure legal status, and the commodification of intimacy intersect in the production of what my informants experienced as dislocations. On the other hand, I use it as it was explained to me when women described feeling out of place (*fuera de lugar*). They talked about themselves in London as women who were not themselves (*no soy yo misma*, which translates as "I am not myself"). This sense of self stood in opposition to what they thought of themselves before migration, that is, *la que realmente soy* ("who I really am").[3] By using the *same/myself* evaluative frame (implying "as before"), women reveal a fracture between the women they were before and after migration; a dissonance between the present, the past, and the future; a future in which they believed they could recover their old personhood, *la que realmente soy*.

By discussing women's dislocations in this manner, I not only follow their own understandings of themselves, but also avoid the projection of a whole, unitary subject. I engage with a conception of the self that, as Trinh Minh-ha argues, is composed of "infinite layers" and therefore cannot be understood as a "unified subject, a fixed identity" (1989, 94). By taking my informants' sense of inner fractured worlds into consideration, I contribute to anthropological discussions of the Western person that argue that subjects are not unitary or bounded, but relational (Carsten 2004, 98) and immersed in the performance of simultaneous multiple roles (*personnages*, as Michael Lambek [2013, 838] calls them) in their various social relationships.

My informants' experiences of dislocations resemble those found by Parreñas (2001, 31) among Filipina middle-class domestic workers in Rome and Los Angeles. Like her, I examine dislocations as challenges that women migrants encounter as they navigate through the social processes of migration. Taking this into consideration, I further the analysis by using my informants' dislocations as a critical lens to understand wider conditions of subordination, resistance, and subject formation.

Selling Care in Neoliberal Times

Globalization weaves together the lives of Sabrina and Eva, along with many others who have migrated to the United Kingdom in search of opportunities for themselves and their families. This story starts and ends with neoliberalism and its influence in the expansion of a feminized global

Theory

care/intimacy market in the Global North that has consistently pulled migrant women workers from the Global South. A global phenomenon, neoliberalism is an economic system based on the idea that privatization, austerity, deregulation, and the free market can substitute the state's provision for public welfare. In this model the protective arm of the state shrinks from its commitment to regulation and social welfare. The model assumes that self-sufficient individuals, who are free to make their choices in the domain of the economy, are responsible for their own well-being. This economic model challenges the tacit links that exist, or existed, between care and welfare; care is no longer a social right, but it is a matter of choice for some and of worthiness for others.

This economic model has had disastrous results for people in the Global South. In Latin America in the 1990s, financial institutions pressured states to cut back or eliminate public services such as health care and remove subsidies on necessary items such as food, fuel, and other social services in the name of structural adjustment. These neoliberal austerity measures increased levels of debt across the region and, together with the slow disintegration of the industrial sector—replaced by cheap imports under the new open-markets doctrine—caused a contraction of employment (Portes and Hoffman 2003, 50). By diminishing the security of formal wage employment, unionized industrial labor was replaced with low-wage, precarious service-sector jobs, as well as informal manufacturing work. These changes have had sharply gendered implications (Tronto 2001). On the one hand, it is often women who absorb the loss of state-funded social services by shouldering more reproductive unpaid labor.[4] On the other hand, the new sources of livelihood—which are informal, flexible, and low paying—are often feminized, including, for example, domestic service and sex work, among many others.[5]

Although neoliberalism has been notably devastating in the Global South, it has interrelated repercussions among women in the Global North. Nancy Fraser (2016, 113–14) explains that under the dominant imaginary of a *gender-egalitarian* system, neoliberalism has promoted women's ongoing struggle for professional equality by recruiting them into waged work while reducing real wages and diminishing public provisions. These structural conditions of inequality exist parallel to the lack of state policies designed to provide, for example, an adequate structure in the provision of child care to help dual working households. This situation has raised the number of paid working hours needed to support a family, which, in turn, generates what Barbara Ehrenreich and Arlie Hochschild (2002) have called the *care deficit*. That is, without appropriate state support for social reproduction, women's insertion into a "professionally equal" labor market generates a care gap that pulls poor, less advantaged women to do the care work they no longer have the time for in exchange for low wages. There is a further aspect to consider. The gender-egalitarian ideology behind women's insertion in the labor market is still embedded in the patriarchal cultural models that enable its existence. A latent historical hegemony of the male authority—along with a naturalized heteronormativity—has secured the persistent inequalities that prevail within, and outside, the household in terms of reproductive labor. According to the Institute for Public Policy Research (PPR), in the United Kingdom, men's lack of involvement in household care work is informed by a continued belief that domestic tasks are women's work 2012).[6] These attitudes and practices are woven into the traditional dynamics of social reproduction and into the organization of sexuality that normalizes the male breadwinner/female caretaker model of the family. This sexual contract devalues care work, assuming that compensation is based on "love," as a realm of morality, and not on money, as a realm of the economy (Barker 2012, 549).

While under the logic of global neoliberalism the increase in supply and demand for care workers (cleaners, nannies, and elder carers, among others) seems straightforward, the supply and demand for sex workers is less so. However, gendered perceptions of migrant women as gifted care-givers "thought to embody the traditional feminine qualities of nurturance, docility and eagerness to please" (Ehrenreich and Hochschild 2002, 9) make their role as sex workers additionally desirable. These perceptions are combined with the fact that sex work is increasingly becoming a source of livelihood for women (and men) who are trapped in a system that favors low-income jobs and offers very few prospects. Similar to those migrant women who "choose" domestic work as an option, migrant sex workers choose sex work in the face of a lack of realistic alternatives.[7]

The expanding sex market offers better financial opportunities to save and send remittances back to home countries than does domestic work. As Wendy Chapkis argues, "Most women's choices are severely limited by their disadvantaged position within hierarchical structures of sex, race, and class: gender inequality, coupled with extreme differences of wealth within and among nations, creates tremendous pressure on women to engage in any available form of employment, including sex work" (1997, 52). Sex work is also an avenue to pursue dreams and socioeconomic aspirations; in some cases, it also offers love and the prospects of romance and family life.[8]

The insertion of women migrants in the global economy of caring labor encompasses important contradictions embedded in the conjoined effects of neoliberalism in the Global North and the Global South. While these economic forces shrink women's prospects in their own countries, they inflate a racialized, gendered caring labor market in the Global North that provides new livelihoods for those from the Global South. As I will show, this efficient market enables the existence of an informal relational affective economy that remains cheap, flexible, and unlimited in its resources. This book is a story of those trapped in the middle of a care crisis that oils the engines of global neoliberalism, whereby women from the Global South seek to address their precariousness by feeding the needs and gaps created by the neoliberal policies in the Global North.

Latin American Migrants in London

The women in this book are part of the myriad of cultures that form the diverse social and racial landscape of London. Although most migrants come from countries historically connected to the British colonial endeavor, global cities like London have received a steady flow of migrant labor from all over the world that sustains the economy of the country. Since the sixteenth century the British Empire, as with many other colonial projects in Europe, became rich by extracting human, natural, and economic resources from various colonies in the south, leaving behind a trail of dispossession and precarity. Although by the beginning of the twentieth century Britain had lost most of its power, during the First and Second World Wars the country opened its borders to its colonial subjects to recruit enough people to serve in the armed forces. Later, these migrants became the workforce of the country and took part in the furnaces and forges of the manufacturing industries, as well as in service-sector jobs (porters, cleaners, drivers, and nurses) that paid badly and were generally rejected by white people. The country's economic power was the result of a combination of colonial dispossession and the support of an economic model that enabled its continuation.

A century later, a new postcolonial logic based on a neoliberal global economic regime continues to pull a migrant workforce that is much needed for the maintenance of the country. In this regard, migration from Latin America is the result of an international market in which global cities attract a multitiered division of labor, whereby highly skilled professional managers from developed countries sustain the global financial institutions and low-cost "unskilled" people from the developing world sustain the infrastructure of these cities through their manual and invisible labor. This is reflected in the United Kingdom's immigration policies, which switched from providing visas for political refugees and displaced persons from Chile and Argentina fleeing repression at the hands of military governments (1960s and 1970s) to promoting visas for work in the service-sector industry (in hotels and restaurants and as cleaners) for Latin Americans, particularly Colombians who were leaving their country because of war and conflict (mid-1970s).[9] Later, throughout the 1980s, Ecuadorians began migrating to the United Kingdom, with many claiming asylum. The 1990s and 2000s saw Latin Americans continuing to settle in the United Kingdom as students, refugees, or economic migrants mostly working in the service sector. During this decade the migration of Ecuadorians and Peruvians increased, and in the early 2000s Bolivians and Brazilians joined the list. In 2013, there were an estimated 145,000 Latin Americans in London and just under 250,000 in the United Kingdom as a whole (McIlwaine and Bunge 2016, 14).[10]

Latin America, with its historical economic and political crises, today remains the region with the most strikingly unequal distribution of wealth in the world (Portes and Hoffman 2003, 55). The introduction of structural adjustment programs in the 1980s and the subsequent neoliberal economic policies throughout the 1990s led to a contraction of formal employment, enhanced economic divisions in the region, and influenced the migration flow to the United States and Europe. Besides the economic and political conditions of the region, two further structural aspects must be considered when analyzing these migration trends. First, the migration of Latin Americans has been influenced by a series of severe restrictions that the US government imposed on immigration, especially since the 1990s. Border controls were further tightened after 9/11 in 2001. These measures impeded the access of thousands of migrants to the country. My informants expressed a desire to go to the United States as their first choice, but found it impossible because of visa restrictions. Europe was, for many, an unknown imagined territory, but thanks to fewer migration restrictions in comparison to the United States and to increasingly well-established social networks, it offered a viable alternative. This is reflected in the fact that in 2017 Europe hosted 78 million migrants (of a total of 258 million), of which 8.8 million lived in the United Kingdom.[11]

Second, the financial and economic crisis in 2007–8 pushed thousands of Latin American migrants out of Spain and Portugal in search of work in other parts of Europe. For instance, the number of Brazilians legally resident in Portugal in 2005 was more than 80,000, making them the largest single foreign group in the country (Padilla 2007, 69–70). In Europe, Spain was a popular initial destination for Latin American migrants because of the language and, in some cases, the possibility of claiming nationality by proving Spanish ancestry, thus ensuring legal permanence. The growth of the Latin American population in Spain drastically increased from 13,500 to 200,000 people between the end of the 1990s and the beginning of the 2000s; the number of Latin Americans reached 1.5 million by 2006 (López de Lera and Oso Casas 2007, 34–35). Before the global economic crisis in 2008 many Latin American migrants were attracted to Spain because of its rapid economic growth, which resulted from a flourishing real estate market.[12] This meant a steep increase in job opportunities within the construction sector for men and the care sector (particularly elder care) for women. However, the crisis led to the collapse of the real estate market, creating an abrupt rise in unemployment and enormous levels of debt.[13] As an illustration of this recent migration flow, from 2012 to 2014 approximately 15,600 migrants moved to London from Spain (McIlwaine and Bunge 2016, 13).[14]

In reference to the total population of Latin Americans in London (145,000 in 2013), McIlwaine and Bunge (2016) indicate that 51 percent are well educated, having attained tertiary level/university education (of which 1 percent are postgraduate); however, a lack of language skills (17 percent) affects people's prospects of finding suitable jobs in the United Kingdom, even when their qualifications are recognized and they hold legal status.[15] Despite their lack of English language skills, the service-sector economy in the United Kingdom, which dominates 91 percent of London's economy, provides plenty of job opportunities for migrants.[16] A quarter of all Latin Americans in London work in service-sector occupations (contract cleaners, porters, waiters, hotel chambermaids, and security guards), with an additional 11 percent employed in caring, leisure, and other services (McIlwaine and Bunge 2016, 20).[17] Because of their educational and class backgrounds, taking up jobs in the service sector often represents deskilling. The women in my research face a paradox commonly experienced by global middle-class migrants: while migration confers a degree of economic independence that improves women's status in the family and achieves the goal of upward mobility in their material and affective lives back home, their trajectories as domestic and sex workers produce a series of dislocations—including contradictory class identifications—that deeply affect migrants' subjectivities. My intention is to offer a picture of those middle-class migrants trapped in a system characterized by a juxtaposition of emancipation and oppression that holds them in ongoing cycles of inequality (Lan 2006, 3).

Middle-Class Dislocations

Attempting to study such a diverse group of women poses potential problems when trying to construct an ethnographic narrative. This book does not intend to be panoptic—it is not a depiction of a self-contained cultural group. Furthermore, it does not pretend to develop general statements of an extremely diverse and complex geographic region. The investigation of multiple national groups foregrounds complexity, but this reflects the natural progression of my fieldwork, as women lived and worked among people who often were not co-nationals. Of key importance is the fact that this group of women, despite differences in terms of nationality and social background, all self-identified as middle class. In their narratives of class identification, they often talked about having had relatively comfortable middle-class lives with access to higher education, property, employment, and leisure time. They shared similar ideas regarding home ownership, education, moral values, and consumption as means through which they could symbolically, materially, and emotionally attain and perform their class identity. However, because of deteriorating economic conditions in their home countries, women experienced a drastic transformation in occupational status and a reduction in wages and in opportunities to improve their social status through university education. They found themselves facing increasing levels of unemployment and debt and dwindling opportunities to not only achieve economic security for themselves and their families but also advance their middle-class aspirations. In this book, I offer a faithful representation of middle-class migrants whose dreams had been shrinking and all but disappearing within their own societies, leading to their migration.[18]

In trying to locate the middle classes in Latin America, some scholars explain that this class began to arise in the mid-nineteenth century as part of a creolization project based on an ideal bourgeois European lifestyle of modernity. There was a drive to create *gente culta* (people with culture) who would promote and disseminate a particular Western morality.[19] Although not fully specified as middle class, these new subjects were located somewhere between the elite (those with white European backgrounds) and the poor (those who were indigenous or black). From the late 1940s to the mid-1960s there was special interest in the impact of the growing middle classes in the region. This was because the existing middle class included occupational groups tied to state-supported indus-tries and mushrooming public bureaucracies. They were perceived either as central actors involved in the processes that led to the attainment of democracy, stability, and development or, quite the opposite, as those who, because of their position in the middle, held conservative ideologies and were therefore reluctant to take risks.

During the 1980s, with the extended economic crisis characterized by debt, there was a preoccupation with the effects of the market on pre-cariousness and flexibility of labor and its consequences in terms of social exclusion and poverty. After the insertion of structural adjustment pro-grams, some claimed that the middle classes were doomed to disappear as the economic crisis led to the *proletarianization* of those who had once been the *new middle classes* (those who had been salaried employees since the 1950s). This new middle class was now old and was being replaced by "a new 'new' middle class of self-employed entrepreneurs large and small, particularly in importing–exporting, computing, telecommunications, and services" (Parker and Walker 2013, 13).[20] Still, the new new middle class enjoyed the opportunity not only to have access to consumer goods as never before, but also to improve their social prestige through higher education. The situation nonetheless began to change from the 1990s onward, when university degrees no longer guaranteed a middle-income job. The consequence was the upsurge of a middle class defined less by education and stable employment in the public sector and more by an as-pirational lifestyle. Overall, the socioeconomic changes endured by Latin American societies have created a middle class that has been constantly produced and reproduced through the lived experiences of social stratifi-cation in material and symbolic terms.

The Intersection with Race

Education, lifestyle, taste, family name, and connections are fundamen-tal pieces in the definition of the middle classes in Latin America; how-ever, this complex class identity cannot be fully understood without its historical colonial intersections with race, more specifically with being or becoming white. Race (skin color) plays a fundamental role in the process whereby people position themselves and others within the social pyramid. This is reflected in the fact that those who belong to the elite are white, while the poor and the working class are considered black or indigenous.[21] The history of such identifications dates back to the colo-nial cultural logic that was imposed on the continent, particularly in the nineteenth and early twentieth centuries, when there was a common pre-occupation with race and race mixture in relation to progress, modernity, education, and civilization. By the 1920s and 1930s several countries in the region started constructing their national ideologies around the idea of an all-encompassing *mestizaje* (miscegenation). According to Peter Wade, *mestizaje*, despite its homogenization rhetoric, is in fact an "all-inclusive ideology of exclusion" (2005, 243) that incorporates a de facto racial hierarchy whereby blacks and indigenous people would eventually evaporate through a process of *blanqueamiento* (whitening). According to Theo Goldberg, insofar as racial mixing came to define *Latinamericanization*, it became "elevated by making the mimicking of the European habits the defining aspiration"; even more, it became "the condition of possibility of racial elevation" (2009, 214).

Since its inception, the concept of *mestizaje* as the new mixed modern citizen was highly racialized. Still, as Peter Wade (2010) explains, the differences between *indio* and mestizo were (and still are) not necessarily based mainly on skin color or even physical appearance more generally, but on language, dress, occupation, and place of residence. Indeed, *mestizaje* is more complex in its racial politics of meanings and social implications than its usual rendering as *mixed race*. These historically situated inequalities still exist today, as the racial pyramid in Latin America (with white racial identification at the top) mirrors the social structure and class differences with their concomitant inequalities.

I encountered some vestiges of these ideologies and witnessed the intertwinement that persists between race, race mixture, and class among my informants. As many scholars on race in Latin America have found in their respective studies, my informants used any hint of whiteness, such as a narrow nose, a white ancestor, or sometimes having or claiming a high social status, as a way to whiten themselves.[22] Most considered themselves white (in a few cases they mentioned the word *mestizas*) and referred to others—less white or showing indigenous features—as *morenas*.[23] In the case of Brazilians the term *mulatta* was rarely used among those who had black ancestry. Only one of my nonwhite informants self-identified as mulatta and she explained it in terms of the mixing that existed within her family. The categories black or indigenous were avoided because of their devalued characteristics, even among those who claimed to have had indigenous or black parents or grandparents.[24] They would rather use the intermediate categories *morena* or mulatta because, as Edward Telles and Tianna Paschel explain, these categories "simultaneously emphasize social values of race mixture and proximity to whiteness" (2014, 871).

As I will show, women's middle-class subjectivities were deeply influenced by the white racial (Eurocentric) attachments and identifications that they used, for instance, while homemaking in London and back in their countries or while shopping for themselves and their families, despite the contradictory class positions that they held in London. These identifications were used to locate themselves vis-á-vis other migrants and other nonwhite people.

Understanding Middle Class

Much has been written about the emergence of a global middle class and the ways in which people assume and perform such class. As complicated as it may be to generalize about the common characteristics of this so-called middle class, most scholars agree that middle-class people appear to share similar expectations of a particular lifestyle grounded in certain values, patterns of consumption, and a desire for a particular status. As Deborah James (2015) suggests, across the world the identity of the middle class presents an in-between status. It is characterized by people's efforts to attain an upward identification and aspirations to become culturally and socially superior even if they do not seem to possess the material attributes or background that implies.

From a classic Marxist perspective there is no such thing as the middle class. There are fundamentally two classes: the owners of the means of production and the workers. Therefore, the study of the middle class poses a problem when trying to analyze class beyond labor, capital, and histories of class struggle regarding modes of production. The main peculiarity of the middle class is that it appears to be between being in control and being exploited, hence the slippery boundaries for a strict definition. As a way to move beyond material explanations, scholars like Ollin Wright (1997) take a Weberian analysis of status to explore class subjectivities constructed on social mobility and life chances.[25] This approach takes into account the role of education, occupation, social networks, and a community's relationship with the market as the means whereby people construct and maintain their class identity. Pierre Bourdieu (1984) combined the material conditions of class with status concerns and provided a parallel approach to the analysis of class. This approach allows for the study of class as part of the social structure and as an embodied disposition that individuals acquire in practice throughout their lives. For Bourdieu, class identity depends not only on economic structure and assets, but also on an individual's position and accumulation of capital—economic, social, and cultural—that will produce and reproduce class identities and status differentiations. Bourdieu's analysis places class in social space defined by capital, at the same time explaining how class positions engender representations of privileges and social differentiations.

Drawing on Bourdieu, my work engages with social class as a relational category in which people share similar positions in social space, meaning that they share not only an economic position, but also a set of cultural practices and/or dispositions. My informants identified themselves as middle class, not because they had expendable income or because they owned their means of production, but because they shared a set of characteristics (status, occupation, values, and material culture), claims (respectability, normalcy, moderation, and entrepreneurship), and life chances that shaped their class identities and notions of status. Even though women might have held distinct positions within the middle classes in their own countries (lower middle, middle middle, upper middle), they shared a mutual understanding of their class identity based on the aspiration or desire for a similar lifestyle. I draw on this self-identification as a meaningful material and affective category that women used to make sense of themselves as migrants investing in new socioeconomic relationships to retain and at the same time achieve new middle-class dreams and aspirations.

Taking into consideration that women's middle-class identities had already been modified and affected by the deterioration of the economy back in their home countries, I will show how their migration trajectories reinforced their class and racial dislocations in profound ways. These women had not only joined the flow of people who migrate in search of opportunities for themselves and their loved ones, but also found themselves working in occupations that contradicted their earlier ideas of class, respectability, and status. Instead of hiring house cleaners to work in their middle-class homes, they had become the maids working for middle- and upper-class women or had entered into a sex work market, which challenged their moral values and sense of propriety. Besides having to endure the shame of migration and the stigma of their occupations, they found themselves having to face the reality of being racialized migrants holding undocumented status.

As middle-class migrants, my informants belong to an expanding group of people whose aspirations have been curtailed by the rapidly changing and insecure economy of the current global economic climate. They therefore face increasing anxieties and struggle to maintain their status and values, which are challenged by their multiple dislocations.

As I learned during fieldwork, for women who found themselves dispossessed and placed in contradictory class positions, clinging to an idealized self-perception of a higher status (infused by white Eurocentric aspirations) or longing for "normality" helped them to negotiate their current estrangements. The search for returning to the normal, to go back to who they "really were," permeated women's everyday middle-class subjectivities. This longing to secure a (sometimes idealized) middle-class foothold and to recover a sense of normalcy in their everyday lives informed women's ideals, their present anxieties, and their aspirations for the future, even if their everyday lives as undocumented domestic and sex workers in London contradicted those ideals.

Selling Care

One of the main challenges of writing this book involved combining the study of domestic and sex work. Bringing these occupations together fits with the natural development of my research trajectory because women who were sex workers had been domestic workers when they initially arrived in London. I learned this was far from a coincidence, because the shift from one occupation to the other reflects women's overall precariousness within care work and responds to a wider socioeconomic order. As I will show, the commonalities and connections between female domestic and sex work migrations are intimately related to the inner workings of neoliberal reforms that have, on the one hand, displaced the responsibility for care onto families and individuals and, on the other hand, mobilized gendered sources of cheap labor through the promotion of highly feminized forms of work on a global scale. As I have previously explained, my informants fill the care vacuum that states create and at the same time experience a downward status mobility as they enter a labor sector that is under pressure to deskill and devaluate caring work to keep labor costs low.

Located within the logics of globalization and neoliberalism, my analysis gains inspiration from and builds on the vast literature that examines the global economy of care work (mostly domestic work) in relation to its casualization, labor rights, negotiations, and power relations between employer and employee, as well as on the social penalties that arise when *caring* becomes a form of paid work.[26] Likewise, the range of powerful ethnographies that offer accounts of the lives of sex workers by interrogating women's relations to work, family, law, and the state are significantly influential to my own analysis,[27] particularly the work of Elizabeth Bernstein (2007a) and Wendy Chapkis (1997), which shows that the contemporary sexual economy—within the broader framework of postindustrial transformations—has dramatically changed in terms of its actors (workers and clients), services, and socioeconomic consequences. Sex workers are increasingly providing the same type of services that other care workers offer, such as pampering, empathy, entertainment, and emotional support. Hence, as some scholars have suggested, sex work should be thought of as part of a broader group of service occupations that characterize affective economies and care work in capitalist globalization.

I offer a distinctive analysis of the connections and commonalities between female domestic and sex work migrations and broaden the scope of previous ethnographic studies that focus on one occupation or the other but fail to consider the relationships between them. While much scholarship has considered nannies, cleaners, nurses, hostesses, and sex workers discrete from each other, through the analytical device of *intimate labor* Eileen Boris and Rhacel Salazar Parreñas (2010) have argued that we must consider the connections that exist between these different forms of work.[28] Intimate labor focuses on a range of activities that belong to the service economy, but also takes into account occupations that are ordinarily private or hidden. For them, "a sex worker is clearly an intimate laborer because, after all, intimacy is a euphemism for sexual intercourse. Likewise, a domestic worker because of the access to the intimate space of the home and knowledge of its inhabitants' habits would be an intimate laborer" (2010, 5). Intimate labor encompasses a range of activities, including personal and family care, household and bodily upkeep, and sexual contact, but more important, it places the categories of care, domestic, and sex work in a continuum. It includes those activities that do not necessarily require face-to-face interaction, but involve different forms of intimate knowledge. Following this analytical category, I explore how middle-class women—who move from one occupation to the other—experience similar conflicts and conundrums when working as domestic and sex workers in London. I show how their intimate work entails the performance of activities that are intrinsically relational and affective and, more important, needs the performance of a particular gendered emotional labor.

In her seminal work with flight attendants, Arlie Hochschild (2003) reveals the pivotal role that emotional labor has on the service-sector industry and its concomitant feminization. She argues that the increasing participation of women in service-sector jobs that demand emotional labor is far from coincidental because they have been traditionally considered better than men at creating feelings of well-being in others as a result of their natural caring dispositions. Emotional labor includes face-to-face interactions in which workers must induce particular feelings in the client or customer while managing their own emotions. Hochschild (2003) explains that the worker can engage in *surface acting* and/or *deep acting*. In surface acting, "the action is in the body language, the put-on sneer, the posed shrug, the controlled sigh"; in other words, one merely pretends to be the character. By contrast, deep acting is a "natural result of working on feeling; the actor does not try to seem happy or sad but rather expresses spontaneously" (2003, 35), thereby becoming the actual character.

In my own research, most women performed surface acting by forcing a smile, staying docile and patient or disguising fatigue and frustrations in front of demanding and capricious employers, or simulating love, romance, and pleasure, as well as providing affectionate support for clients on a daily basis in strip bars, brothels, and flats. No client wants to deal with a dreary and indifferent sex worker, just as no mother of a household wants to deal with a surly and peevish nanny or cleaner. In other words, women found themselves constantly performing gendered emotional labor that was difficult to sustain in the long term, but that was nonetheless necessary for the success of their work. Maintaining surface acting in their everyday work and relationships with employers and clients was draining and could lead to strain, yet for many, it was necessary to deal with the estrangements that the work produced and the exploitation that it entailed and to avoid the uncomfortable commodification of intimacy.

However, matters were further complicated when women engaged in deep acting and manufactured authentic (even if fleeting) emotional ties with clients and employers because it could lead to either the development of emotional intimacies or further exploitation and inequality. The desire to signal authentic emotional ties and satisfy employers and clients using emotional intimacy relates to the intertwinement of structural and individual circumstances. On the one hand, it is a consequence of the increasing demand for *immaterial labor* under neoliberalism and the growing diversity of services offered in the care work market that places an emphasis on emotional labor and the management of emotions (Freeman 2014, 138). On the other hand, this quest for emotional intimacies speaks of women's personal investments and desires for authenticity that correlate with their own desires and aspirations for the future.

In other words, the intrinsic affective dimension of domestic and sex work, combined with the performance of gendered emotional labor and women's personal choices, can be conducive to the development of emotional intimacy and care. In this complicated set of transactions, it was then not unusual for women, clients, and employers to find themselves in a state that oscillated between work, care, and intimacy. As a result, women found themselves in constant need to find the best way to manage the commodification of intimacy. Following Viviana Zelizer's work, I focus on the ways in which women effectively dealt with the often-delicate issue of mixing economic activity and intimacy by differentiating meaningful social relations and appointing certain sorts of emotional and economic transactions appropriate for each relation (Zelizer 2012, 152).[29]

As I will show, these transactions were not always successful, and the women found themselves trapped in a system that undervalued their labor and perpetuated inequality. Still, their socioeconomic, emotional, and ethical calculations allowed them to adapt and even take advantage of their liminal positions. By focusing on the dislocations created by women's intimate labor, I show migrants not only as economic actors but also as individuals involved in a process of commodified intimacies that are central to their making of the self and the construction of their subjectivities. I explore the mechanisms that women used as attempts to build practices of resistance in opposition to their precarious, fractured realities. These practices, I argue, were based on the women's morality and ethics.

Ethics of Care

So far, I have explained how economic conditions, class and racial identifications, insecure legal statuses, and women's occupations intersect in the production of what my informants experience as dislocations. My understanding of such estrangements includes an equal consideration of women's tactics to counteract them. I explore those counteractive tactics by focusing on ethics, particularly on ethical practices of care that women engaged with while working, while sustaining kinship relationships, and while dealing with their fractured selves. I use the term *ethical* in its broader sense, "referring to the field of action or practical judgement, rather than to what is specifically right or good" (Lambek 2010, 9). Although I do not draw a sharp distinction between ethics and morality and use the terms interchangeably, I acknowledge those moments when women talked about morality specifically. Morality was explained to me in relation to particular *values* they associated with being a good mother, daughter, sister, wife, or friend.[30] Notably, all of these are social identities with important gendered dimensions, constructed around notions of care and responsibility for others. Following this logic, one could argue that women's discourses of morality served as a gendered structure that gave some sense of order (Durkheim [1906] 1974), while ethics functioned more as agency, as intention, or, in a way, as resistance.

My interest in ethics serves as fertile ground to show the connections between caring—as an ethical as well as an economic regime—and neoliberalism. As an economic regime, caring is transformed into an uncomfortable, undervalued commodity infused with affective features; however, as an ethical practice, caring can potentially manage the consequences of the commodification of intimacy, providing meaning at moments in which social relations appear to be strained and becoming a mechanism to resist the inequalities created by the economic regime of care. In this regard, a focus on the ethics of care offers a framework to comprehend the fractured subjectivities of women immersed in various relationships across economic and social divides.

My inquiry builds on and contributes to recent literature that investigates the connections between morality and neoliberalism through regimes of care.[31] Many of these studies have focused on the techniques and modes of self-fashioning and self-subjugation through work, entrepreneurship, sobriety, and thrift.[32] As Andrea Muehlebach suggests, the morality of neoliberalism hinges on a particular kind of ethical caring subject (2012, 7). This subject engages in acts of care in a Foucauldian sense by engaging in "technologies of the self which permit individuals to effect by their own means or with the help of others a certain number of operations on their own bodies and souls, thoughts, conduct, a way of being, so as to as to transform themselves in order to attain a certain state of happiness, purity, wisdom, perfection or immortality" (Foucault 1988, 18). As Wendy Brown argues, neoliberal morality is solely measured in terms of individuals' ability "to self-care—to provide for their own needs and service their own ambitions" (2003, 15). This, in her view, reconfigures morality as a matter of rational deliberation about costs, benefits, and consequences— all of which are directed toward the self. This sort of morality appears to be solely animated by instrumentalist, utilitarian, and calculative rationality.

However, neoliberalism imposes a paradox that allows for the simultaneous existence of apparently opposing practices. Building her analysis on an economy of voluntarism in Italy, Muehlebach (2012) shows how neoliberal morality scrutinized beyond market rationality entails a productive tension. This tension becomes clearer if one moves away from an analytic of self-fashioning toward an ethics that is "other-oriented" (2012, 24), hinged on an ideology of care and empathy, on affect rather than rationality (Robinson 2013). Although my case originates from a radically different situation, because my informants were involved in market transactions that included caring as an economic arrangement, I found similar ethical practices that were not merely oriented toward the self or market-driven calculations. In many instances, caring as an ethical practice was structured around the recognition of others and the responsibility toward others in situations of commodified and noncommodified intimacy.

By saying this I am not suggesting that self-fashioning is absent from my analysis. On the contrary, the neoliberal regime places women in a position in which they must fit a particular subjectivity that exists in the middle of self-care and strive for personal fulfillment despite structural constraints. For instance, I show how migrants, despite experiencing class and racial dislocations as a result of their undocumented realities, self-fashion as respectable middle-class people. I also pay attention to the subtler forms of self-fashioning that women engaged with to become successful intimate laborers, as well as how women transform themselves into distinctive and caring consumers and homemakers within precarious realities. Yet, the point of these practices is not mere self-care, but the situating of women's identities as relational subjects embedded in various relationships that entail affective labor and care (at work and with their families).

Following this, my analysis of ethics is based on an underdeveloped approach to the study of morality and ethics within anthropology,[33] that is, a feminist ethics of care.[34] This approach positions individuals as relational subjects and explains how moral thinking is influenced by people's responses to others and therefore argues for a relational and nonunitary understanding of personhood (Tronto 1994; Cockburn 2005). Its relevance, as Virginia Held suggests, is that it "pays more attention to people's needs as to how actual relations between people can be maintained or repaired" (2006, 28). It places an emphasis on a sense of responsibility toward others (Walker 1998; F. Williams 2001) and therefore allows for the consideration of caring as an economic activity, as well as a moral one. By looking at ethical practices in this way, I am able to establish a link between the moral and the economic within neoliberalism and show that what appear to be oppositional practices—ethics and emotions—are not necessarily so.

These ethical choices took place while women sold care and performed emotional labor with their employers and clients. As I have explained, these commodified intimacies could produce a series of dislocations that questioned women's moral universes. However, by enacting an ethics of care and accounting for the responsibility toward the other, women were able to inhabit cultural referents that were familiar to their identities and personhood. An ethics of care, however, existed beyond the realm of their intimate labor and was also performed at moments when they needed to maintain their kinship roles and identities through different practices.

An analysis of ethical practices of care requires consideration of the structural conditions that permit or constrain its existence. Therefore, my reflection pays close attention to the structural circumstances of inequality in which women engage in such practices. As such, I do not romanticize or essentialize an ethics of care as intrinsically female by naturalizing women's alleged affinity for relationships of care as natural and good.[35] This essentialist thinking contributes to the heteronormative patriarchal model that subordinates women to a system that flourishes as a consequence of such gendered discourses. Furthermore, it masks the nuances, contradictions, and uncertainties through which people navigate to make their own choices. In this regard, my analysis includes the possibility of *not caring* even in situations where it was "socially and morally" implicit to do so. The not-caring choice, I argue, is also an ethical one because it entails agency. By doing this, women were able to recover a sense of control over their own—often alienating—labor and personal estrangements and build practices of insubordination in opposition to their dislocated realities of menial labor. While these practices appear as self-care mechanisms used to protect their racial and class identifications, cultural dispositions, and affected lifestyles, they are also embedded in a constellation of meaningful social relationships and their responsibility for the maintenance of such relations. In other words, the choice not to care entailed a form of self-care and care for others at the same time.

My focus on ethics of care demands an understanding of resistance. I argue that women navigate uncertainty by engaging in an ethics of care as a way to resist situations of increasing dislocation and structural inequality. By saying this, I am not suggesting that they did not make judgments or engage in moral activity before they migrated to London. Rather, I contend that neoliberalism provides a moral framework in which women see themselves as moral subjects engaging in ethics. Following this, I argue that women were suddenly propelled into becoming acutely conscious of themselves not only as fractured subjects but also as moral and ethical actors in a way that had not characterized their previous lives.[36] These choices, then, emerged from personal reflections and judgments of their imagined world (their past lives) in conjunction with the contradictions of their daily lives in the present. In showing this, the book reveals the creation of new complex ethical subjects longing to recuperate an ideological notion of who they were while weaving creative alternatives across their ruptures. By doing this, women generate a moral worldview that is central to the recognition of themselves as ethical actors.

Overview of the Book

Why did I come to London? was one of the questions women repeated after I asked them about their migration journeys while I listened to, recorded, and pieced together their journeys during fieldwork. Chapter 1 uses a close appraisal of women's narratives to show how migration is not only a matter of push–pull economic factors, but also a matter of love, debt, care, family, adventure, security, and escape. These stories demonstrate how, through their migration journeys, they are trying both to care from a distance and simultaneously to emancipate themselves from normative kin pressures and fulfill personal aspirations.

Having explored women's journeys, the book deepens the analysis of the everyday experiences of migrants by focusing on documentation and illustrating the precariousness of migrants' legal statuses. Chapter 2 follows personal narratives that show how *illegality* is predicted long before arriving. This is ironic, given that the women I worked with entered the United Kingdom with the proper paperwork and visas. It was only later, once they overstayed their visas and disappeared from the system, that they became undocumented. By looking at migrants' experiences while manipulating documents, working in clandestine occupations, and encountering the state, this chapter reveals how illegality is not a cut-and-dry legal state, but a way of being that is learned, embodied, and performed. Once in London women became part of the service-sector economy of care, Chapter 3 discerns the traces of everyday dissatisfactions, as well as conflicting satisfactions, among domestic workers. On the one hand, women's dissatisfactions reflect a prolonged but more or less concealed struggle over the norms and inequalities of the labor process. On the other hand, women's satisfactions paradoxically ensue from the emotional labor and care that they provide at work. Considering this dilemma, the chapter is concerned with the exploration of personal negotiations while caring, including moral considerations and ethical choices. The chapter presents the ways in which women structured their emotional lives to navigate their occupations and regulate their intimate labor relationships.

Chapter 4 presents the cases of women who, after having been domestic workers, made the decision to become sex workers as a way to achieve financial security, to gain new experiences, or to fulfill desires of transnational love and romance. It explains how women, who provide various kinds of sexual intimate services within sex work, deal with the often-blurred boundaries between labor, care, sexual intimacy, and money. It shows how, in the face of commodified intimacy, women make ethical choices in their everyday relationships with clients as a way to re-configure a sense of self. How do people deal with the challenges generated by the perilous proximities and inequalities that are created within care work? Chapter 5 answers this question by exploring gift exchanges within domestic and sex work. It brings together classic and contemporary anthropological literature on the gift, exploring the parallels and differences of gift exchanges in both occupations. Gifts are used as a tool to cope with uncomfortable intimacies, to manage the inequalities that exist in both occupations, and to transcend the constraints and contradictions of these labor relations in favor of women's desires and aspirations. Gifts are used as mechanisms to locate new social relations and to normalize the somewhat uncomfortable emotional intimacy that is embedded in both occupations. Chapter 6 expands on the different strategies that women use to negotiate the tensions that arise between recuperating a sense of normality and migration as a process of radical change. I explore these tensions by examining how women aim to recuperate the normal by imagining and constructing home at a distance. The ethnography shows how they use consumption as a tactic to display middle-class taste and use social events as spaces where they can display and reclaim their lost status. Given the focus on wanting to retrieve a sense of being normal, this chapter critically questions the *real* self and asks whether this notion is more an ideological construction than a real reflection of their pasts.

Where are these women now? Is the future (now the present) as bright as they wanted it to be? Are they enjoying the world they hoped for and imagined back in 2009–10? The future, which presents itself at times as a moment of hope and aspiration and at others as a time of doubt and uncertainty, is an intrinsic part of the migrant experience. To give some closure to the life histories that I have presented, the conclusion sketches what happened to the women after the period depicted here. It shows how all of them, in diverse ways, continued to dream about a better future. This imaginative practice was a key feature of their lives in the present; it was not a fantasy, but a modified possibility of reconstructing the life and the person they felt they had lost as part of the migration process.

A Note on Methods

This book is based on twenty months of fieldwork research in London between August 2009 and April 2012. My main research method was based on participant observation; however, toward the end of my fieldwork period, having developed close relationships with my informants,

I dedicated some time to recording their life histories. This reminded my informants of my position as a researcher and gave them the space to construct personal narratives of their journeys. Gathering life histories, I found, served as a way in which women were able to reflect on changes over time. From the beginning of my research I disclosed my role as a researcher and explained the nature of the work. Throughout fieldwork, consent was sought from and given by my informants, who were aware that their identities and the information that they shared with me would remained protected throughout my fieldwork and writing process. All names in this book are pseudonyms, including names chosen by the women themselves, and to protect their identities I do not reveal the exact places or cities they were from.

Field Site and Access

London proved to be a complicated place to do fieldwork since the urban field site is not a given space but must be found and produced; doing fieldwork in the city requires constant effort and complicated logistics. My informants lived and worked in various areas of the city; they shopped, visited friends, went to church, and spent leisure time at different locations. As a result, I did not simply hang out, observe, and wait for life to unfold in front of me; rather, I needed to elaborate a daily plan that included juggling various meetings across the city. My everyday work responded to the hectic lives of the women and the variety of locations they inhabited in London. This forced me to move around several sites. In contrast to more traditional anthropological fieldwork, I accessed and reentered my field site on a daily basis. I was performing research on the move via the metro, buses, and trains. Sometimes these were field sites in themselves, since it was while commuting in London that my informants and I had the opportunity to talk and share the trials and tribulations of the day.

My project was originally intended to focus on the lives of Latin American domestic workers, but thanks to the insights of my supervisor, Olivia Harris, who wanted me to broaden the scope and offer a fresh view on Latin American migration in the United Kingdom, we decided to investigate two occupations that appeared to be stereotypical among Latinas in London, that is, domestic and sex work. It started as an experiment that began in the summer of 2009, before I officially began fieldwork. My first contacts with people started before fieldwork. In the summer of 2009 I got in contact with a local project that works with sex workers in London. It is run by a mixed group of white middle-class women, some of whom are postgraduate students. As activists, they shared the experience of working or having worked in sex work. I told them about my research, my interest in their work, and my availability to become a volunteer. I volunteered for two months. The work was exciting because I met women from various parts of the world who worked in the sex industry in London, which gave me an initial insight into the trade. After a while, however, the activists running the project began to find the presence of an anthropologist—who was not and had not been a sex worker—intrusive and problematic because of the power dynamics this entailed. According to some of them, I would never be able to understand the reality of sex work because I had not experienced it. While this is true, as a feminist anthropologist working with disadvantaged communities, I am aware of the politics of representation and the power involved in our research processes. Therefore, I would never claim to know how it feels to be one of them or assert some form of universal truth regarding the experiences of my informants.

The activists offered to let me interview some of the sex workers who attended the project, but I explained that the nature of my research was based on long-term participant observation that would require more than interviews. I had already talked to some women about my research who seemed interested in participating; however, the gatekeepers worried that I was getting too close to some of the women and wanted to limit my contact and relationships with them. They decided they did not want a researcher present for that long or, for that matter, establishing close relationships with women who worked in the sex trade.[37] While I deeply respect the work that this group of activists does, there was a level of power taking place that they were not able or wanting to see. As middle-class, educated, white women, these activists had the choice to enter and exit sex work as they wanted. They were not undocumented migrants from Third World countries forced to make a choice because of a real lack of opportunities. Although I defend choice and believe that sex work should be decriminalized and recognized as a form of work, I also acknowledge that there are important nuances while advocating for it.[38]

Once I left the project I started to develop my own independent contacts. The internet proved to be an infinite source of potential contacts that eventually became worthwhile and rewarding. I went online and found sites where different women offered services that were branded as escort services or disguised as masseuse services. Although I knew it was a gamble, I sent emails to several women in which I explained my research in Portuguese and Spanish. Two women responded, one of whom does not appear in this book because we only met twice. However, by fortuitous opportunity, the other turned out to be Sabrina, who became a key informant. We spoke on the phone before meeting because she wanted to make sure I was not a client in disguise. A few months later she told me that she had wanted to hear my voice before meeting with me to see whether she could trust me. I found during fieldwork that this was a common tactic Sabrina used to evaluate whether a client was safe. "It is all in the voice," she said. Her technique proved to be accurate most of the time, but not infallible. Immediately after our first phone call, she sent me her address and I visited a working flat for the first time in my life. Sabrina became the woman who opened the world of sex work to me in this second phase of my research and gave me access to other sex workers.

In parallel with the advocacy work with sex workers, I looked for Latin American events around London that would offer me the space and opportunity to meet other women. My access to domestic workers evolved in a completely different fashion. It was a stroke of luck and went much more smoothly. In late June 2009, I made contact with a woman from Peru who later became one of my main informants. It started at a bus stop in south London while en route to a Peruvian party celebrating Independence Day. As I was standing at the bus stop talking to a friend of mine in Spanish, a woman nearby asked us for bus directions. She spoke Spanish and she was going to the same event. We spent the rest of the evening in each other's company and at the end of the night she gave me her contact details. I explained what I was doing in London and asked whether she would mind me contacting her in the future. Eva became my gateway to other Latin American women who worked in domestic work. As is common in anthropology, it was a *snowball effect*, which led me from one story to the next.

After establishing initial contact with my informants, relationships with them quickly developed. All of them, without exception, invited me to their homes soon after we met. I spent hours with women in the rooms and kitchens of the flats where they lived with other migrants, where we gossiped, cooked, ate, and shared moments of commensality. In addition to conducting research in women's homes, I also had the opportunity to accompany them to the houses where they worked and to learn about their daily intimate labor while cleaning empty flats and houses. I cannot claim to have experienced the burdens of the demanding work that they did, but spending time with them at work gave me important insights into their work and created solidarity between us.

I also spent time at working flats, flats where sex workers both lived and received clients. I would sometimes stay there for several days at a time. Participant observation in these spaces was of a different nature.

I did not engage in any form of sex work, but through long periods of spending time together I did develop an understanding of the everyday workings of prostitution. Days at these flats tended to involve lengthy periods of waiting for my informants while they attended to their clients. During these periods I experienced the pace of life that evolves in such spaces. Some days were busy, with clients arriving around the clock until midnight. We always, however, had time to eat, talk about the day, watch a film, and go to bed. Other days were the "lazy days," when women would only have a few sporadic clients, so we would spend the entire day talking and hanging out or running errands. I also met several clients and spent time with them, along with my informants—going out for dinner, to a concert, on a short trip outside London, or at the flats.

Spending time in these flats was also stressful. Before I knew it, I began to have a more active role in my informants' everyday work. I became efficient at helping them change clothes between clients and ready the bed and other services, such as clean towels, toothbrushes, and water. On some occasions I became a kind of gatekeeper who would check on suspicious clients through the windows before they entered the flat. Flats were also potentially dangerous places where women were under a constant threat of abuse and violent attacks. I shared this experience of fear and uncertainty with them each time they opened the door to a new client. After one of my informants was brutally attacked, I started hiding a kitchen knife under my seat while I waited for my friends to finish their sessions with clients and stayed in a constant state of alert with the phone ready in case there was an emergency. I learned to always keep the television on or make some noise as a sign to potential offenders that they were not alone in the flat. Despite the potential danger of these places, spending time in these flats gave me valuable insights into sex work, enabling me to witness the trials and tribulations of prostitution behind the scenes and to develop close relationships with the women.

In addition to spending time with women at work, I was also part of their social lives. I attended weddings, baptisms, and birthday parties and even became a *comadre* (godmother). I became part of their families and they became my friends and family in London. I answered their phone calls in the middle of the night after they had experienced violence at the hands of clients or when they were in need of an abortion. I translated texts for clients and employers and wrote applications for visas and tax credits. I wrote invitation letters for immigration officers and answered phone calls when women needed translations. I went with them to the doctor and translated their pains and their sorrows for the medical staff. I held their hands during chemotherapy and cried with them after talking about the impossibility of the future and their broken dreams. I cried when they left and when they died. I was Anita, the anthropologist who was always ready to listen to their stories, their sorrows, their fears, and their joys, without judging their choices or the contradictions in their lives.

My Position

As a non-British, non-European woman I was not "at home" during fieldwork. I was in an intermediate place. I was a foreigner in the city of London, just like my informants. We were all migrants, all women from Latin America, and yet the distance and the differences between us were immeasurable. Being a Latin American migrant woman without doubt eased my initial access. I was considered a sort of insider who shared a similar cultural background. However, although I am Latin American, I "did not look Mexican"; according to them, I looked more like a gringa. Therefore, my background was a continuous source of comments, queries, and speculations. Ironically, my middle-class white identity, because of its advantageous position in the racial and social pyramid in Latin America, helped me navigate and gain quick access into their lives. However, from the beginning of my research I was aware of my position of power in our relationships. Not only there were significant differences between us in terms of class, race, education, and legal status, but also my status as a researcher played an important role in how our relationships evolved.

Acknowledging the relations of power that are intrinsic to our work and considering the predatory nature of our research enterprises, I decided to engage in acts of reciprocity with my informants. As my relationships with them unfolded, I started becoming an asset that they could use. As non-English speakers, my informants were in constant need of a translator. Throughout fieldwork, I provided my services and became a quasi-mediator between them and the non–Spanish speaking world. I became their English voice. I went with them on visits to their doctors, dentists, lawyers, employers, landlords, clients, and pimps. I also helped them with negotiating phone accounts, setting up bills, filling out forms, and visiting state bureaucratic offices. The demands were constant and sometimes overwhelming, yet I saw these exchanges as my way to reciprocate. I do not claim that this erased the inequalities between us, but as a feminist scholar who was already conflicted over the gender inequalities in the lives of these women, I did not want to extract yet more labor from them without giving something back. It was an ethical problem to me.

The nature of my research brings up various other ethical concerns. First, my research entailed working with migrants who were potentially undocumented. Although undocumented migrants were not the focus of my project, there was a strong possibility of finding people who were in a precarious legal situation. From the moment I met women who were undocumented in London I remained highly sensitive and careful to keep the women's legal status protected from authorities, co-nationals, and others. While writing field notes I never referred to their legal situation and I did not record any information that could disclose their identities.

The second issue of ethical concern is that my research involved working with women in labor markets that are informal, illicit, and highly exploitative. When working with sex workers, I had to be very careful about not sharing any information about my informants, even with those who were considered friends. Working with sex workers is a difficult enterprise because of the stigma attached to the occupation and its illicit legal connotations. I had to learn how to protect women's identities, including names and biographies, from people outside the trade, from family, and from other sex workers. Although it was difficult to understand how their lives unfolded within a trade in which they must juggle several identities, personas, truths, and lies, after a while I learned how to keep their stories straight, follow the flow of their narratives when accompanied by other people, and protect their various identities in London.

My work with domestic workers was similarly challenging in relation to their biographies. Here I am referring not only to women's undocumented statuses, but also to the fact that because of their downward status mobility, women created alternative narratives of their lives. These narratives were not always consistent and were filled with contradictions. It was hard to follow which story they wanted people to believe. I believe that this is not unique to my research and that any social scientist doing long-term fieldwork eventually faces this sort of issue. However, these alternative life stories were far from being gossip or white lies; they were part of who they needed and wanted to be in front of others in London.

The size of my sample is small. Although I met many people while doing fieldwork, in this book I focus on the stories of a handful of women. I am not claiming that they are representative of the Latin American community in London. I do not intend to homogenize them or to pretend that it is possible to present a coherent picture of their lives and practices in London. This book is about the intimate experiences of particular individuals who are very different from each other but who nonetheless experienced and engaged in similar personal, social, and economic struggles as migrants. As Michael Herzfeld argues, "Bringing people of widely divergent classes and cultures into a common framework allows us to render visible aspects of social life that rely on, or even consist of, invisibility in their individual contexts" (Herzfeld 2015, 19). The value of focusing on a small group of people lies in the possibility of delving deeply into the details of people's lives "to extract hidden and significant social realities in tiny local details" and to "recognize in those details the enduring, lived consequences of events taking place in the centers of power" (19). After all, as anthropologists we aim to understand wider social problems from the point of view of those who find themselves stranded within the system that oppresses and exploits them; the trick "is to keep both the detail and the larger picture in focus" (19). I start this anthropological endeavor by introducing the reader to the migration journeys of the group of women who made this book possible. I hope that my focus on their life trajectories in London can render visible the way in which people around the world not only experience everyday inequalities and dissatisfactions, but also find mechanisms to overcome them and fabricate hopeful alternatives.

PART I

Personal Dislocations

CHAPTER 1

"Why Did I Come to London?"

Narrating the Migrant Self

Why did I come to London? The question was repeated after I had asked my informants about their migration journeys. Women's narratives of migration were more than just stories. To some degree, the narratives gave coherence and meaning to their decisions and projects; they helped them understand their own experiences in London. In considering the different personal stories and backgrounds of the women in this book it is important to focus on the recurrent themes that appear in the narratives of their journeys because they shed light on structural systems of inequality that affect global mobilities. Their moves are not necessarily circumscribed by the *push–pull* phenomenon, whereby migrants are pushed by domestic poverty and pulled by wealth in developed countries. As Pei Chai Lan argues, "reasons are propelled by 'intersecting circumstances of vulnerability' that may include financial distress, family dissolution, and lack of direction and choice in their homeland" (2006, 126). Migrant women, as she further suggests, should not be seen merely as victims or commodities in the international labor market because their journeys "assert meanings and exercise agency against the imposed cultural constraints" (126). The stories in this book show that migration is a personal process that is inextricably linked to the political economy of countries of origin and to the dynamics of wider trends of international female migration; at the same time, the stories demonstrate how women's decisions are guided by their personal desires and self-transformation.

The themes that populate the narratives of migration speak of global struc-tures of inequality that affect the everyday lives of people around the world. My intention here is to use these stories to build on the aspects women themselves pointed out as relevant parts of their identities to comprehend the lives of women as they unfold in the global economy of care.

Drawing on the life histories of Latin American women in London, this chapter serves as an introduction to the reasons, motivations, and expectations of my informants in relation to migration. By examining the personal narratives of women, I show that international migration is not merely an exogenous process shaped by economic reasons; rather, economic factors are embedded in broader social settings that articulate individuals' dreams and aspirations for the future.

Narratives of Debt and Inequality

As Saskia Sassen explains, "migration is not simply an aggregation of individual decisions, but a process patterned and shaped by existing politico-economic systems" (1999, 155). In the case of Latin America, ongoing economic reforms have dramatically affected the livelihood of the lower- and middle-class people who are increasingly facing a short-age of job opportunities, rising unemployment rates, insecurity, and violence. In countries already characterized by weak institutions and very little social welfare, the effects of neoliberalism augment the state's lack of responsibility and obligation to care for its people. It is in the hands of individuals, as autonomous economic actors, to be responsible for their own well-being, in other words, to become entrepreneurs to advance their own dreams. Entrepreneurship as a mechanism of self-employment and a vehicle for income generation emerges as one of the few strate-gies to survive in precarious economies. I examine the consequences of neoliberalism and its signature element of entrepreneurship as a gateway to indebtedness that prompted women's migration journeys. In many cases, debt originated in the bankruptcy of businesses generated by economic instability and the associated aspects of state collapse, including unem-ployment, excessive costs of health care, and insecurity. Eventually, for some, the global crisis of 2008 pushed them over a threshold, compelling them to move to a new country for the second time in quick succession.

"At least we have managed to pay the debt we had back in Honduras," Sarita once told me when we were at her London flat, eating tacos and homemade tortillas in the company of her husband and daughter. Forty-seven-year-old Sarita from Honduras, mother of three, had migrated to

Madrid at the beginning of 2005 to settle a debt of $60,000 that she and her husband had accumulated over the course of two years in Honduras. Sarita's initial debt consisted of a $20,000 bank loan to set up a carpentry workshop for her husband. The money was also invested in a stand provided by Coca-Cola where she sold Mexican food outside the workshop. "We were doing well, Jesus had plenty of orders but not enough cash. We could not risk losing clients, so we started using our credit cards to meet the demand. The situation got bad when clients started asking for credit or paying by installments. Before we knew it we had a debt of $60,000," she explained. With no money to pay off the bank or credit card interest, they had no choice but to mortgage their house to take out a second loan. Matters were further complicated by the presence of gangs that controlled the area and collected "war" money from local people, money they had to pay. These gangs of young men flourished thanks to the lethal combination of unemployment, increased drug trafficking in the region, and the mass expulsion of migrants from the United States, placing Honduras in the center of a violent war.[1]

Amid structural violence and increasing insecurity, Sarita and Jesus were unable to repay their debt and risked the repossession of their home. The solution to their financial predicament was for Sarita to go to Madrid to join her brother, who had told her about job opportunities in domestic work. Still without enough money to repay their debt by the end of 2005, Jesus migrated with their youngest daughter to London, where his sister lived, as a way to secure a steady income. Sarita joined them immediately afterward. Using a false Spanish passport, she started working as a cleaner for a company where she earned £220 per week, plus the extra money from her domestic work. Jesus managed to find sporadic carpentry jobs with the help of a Portuguese man who owned a workshop. After five years, thanks to their joint income and by sending £700 per month to Honduras, they cleared their debt.

Sarita explained that the worst aspect of being in debt was not the economic restrictions but the moral burden. She could not help but think that they had failed to succeed in their entrepreneurship project; their debt had accumulated as a result of bad financial decisions. Instead of producing furniture to be sold for cash, Jesus kept working under a credit regime that continuously produced debt. Still, there was something honorable about their indebtedness: "Our debts had nothing to do with wasting money by spending it on clothes or unnecessary things. Our debts had been incurred because we wanted to save our business, save our house and improve the lives of our children." Credit, as scholars have discussed, may be the only way for people to maintain basic necessities: housing, food, utilities, and their business (B. Williams 2004; Di Leonardo 2008; Collins and Mayer 2010). This was indeed the case for people like Sarita and Jesus, who defined themselves as hard-working, middle-class people with a relatively comfortable life (they had their own house, cars, and a small business): "We were not poor, not really, more like middle class but really struggling to maintain our business and save enough money to send my daughter to university," she said.

Unemployment and lack of state support compared with rising living expenses create difficulties in making ends meet. For instance, in Bolivia, poverty and lack of employment pushed out one million migrants after 2000. In 2002, 65 percent of the population was living in poverty, of which nearly 40 percent were in extreme poverty. Bolivia remained one of the poorest and most unequal countries in Latin America, and the opportunities for income generation among the poor, particularly the poor indigenous population, continue to be a critical issue today.[2] Later, with the emergence in 2003 of social movements against the reforms of President Mesa, Bolivia was plunged into a period of political upheaval and social insecurity until Evo Morales won election as the first indigenous president of the country in 2006. This eventually led to further political and social problems that deeply affected the middle class. "Not even those with higher education could get a job back then," Lourdes (forty-seven) from Bolivia told me when referring to the economic crisis.

During this period, Pedro, Lourdes's husband, had lost his job at a research center at a university because of state cuts and was unemployed for two years before going to London. As a result, Lourdes became a small-business entrepreneur and rented a market stand where she sold conserves, fruit preserves, and other tinned goods and became the breadwinner for the family. But the money from her sales was not enough to support a family of five. With very little income from the business, they were forced to mortgage their house to obtain a bank loan, hoping that Pedro would soon find a job. When their debt accrued to $20,000 and they found their house in danger of repossession, Pedro decided to migrate to the United Kingdom. He stayed in the United Kingdom and managed to send enough money home to pay off half their debt, until he was deported in 2004. He found his way back within the year, this time with his family. By moving to the United Kingdom, they hoped they would be able to catapult their children into professional or white-collar jobs with social prestige. Pedro, as a middle-class professional, was aware of the difficulties in maintaining the lifestyle they wanted and climbing the social ladder in Bolivia. They needed $6,000 for the trip to England, money Lourdes obtained from a moneylender/loan shark (*usurero* or *prestamista*). This debt, according to Lourdes, was paid off over two years.

Similar stories were told by Jovanna (thirty-eight) and Cecilia (thirty-seven) from a city in the east of Bolivia. They were both unemployed, both had mortgages to pay, and they had very little prospect of finding jobs, despite having university degrees. As an accountant, Cecilia used to earn enough money to lead a comfortable life and help with the household expenses at her parents' home. However, in 2003 her father suffered a stroke, and with no medical insurance Cecilia and her brother incurred considerable debt because of medical bills from a private clinic. With debt and the significant risk of her father relapsing, they mortgaged their house to finance his treatment. Cecilia was then made redundant in 2005 and could not find a job because of the general economic crisis. She was desperate: "I could not sleep, I could not breathe anymore thinking about the money and my father's health. I had an acquaintance who had come to London and started making good money at a cleaning job. It was a difficult decision to leave Bolivia, but it was my only choice," she told me.

In a similar vein, Jovanna, a single parent of a ten-year-old girl (by the time I met her), had worked as a computer technician and information technology teacher but lost her job in 2001. While narrating her story, she told me that the situation in Bolivia had become unbearable; she was unable to find any work, her father's house was about to be repossessed by the bank, and her ex-partner refused to pay any child support. "The day I found myself with no money to buy milk and diapers for my baby was the moment when I decided to come to London," she said. Although her family was not rich, her father had offered them a comfortable middle-class life. They owned their own home, had cars, went on vacation occasionally, and, more important, all went to college. Her brother was a lawyer, her sister was an accountant, and her mother had been a housewife who never had to work.

But life as she knew it was over. She had a child, debts, and no job prospects; her only choice was to migrate. She found it very difficult to cope with the idea of migrating and working as a cleaner, but it was the only solution to her problems. Once she decided to go to London in 2002, Jovanna asked for a $5,000 loan from a moneylender to pay for the flight and initial expenses. According to Jovanna, this debt was paid off in the first fifteen months she worked in London, including the interest; however, she was unable to pay the mortgage and avoid repossession of her father's house. At this point, Jovanna's sister, Karina, came to London in 2006 to work as a cleaner. With their joint salaries and their brother's help, they were able to settle their father's debts and invest in the purchase of a plot of land for the construction of a new house.

Jovanna's original plan was to stay in London until 2007 because she wanted to go back to Bolivia to her daughter, whom she had not seen in four years. However, in June 2006 she was diagnosed with breast cancer that initially required chemotherapy and two operations. With the high prospect of relapse, it became unimaginable for her to go back to Bolivia because she did not have any form of social security or health insurance to treat her illness.

> I wish to stay in the UK to continue my treatment. I would not be able to get this type of medical service if I went back to Bolivia, not without money. Many people in Bolivia go abroad for medical treatment—for example to Chile or Brazil. My cousin is an oncologist who works in Brazil. When I told her about my diagnosis, she told me that the best thing for me was to stay in the UK.

Although Jovanna did not want to migrate permanently, her life circumstances, combined with the lack of resources in Bolivia, a nonexistent public health care system, and no support for single mothers, prompted her to bring her mother and daughter to join her in the United Kingdom. Jovanna's illness and the possibility of accessing medical treatment became her main reasons to consider staying permanently.

Distinct types of economic crises and economic investments pushed women into debt at different periods of time. When I started doing fieldwork in 2009, I witnessed an increase in Latin American people coming particularly from Spain (but also from Italy and Portugal) to find work in London. Many of my informants liked to call these migrants "*los 'españoles' desplazados*" (the displaced Spaniards). They were Latin Americans with European passports who were experiencing the consequences of the financial crisis in Spain.

Take Amelia, who moved to London in 2009 after the bankruptcy of her business in Madrid. Fifty-three-year-old Amelia was born in Spain but migrated to Venezuela with her family when she was only nine years old. After having carved out a life in Venezuela, she returned to Madrid in 2000 (forty years later) to take care of her elderly mother, who had returned to Spain. Her migration was also related to what she liked to call "the Chávez effect" and the political polarization and economic instability that resulted from it.[3] According to Amelia, Hugo Chávez's socialist policies had created not only an economic crisis in the country but also anxiety and distress among the upper and middle classes, which were targeted in favor of the popular classes, the classes that had been the scapegoats for Venezuela's economic failures (McCoy and Myers 2006). Because Amelia had a Spanish passport, she did not have to suffer the *Chavista* state. In Madrid Amelia easily found work thanks to her experience in real estate and the booming construction industry. With the business flourishing, she decided to set up a convenience store in 2006 as an investment in her future.

In Amelia's view, entrepreneurship was not a risk but a sign of success. It implied, as Carla Freeman argues, "an independence in which the individual is defined as a self-propelled, autonomous economic actor, ever responsive to a dynamic marketplace, and simultaneously encouraged to seek introspection, self-mastery and personal fulfilment" (2014, 20). Founding a small business asserted her status as a businesswoman experiencing upward mobility that would allow her to have the means, flexibility, and time to live as she wanted, that is, between Venezuela and Spain. Thus, with a proportion of her savings and an initial bank loan of €25,000, Amelia opened the store in Madrid. The business was doing well and even though she reinvested most of the profits into the store, she was earning enough income to live comfortably, be her own boss, and repay her debt. However, with the collapse of the Spanish economy, Amelia lost her business and found herself with a debt that she was not able to settle. After much deliberation and reluctance on her part, she migrated to London and started working as a live-in domestic worker for a rich Spanish family. It was the only way to pay off her debts without anyone in Venezuela knowing what she was doing.[4]

Narratives of debt are linked to the failure of entrepreneurial projects within structural conditions of economic inequality and precarity. On the one hand, these projects were embedded in a morality that was related to the self-fashioning of independent subjects looking to achieve upward mobility. On the other hand, they were intertwined with women's roles and obligations within their families. In this regard, it could be argued that debt entails a productivity for self-making, performing affective labor and maintaining social ties. Nonetheless, because of the dependencies and asymmetrical social and economic relations that debt creates, on an everyday basis it was remembered and lived through with shame. This is particularly relevant among middle-class people because of the morality behind debt that sustains the obligation to settle it (James 2015; Graeber 2012, 122–23). It is important not only to hide one's indebtedness but also to ensure that the process of repaying it can be done swiftly, in an individualized way.

For some of my informants, settling their debt was much needed to save face, protect the reputation of their families in their home countries, and recover some of the reputation that they had lost as a result of their migration. Furthermore, it was only by canceling their debt—which belonged to the past—that women could restore the ideological construction of their present and hence their future.[5] Investment in their future was restricted by their state of indebtedness, but migration and their lives in London offered the opportunity to imagine other possibilities.

Indebted Aspirations

Although structural conditions of neoliberalism affected women's indebtedness, it is also important to pay attention to women's personal aspirations for social mobility as factors that prompted their indebtedness and migration. In 1991, Eva saw migration as a way to escape the collapse of the Peruvian economy in 1990 and the rampant violence that the country went through, particularly following the upsurge of *Sendero Luminoso* in the 1980s. Migration, however, also meant the possibility to begin a new life for herself and her baby. After borrowing $8,000 from a moneylender, she went to Madrid knowing that she would easily find a job in the care sector. The 1990s witnessed an increase in Peruvians migrating to Spain because of labor opportunities for domestic work, nursing, and construction (Escrivá 2003, 9). The job opportunities in Spain were a solution to Eva's problems in Peru: "I made the decision to migrate seventeen years ago before my daughter was born. I was not only running away from the everyday insecurity and violence, but also wanted to avoid the shame of being associated with the indigenous background of Maria's father." He was, according to Eva, "*de lo más profundo del Peru*" (from the deepest part of Peru), an implicitly racist remark that suggests having an indigenous background. Fortunately, from Eva's perspective, her daughter had inherited her "white" genes and not the "indian" ones of her father, an aspect that automatically put her on top of the racial pyramid. This whiteness combined with a European nationality secured her daughter's future until 2008 when Eva, because of the economic crisis in the country, decided to embark on a second migration. To achieve this, Eva asked for a loan of €10,000 from a Bolivian loan shark in Madrid. This amount, she said, was needed for the initial expenses for the trip and also represented a safety net in case she could not find work in London immediately. "I was not going to live in a shit hole with my daughter. Even if I had to pay more money I wanted to find decent accommodation for both of us, at least until we found our way in London," she explained. London represented the opportunity to achieve middle-class aspirations that included, first and foremost, having a home (by getting housing benefits), followed by providing a university education for Maria, learning English, having access to better paid jobs, and finding a European partner. According to Eva, it was "just a matter of time."

In a similar vein, forty-six-year old Sonia (mother of three) had a relatively stable middle-class life in Bolivia where she owned a pharmacy, taught at university, and worked part-time at the local hospital. Her case is a remarkable illustration of middle-class people who, to actualize expectations reserved for the wealthy, became entangled in a cycle of borrowing now and paying later. When her daughter Paulina wanted to travel in Europe, Sonia did not hesitate to borrow money to make the dream come true. To pay for Paulina's trip, Sonia asked for an initial bank loan of $4,000. Paulina flew to Madrid on March 11, 2004, the day of the terrorist attack in the Atocha train station in Madrid, so her plane was sent home. After the failed trip and with $2,000 less in ready cash, Paulina again insisted on going to Europe, this time to Italy. To please her daughter, Sonia asked for a second bank loan; she borrowed $2,500 from one bank and $500 from another.

On this occasion, Sonia and Paulina agreed that Paulina would repay the money once she found a job. Once in Italy, however, Paulina was not only unable to find work, but also fell in love and became pregnant. Although Paulina's pregnancy represented a financial problem, Sonia's main disappointment was that her daughter had fallen in love with a Bolivian—"*un indio ya ves*" ("an indian, you see")—and not a white Italian who would have given her documents and "white babies with blue eyes—pretty babies," she told me. Theo Goldberg explains how the idea of becoming whiter, or lightening the race, goes hand in hand with the notion of upward mobility, which is intimately articulated through race, class, and gender (2009, 216). Indeed, Sonia's aspirations of elevating her family's social status by whitening her grandchildren were frustrated by her daughter's choice of partner (see Telles and Paschel 2014, 870). Even more, because of Paulina's pregnancy, Sonia had to entirely absorb repayment of the debt. Sonia said that before she realized it, she found herself in a serious predicament: "I was borrowing from one bank to pay another. I was up to my neck in debt" (*con el agua hasta el cuello*).

> As I ran out of stock in the pharmacy, it stopped becoming financially viable and my economic situation became critical. Then a friend told me

that if I came to England and worked for a while I would be able to pay off my debts in no time. I did not even know where England was, but I had to do it as my debt had increased to $18,000 due to the interests. On top of this I still needed an extra $6,000 to pay for the trip.

As Sonia recalled it, her debt had been a result of spoiling her daughter combined with the various sources of credit, which only patched up other debts. She entered a pattern of self-lending from earlier sources of credit, getting herself into an endless cycle of debt. Migrating to London was the only solution to her indebtedness and to help her regain some of the respectability she had lost as a result of the bankruptcy of her business and debt.

Narratives of migration to repay debt, including further debt accumulated for the purposes of traveling abroad, loomed large in women's accounts. They were mortgaging their present through debt while using the promises that migration offered in anticipation of a valuable future (Bastia and McGrath 2011). In this future they would be no longer indebted, but they would have to engage in forms of menial labor that stood in contradiction to their previous class identifications. Although debt appears as a metanarrative that gave coherence to women's decisions to migrate, its origin was rooted in family obligations and an ethics of care. In other words, being good mothers, good daughters, or committed family members were unspoken reason for women (and in some cases their partners) to incur debt.

Obligation versus Escape

When I initially talked to women about their reasons for migrating, obligations toward children and other family members dominated their stories. This is hardly surprising, considering the common assumption that women are naturally predisposed to serving their families. Gender in Latin America is strongly reinforced by cultural norms, partly under the influence of Catholicism, which places motherhood and other kinship roles as powerful referents in the construction of the female identity (Molyneux 2002; Chant and Craske 2003). Scholarship on female migration has explored the roles that women must perform at a distance when they leave family behind; regardless of the distance that they travel, they are still bound by obligations of care toward family (Hondagneu-Sotelo 1994). In my research I encountered a few women who left children back home; some had grown-up children, others migrated with their children, and some did not have any children.

Amanda (thirty-six) described her life in Brazil as relatively comfortable. She was a schoolteacher and, as a middle-class white woman, occupied a somewhat privileged position within the extremely unequal social structure. However, as the single mother of two children, she was facing some financial difficulties in providing the type of life she wanted for them.[6] Her son Fernando suffered from chronic depression, which represented a huge financial burden. Although her father helped her with some of the expenses, she could not cope with the economic pressure. After finding herself with unpaid bills mounting up and with the feeling that she was failing as a mother—because of her inability to improve her son's psychological condition—she decided to migrate to London in 2008. She worked as a domestic worker in London for some time but was not able to save enough money to look after Fernando. In the face of a lack of realistic alternatives to make money and after weighing financial benefits, Amanda moved into sex work. The money she made from sex work would go toward looking after Fernando by paying for his treatment and ensuring that both of her children attended good private schools. "My plan is to stay in London until I make enough money to pay for university for both. Education is the only thing that I can actually offer them to improve their lives in the future," she told me.[7]

Women used narratives of care—of providing for family members and giving them a better future—to justify their trajectories and choices. However, once our relationship became closer, they started disclosing other reasons that, in their minds, were less socially acceptable. Behind their real obligations and the social pressure as members of tight kinship networks, migration offered some respite in their lives. It was a breathing space where they were able to resist the social pressure to stay at home and accept their lot in life. Nevertheless, women's narratives were tainted by an uneasy mix between caring for the family and experiencing freedom for the first time in their lives.[8] Amanda mentioned how much she missed her children and how sad she felt about being so far away; nonetheless, she found comfort in knowing that they were in good hands—sometimes she even remarked that they were "in better hands"—because they were under the care of their grandparents. Despite the clear sadness caused by the separation, she said that she was constantly confronted by "selfish" feelings of freedom or emancipation. For the first time in a long time she had the opportunity to travel, to go out with friends, to do things she had been denied—because of being a single mother—in Brazil. Although she was not denying moral conundrums, she felt free and was understanding slowly who she was beyond her role as a mother.

Monica (thirty-six) and Giselle (thirty-eight), both from Brazil, left the country to start a life away from kinship obligations. They did not have children, but they were both the main carers for their aging parents in Brazil. Being young and single—and living at home—meant that they had to fulfill duties of care and be "good daughters." This meant that a big portion of their salaries was destined to support their parents. However, as a secretary, Monica was finding it increasingly difficult to pay the bills at home and try to save some money for herself. "I feel obliged to stay in Brazil because of my parents; they are old and they need my help. But I am also young and want to live my life and find love. After much deliberation I decided to come to London so I could help them by sending money and in the meantime enjoy my life," she told me.

While telling their stories, both women described feeling guilty for being away, but at the same time they felt relieved of daily care for their parents. After working for some time as cleaners and not being able to earn enough money and enjoy their new freedom, they slowly moved into sex work. For women who did not have children back home, sex work, as I will show in the following chapters, represented a way not only to achieve economic goals but also, most important, to fulfill transnational aspirations of love and romance. Even though they had escaped everyday obligations to their families, they both bore the responsibility of maintaining a flow of money to Brazil. They cared from a distance and thus fulfilled their roles as filial daughters without entirely changing previous gender structures.[9] At the same time, however, they were able to explore the possibilities offered by their newfound freedom.

In a rather different vein, yet with some similar echoes, Juliana (fifty-one) used to work as a switchboard operator in southeast Brazil and earned just over the minimum wage (R$415,00 [approximately £117] per month in 2008). At that time she and her partner were constructing a house. She envisioned the house as the place where she would grow old and eventually retire—it had space for animals and an orchard and was away from the city. "I wanted to finish the house but we did not have the money to do it. With my sisters in London I knew I could go for a few months to work and make substantially more money to finish the house." With three grown sons and most of her family living abroad, over the years Juliana had been in charge of caring for her elderly mother. She explained that the task was tiring because she was required to juggle ensuring her widowed mother had everything she needed with attending to the needs of her partner, as well as dealing with her job and other daily hassles. Although she felt guilty about leaving her mother behind, she felt the need to "take a vacation from family" and in the meantime earn the money to achieve her dream. For Juliana having the extra time for herself was a luxury she had not had before: "If I want to stay in my room listening to music or reading I can actually do it without having anyone asking for something all the time." The burden of guilt was ameliorated by seeing migration as a temporary experience that gave her the opportunity to accomplish her long-term goal.

What these stories suggest is that regardless of women's statuses and roles within their families, they found themselves trapped in traditional female roles that are structured around notions of care. Women's sense of guilt and ambiguous locations in their newfound freedom speak of wider gender ideologies that place women's identities as relational and never as individuals. Their obligation to care for and sustain their families both economically and emotionally influenced their decision to migrate; paradoxically, this decision also emancipated them from those constraining roles. In this regard, migration for some women not only offers the opportunity to sustain their families and maintain their kinship bonds, but also becomes a legitimate and ethically justified way to be relieved of the burdens of family.

New Beginnings

The possibility of imagining that life could be better somewhere else encouraged women to start long journeys that deeply affected their lives and their persons. Some women's narratives described a quest for new adventures, but others revealed painful memories. Both types of narratives are ultimately flip sides of the same coin. These stories show how migration functioned to cope with the past for the sake of the future in a personal, intimate, and sometimes painful way.

Exemplifying this is the story of forty-three-year-old Sabrina from Brazil, who, after ending an eleven-year marriage, wanted to make a fresh start with her adopted son (then age nine) in London. With a job that did not allow her to provide for her son and no marriage holding her back, Sabrina saw migration as a temporary state in which they could solidify their relationship of mother and son. She arrived in London in 2007. She was employed as a domestic worker before moving into sex work, at which point she was forced to send her son back to Brazil to live with her aunt and mother. Sabrina's dream, which initially included her son, transformed into a personal challenge—though still linked to his future—to earn a million *reais* before returning to Brazil. The financial success that migration offered was driving her away from her son; ironically, what began as a journey of kinship recognition resulted in long-distance separation that could have short-term repercussions. In the long term, however, Sabrina was convinced that the separation from her son would bear fruit that they would enjoy in the future—this would justify her absence.

Some women go abroad to escape unhappy or abusive relationships. Angelica (thirty-two) from Brazil left her twelve-year-old daughter after a painful separation from an abusive partner. With no job, suffering from depression and struggling with the repercussion of having been in an abusive relationship, she wanted to make a fresh start. When she decided to migrate, her ex-husband asked for custody of their daughter and took her under his care. Angelica initially migrated to Portugal in 2003 and then, after being deported in 2005, found her way to the United Kingdom. It was painful for her to think and talk about her daughter back in Brazil, but she constantly said that it was probably for the best because she thought of herself as a bad mother. Angelica's narratives were painful to listen to; they were filled with sorrow and guilt: "I know I came to Europe to escape from my life in Brazil. I could not see another way out of my relationship, but I think about my daughter every day and I know that she might not forgive me."

The combination of the deterioration of economic conditions and the continuous search for strategies to patch up and cover up painful pasts is illustrated by the story of Cristina (fifty-five) from Ecuador. Cristina had migrated to Madrid more than fifteen years earlier and, after having secured a home and an income, she brought her two daughters and her son to live with her. Cristina's migration to Europe was fueled partly by the economic crisis in the country and by being trapped in an abusive marriage.[10] Following Ecuador's financial collapse in 1999, outmigration grew exponentially. Until the early 1990s it averaged 20,000 Ecuadorians annually, mostly traveling to the United States. In the years prior to and immediately following the 1999 crisis, the number grew sixfold, averaging 130,000 migrants a year between 1999 and 2003 and peaking at nearly 176,000 in 2000 (FLACSO-Ecuador and UNFPA 2008). Although most migrated to the United States, there were an estimated 300,000 Ecuadorians in Spain who often came from lower middle- to middle-class families (Portes and Hoffman 2003, 70).

"I had a comfortable life in Ecuador where I had a house, my family around and my children. But I was in an abusive relationship and I knew that the only way out of my marriage was to put an ocean between the two of us," Cristina explained.

However, her sacrifice bore fruit, as her children grew up in Spain, had Spanish passports, and now, as adults, had the opportunity to choose what they wanted to do with their lives. Nevertheless, for the second time in her life, she decided to migrate to offer her youngest daughter, Jasmine, better opportunities for her future in London. Claiming that Jasmine was starting to get into trouble in Madrid by mixing with the wrong people, Cristina decided to leave and take her daughter to London to teach her a lesson on, as she put it. "If Jasmine does not want to study, she will have to work, and if cleaning is the only thing she can do right now, cleaning it is," she said. She remembered how painful it was to see her daughter working as a domestic worker, but she felt this was a necessary lesson for Jasmine to mature and appreciate the sacrifices her mother had made for her children.

Cristina expressed her migration to London in terms of "starting from scratch, doing it all over again." Even though it was a hard choice, she said that going to London offered a twofold advantage—a better life for her daughter and a new beginning for her.

> It is a second and final chance to make things work. This time I need to take care of myself and make arrangements for my future. I am not a young woman anymore and even though I have worked all my life I do not have a pension. Now it is time to save money for my future.

Her plan was to save money, go back to Ecuador, construct a rustic eco-hotel on a plot of land by the beach that belonged to her family, and win back some of the life that she had lost.

The possibility of a hopeful future was intertwined with leaving the unpleasant past behind. The past was inhabited by painful experiences that my informants preferred to keep hidden. Most of those narratives, as a consequence, remain unspoken and have been omitted from my own narrative. As Angelica once told me, "we all carry our ghosts with us and even at a distance they sometimes keep on haunting us." If a painful and conflict-filled past became a pivotal reason for migrating, hopes in investing in a different future certainly reinforced their choice to migrate.

New Adventures

In the collective imaginations of many of the people that I encountered during fieldwork, the United Kingdom was portrayed not only as a place of opportunities but also as a place where one could learn what many of my informants called *real English*. In Latin America, learning English is regarded as a skill that can improve job prospects, especially among the middle classes. English schools are powerful magnets that attract international students of all ages from all over the world. Moreover, until 2012, English students were able to work part-time on their student visas, a policy that opened opportunities for thousands of migrants to the city.[11] However, very few of my informants, who started with negligible English language skills, realized their ambition of improving them. Even those who had managed to learn some English were far from fluent. But women kept their hopes up and invested money in trying to learn.

Mariana (thirty-eight) from Brazil used learning English as an excuse to travel in Europe and the United Kingdom and leave a broken heart behind her. In Brazil she had worked for a marketing firm. She was satisfied with her work and did not have any real economic problems—however, as a single woman in her late thirties in Brazil, she was feeling the pressure of not being married. She had had a difficult break-up with her previous boyfriend, who proceeded to marry someone else immediately after their relationship ended. "I was heartbroken—it was really hard for me to know that my ex was marrying someone else and that I was single. I felt I had no reason to be in Brazil, I needed a change, at least for a while." Since Mariana had an Italian grandmother, she initially migrated to Italy to sort out her Italian citizenship. She said that she did not intend to stay there, but while she was waiting for her papers to be arranged, she decided to make the most of it. She took some Italian lessons and sporadically worked as a waitress to make some money to cover her daily expenses. In the meantime, Mariana met a Colombian man, Ricardo; they fell in love and were married four months after they began dating. As Mariana recalled it, her life had taken a 180-degree turn: from being single in Brazil, she had become a woman married to a foreigner in a foreign country.

However, because of the economic crisis in 2008, Mariana decided to move to London to work, learn English, and save some money before returning to Brazil. The plan included her stepdaughter, twenty-two-year old Clara, and her husband Ricardo, who was also struggling because of increasing unemployment in Italy. They had agreed to meet in London after Mariana and Clara had found jobs and a place to live. I met Mariana just after she arrived in London. She was working eight hours a day as a domestic worker/nanny at the house of a Brazilian woman. She did not have the time or the interest to continue with English classes. Although her intention was to return to Brazil, London offered her the possibility of a life that was quite different than she had originally planned. Mariana's dreams and aspirations changed the moment she found herself in love—without expecting it, she achieved an entirely different dream.

Twenty-seven-year old Vanessa did attend English classes in London. After two years, she managed to understand and speak some English, although not fluently. Vanessa came from a middle-class family in Colombia that supported her dream of going to London. Her father paid for her studies and expenses in full because he thought the language would help his daughter find a better job once she returned to Colombia. As an English student, Vanessa had a student visa, so she could work part-time. Like many other Latin American migrants, she initially worked as a cleaner for a few months until she realized that London was full of options for a young, attractive woman like her. Convinced by a friend from work, Vanessa started working as a stripper and then slowly moved into sex work. Her work gave her the opportunity to have new experiences, have fun, earn good money, and— with a bit of luck—meet a white European partner. Despite being new to the trade and knowing that she could do it because she was away from family and friends, she enjoyed being "on the game" and receiving constant attention from men. Although her current profession surprised her, she made the most of it. According to Vanessa, being a sex worker in London had changed her life forever.

Conclusion

The migrant self is constructed on narratives that contain remembrances of the past as well as the experience of the present; in some cases, they are also colored by hopes of the future. They provide multicolored and multidimensional portraits of the faces behind migration. Those faces often blur and disappear in transit. Women's narratives unfolded at several times during my fieldwork. I have explained their motivations to migrate as they were explained to me. By following the narratives, my intention has been to solve the problem of analyzing the conjunction between structural and personal factors. While acknowledging the difficulties in trying to avoid falling into the trap of offering a simplistic push–pull explanation or an understanding of migration as based on rational individual choices, I take both perspectives into account. Reducing women's stories to either rational individual choices or purely economic forces ignores the fact that—even when economic reasons are significant—those migrating are not necessarily always those in dire need. It also overlooks the fact that people sustain hopes and dreams within their migration projects that are not always entirely "rational" or functional.

By focusing on the narratives of women's journeys, I have sketched the empowerment that results from migration. Mothers, daughters, and married, divorced, or single women found various degrees of freedom, first when they made the decision to migrate and second when they started either solving and paying off their debts or creating new lives in London. Yet there is an important paradox in their lives because they became empowered by performing the same gendered roles that constrained them in the first place. As Lan argues, "the feminization of domestic labor enables women's emancipation and concomitantly sustains gender subordination in the context of global migration" (2006, 126). I will show in the following chapters the ways in which women make sense of this paradox and reconstitute the meanings behind their various gendered roles.

CHAPTER 2

Becoming an "Illegal" Person

Waiting for the bus, Sarita looks all around her, constantly checking that there are no police officers in sight. She talks to me in a faint voice, almost whispering. She asks me the day of the week. "It's Wednesday," I reply. She asks if I am sure. I say yes and ask her why she is worried about the day of the week. She says she has paid for a weekly bus pass that she updates every Monday, but she is always worried about forgetting to top up her travel card and not having enough money to make her journey. She adds that she has heard from friends that many *ilegales* (illegals) are caught by the police and sent to detention centers for not paying their bus or train fares. After waiting ten minutes, the bus arrives and Sarita gets on, her travel card in one hand and her bag in the other. She taps the card reader without looking at the driver and climbs to the top deck. We find two seats together and sit down. I try to ask her about her day at work, but her eyes dart around, her air guarded and distracted. Sometimes she crosses herself and murmurs for God's help.

Like many other migrants, Sarita found traveling around the city a tense experience in which she was exposed to the glare of the public eye and the threat of potentially encountering the police. For most migrants, commuting was an ongoing source of anxiety because of the presence of the Transport for London inspectors who occasionally board buses to carry out random checks on tickets and travel passes. If they found someone who had not paid the right fare, inspectors would ask for identification, leading to other questions that could expose migrants' vulnerabilities and ultimately serve as gateways to deportation.[1] It is not surprising, then, that for women like Sarita taking the bus was a huge challenge that affected her mental state and physical body. She modified her behavior on public transport by whispering or not talking at all. She sat in her seat in silence for the duration of the journey; even her body seemed to sink into her seat, as if she wanted to reproduce a mimetic exchange with it. The mere thought of being asked for her bus pass terrified Sarita. She talked about feeling that her face would reveal that she had no papers. She sometimes felt as if the word *ilegal* were tattooed on her forehead.

In this chapter I move from reasons for migration to exploring migrants' initial engagements with their new homes. My analysis focuses on one of the most salient dislocations in their new lives[2]: their undocumented status. I argue that becoming undocumented is not only a juridical status or a sociopolitical condition, but also a mode of being-in-the-world. Explained by Martin Heidegger (1972), being-in-the-world refers to a mode of being-in that we might call dwelling or inhabiting. For Heidegger, a human being cannot be taken into account except as being an existent in the middle of a world among other things (Warnock 1970). In other words, we and our activities are always in the world; therefore, the interpretations of our activities and the meanings that we attach to them emerge from our contextual relations to things and to others in the world. In London, Sarita existed in the world as an illegal person; therefore, the interpretation of her activities and its meanings emanated from this way of being. As I will show in this chapter, being undocumented and experiencing illegality affect migrants' physical and emotional well-being, shaping their experience of space, time, sociality, and self (Willen 2007, 9–10).[3] In other words, everyday illegality becomes a way in which undocumented migrants inhabit the world, a way of being-in-the-world.

These experiences are compounded by the fact that being illegal represents a decline in status experienced as a class and racial dislocation in the new place. To my informants, an illegal was someone who lived very far away from them, was extremely poor, and hence was forced to cross the river or desert and needed to use *polleros* or *coyotes* to enter the United States. Because of their middle-class identifications, these women saw themselves as higher in status than other illegal migrants, like those who cross the border of Mexico to get to the United States.[4] As Jovanna told me once, "At least I had something to eat, I had a house, not like the people from your country (referring to Mexico) that have to flee in order to survive." In London, the illegals were given a different name and had a different skin color—they were the *sin papeles* or *los africanos*, those who had managed to find their way into the United Kingdom clandestinely.[5] My informants, in contrast to those who Jovanna thought of as illegals, had entered the United Kingdom by plane and had been granted tourist visas at the point of entry. For them, becoming *undocumented* took time. But regardless of their ideological class, race identities, and differences from the "others," they had to slowly learn and embody the category they had initially rejected.

For women with relatives in London, undocumented status affects the whole family. As several scholars have shown, women and men experience illegality in particular ways that are related to gendered expectations (Abrego 2009; Hagan 1994; Menjívar 2000). For instance, illegality prolongs family separation, blocking mothers from providing care for their children as they would like and as is socially expected of them (Abrego and Menjívar 2011). Likewise, it prevents undocumented fathers from fulfilling their roles as breadwinners in the family.

Although my research was with women, in this chapter I consider the effects that illegality had on women's relationships and on their families. I offer a picture of women's lives outside work, involved in caring relationships with their families and partners, who also suffered and were required to deal with the daily anxieties and dislocations of having an undocumented status. Not all my informants were undocumented; some of them had obtained European passports before going to London. Still, those who held European passports experienced a phase of illegality when they initially went to Europe as they entered with tourist visas and became over-stayers.[6] Although I refer to the experiences of undocumented migrants, illegal migrants do not live in isolation and it is precisely their dwelling among people with rights that exacerbates their inequality and their vulnerability.

The Journey toward Illegality

Migration is not a singular event, but an ongoing process influenced by temporal factors that allow women to see themselves as traveling from an uncertain present to a future in which they would fulfill dreams and aspirations, but also a future in which they would inevitably become undocumented. This resonates with what Kathy McIlwaine et al. found among Latin Americans in the United Kingdom, where 70 percent of 960 people interviewed had entered the country with a different immigration status than their current one. More than three-quarters had arrived on tourist/visitor visas and another 10 percent on student visas; later they became overstayers. McIlwaine et al. found that 19 percent of the total were migrants living irregularly in London, with the caveat that 93 percent of this group had entered the country legally and only 3 percent of the people interviewed had entered on false passports (2010, 49–50). Only 3 percent entered without valid documents, but 19 percent ended up without them (McIlwaine, Cock, and Linneker 2010, 47–50).[7]

Women entered the United Kingdom with visas; it was only later, once they had overstayed their visas and vanished from the system, that they became undocumented. They did this by planning and developing elaborate lies that included presenting themselves as tourists before entering the United Kingdom. These strategies were used to avoid suspicion. For Jovanna, for example, traveling to Paris before going to London meant having to pay for an expensive hotel that a friend had booked for her without knowing about her economic problems. "When I saw the hotel, I knew I was screwed, it looked expensive, but I was ashamed of confessing the reality of my situation. Every euro I spent in Paris felt like a punch to my stomach," she told me. As I gradually came to understand, maintaining this pretense was her way of locating herself in a new reality that entailed the experience of downward status mobility. Many of my informants traveled to Paris or Barcelona before London, even though this was a considerable economic investment, and eventually entered the United Kingdom by bus or train.[8] By proving at the UK border that they had been traveling in Europe and were now including London in their trip, women felt that they were less likely to be questioned about their intentions. Despite the distinction that the status of tourist offered them, most women explained that facing border authorities and having to lie about their real intentions aroused shame and extreme anxiety. These feelings only increased when they were subjected to scrutiny by border officials—especially because they could not understand any of their questions regarding return tickets, occupations back in their countries, or reasons for traveling because of language problems. As Jovanna explained to me,

> You don't even want to look them in the eye directly because you feel as
> if they can read the truth in your eyes and they will know you are lying.
> This is the moment when you start feeling like an illegal migrant.

In a similar vein, Sonia went to London in 2007 to work and pay off debts back home in Bolivia that amounted to US$20,000. To get to the United Kingdom, she paid US$6,000 to a travel agency that claimed to be able to offer a plane ticket, a work visa, and accommodation in London. These travel agencies were especially clever at bringing migrants through different routes all over the United Kingdom. Sonia's odyssey started in Edinburgh, where her trip involved traveling by taxi all the way to London because, according to the "tour guides" in Bolivia, it was dangerous to travel by train or coach because immigration officers checked for undocumented migrants on public transport.

"The funny thing is that we had our visas; we were not illegal! We were so scared and stupid! Back then I did not even think about the tourist visa I had in my passport, and I am supposed to be an educated woman. I guess we were all scared," Sonia told me while laughing at the thought of it. These tour guides efficiently made use of the discourse and anxieties produced by the idea of illegality to take advantage of the group. After traveling from Edinburgh to Newcastle and then to Manchester, the guides disappeared with the money and left the whole group alone, clueless as to their whereabouts. Lacking knowledge and resources, they asked a minivan driver to take them to the only place that sounded logical to them; they asked the driver to take them to the Plaza Central (Central Plaza) of the City of London. As Sonia recalls, the taxi driver was bewildered by this request and, after several attempts to communicate with them, decided to take them to Victoria Station in central London. Sonia explained that although they were not undocumented, their intention to overstay their visas, combined with the fear that the guides had instilled in them, affected their initial engagements with the city and their future plans.

These stories suggest that an insecure legal status not only is the result of migrants' actions or the legal frameworks that define them, but also, in situations of precarity, can populate migrants' imaginations even before it becomes a reality in their lives. Regardless of their earlier social statuses, educational backgrounds, class identifications, and expectations for the future, as soon as their plans began to unravel, migrants were immersed in the intricate prospects of illegality. It was later, during the process of learning illegality, that the new undocumented person came into being. In the following section, I explore how migrants and their desires for a good life in which they would be able to sustain their middle-class aspirations placed them in morally conflicting positions and, as a result, experienced deep personal dislocations.

Learning Illegality

Once in London, migrants had to learn how to negotiate and coexist with other people while also learning to embody their new legal and social identity as undocumented subjects. To achieve this, women (and some of

their family members) became what you might call apprentices of illegality and learned to negotiate and implement illicit tactics to access various services, especially employment. In particular, they embodied aspects
of their new status through individual actions such as producing false
documents, using other people's National Insurance numbers (NIN) (i.e.,
Social Security number), breaching the restrictions of their student visas,
and engaging in occupations (like sex work) that were already clandestine.
Once migrants' status became illegal, their actions were circumscribed
under this new label. As Jovanna told me, "whatever you do is illegal; we
are trapped."

Acknowledging that these practices were circumscribed by migrants'
precarious economic and legal statuses, following De Certeau ([1984]
2000), I would like to suggest that they are also tactics of resistance.[9] They
function as short-term mechanisms that enable people to adapt to the
environment, to "take advantage of occasions and depend upon these occasions" (De Certeau [1984] 2000, 43); they are not a result of planning, but
exploit creative opportunities in everyday practices. I am interested in the
operations and actions people use every day to resist the ruling structures
and powers, in this case the structure and definitions that the legal system
makes of migrants. I therefore argue that through illegality women were
"resisting" and embodying new aspects of their nonlegal personhood by
way of learning new skills on the margins of the law and creating possibilities for themselves, even though they could not change the power
relations and structures of inequality in which they lived. Paradoxically,
these tactics contain a contradiction because they were moments of both
opportunity and resistance, as well as increased liability for deportation.

Let us return to the moment Sonia was left at Victoria Station. After
deliberating over where to go or what to do next, the group asked a bus
driver about the location of the Latin American *barrio* (neighborhood)
but received no answer. Fortunately, a woman from Ecuador who overheard their queries came to their aid and took them to Elephant and
Castle, an area in south London considered a Latin American enclave in
the city.[10] Once there, after a few phone calls and exchanges of money,
people found accommodation in various houses as well as contacts for
work. Soon afterward, Sonia found a job through subletting the NIN of a
woman who was going back to Bolivia. The NIN is a number used in the
United Kingdom in the administration of the social security system and
for tax purposes. Subletting a NIN means that by paying the holder of
the NIN £80 per month, Sonia could use the document to find work. The
practice of subletting the NIN was known as *dejar los papeles trabajando*

(keep the papers working); it was a recurrent practice among people who wanted to accumulate benefits, pay taxes, and receive a pension later by sustaining their residence in the country. Because the NIN forms part of the evidence of the right to work in the United Kingdom, when Sonia started subletting one, she was able to work in five separate places as a cleaner in central London.

The easy access to and use of NINs was possible because of a mutual agreement between employers and employees that guaranteed cheap labor.[11] This situation, however, radically changed in February 2008 when a civil penalty regime was instituted under section 15 of the Immigration, Asylum and Nationality Act of 2006, establishing tougher penalties for employers who employed illegal migrants. This new regime forced employers to monitor the immigration status of their employees by threatening them with increased fines (ranging from £5,000 to £10,000) for employing illegal migrants. But more important, the civil penalty scheme sits alongside the criminal offense of knowingly employing an illegal migrant worker, which carries a maximum custodial sentence of two years and/or an unlimited fine.[12] This system had a significant impact on the lives of my informants because many of them were suddenly required to provide original copies of passports and visas.

Despite these restrictions, Sonia managed to continue working with her fake papers and was able to pay off half of her debt back in Bolivia. Unfortunately, in February 2009 she was hit by a taxi while crossing Oxford Street on her way to her first working shift. She sustained serious injuries, including two broken legs and a fractured collarbone. It was only during the three months she spent recovering in the hospital that her undocumented status was revealed. However, because of her injuries and her disability, she was entitled to receive assistance from the state. Under the National Assistance Act (1948) local authorities must help people who are in need and/or sick; they are obliged to provide a safety net for people who are unable to take care of themselves for various reasons.[13] The help is provided to people who have, at the very least, an outstanding application at the Home Office (the ministerial department of the government responsible for immigration, security, and law and order). Thanks to this exception to the immigration rules whereby those without status could access support, Sonia received medical treatment from the National Health Service (NHS), a house, and professional care for over a year, time during which her visa application was pending. Ironically the revelation of her undocumented status gave her the opportunity to stop being an invisible cleaner and construct a social life in London with people at the local Catholic Church.

> I was ashamed of being an undocumented cleaner for a long time. I did
> not want to have any contact with anyone in London, but life had differ-
> ent plans for me and thanks to my 'illegality' I was able to make friends
> and feel like a person once again.

For others, learning illegality occurred when they started using false
documents to work. Pedro from Bolivia arrived in the United Kingdom
in June 2002, spurred on by the promise of an agency to arrange a working visa for him and a job at a fruit factory in a small town in the southern United Kingdom. The visa turned out to be a false Italian identity
document that cost him £300. After two years working in the United
Kingdom he was deported, but went back again with his wife, Lourdes,
and their two sons. Once in the United Kingdom, Lourdes applied for
an English study visa that, at the time, would allow her to work in a full-
time job.[14] In November 2004, while waiting for Lourdes's student visa,
UK Border Agency officials came to search the flat for undocumented
migrants. They discovered Pedro's use of false documents during the
search.

Pedro was warned about the criminal offense, but because his family
was in the United Kingdom, he was given until January 2005 to settle his
affairs in England and return to Bolivia. Pedro and Lourdes knew there
was nothing they could do about their legal situation or the visa; using a
false document was a criminal offense subject to a prison sentence. Their
undocumented legal reality had materialized—they needed to make a
decision and, even though staying in the United Kingdom was risky, they
decided to continue with their plans and fled to London. As Lourdes put it,

> We knew we were doing something illegal as we were running away
> from the Home Office, but we decided that it was better to live covertly
> than to return to Bolivia with empty hands. The solution for us was to
> hide; therefore if you want to disappear from the Home Office, the best
> hiding place is London.

Thanks to the anonymity provided in London, the Home Office ceased to be a
threat and the entire family effectively vanished from the system. Lourdes was
right—in many ways—London was a place where remaining invisible was not
too difficult because the myriad of cultures in the city automatically hid their
racial difference, something that could not be said of the predominantly white
town where they had lived before. However, it was this whiteness that Pedro
and Lourdes found appealing because it confirmed what they had imagined
of the United Kingdom. When they arrived in London, they believed that the
city was polluted by people from all over the world who contaminated and

distorted the English language (even though they did not speak English) and, more important, colored the place with their nonwhiteness.

Facing the reality of a multicultural London became a source of conflict and disappointment because they would have to live among *morenos* (black people) and *Indianos* (the expression people used for Indian people) or *musulmanes* (any Middle East person) and share a house with strangers. In the presence of such diversity they used their previous social, class, and racial differentiation mechanisms within their national groups to position themselves with regard to other people. As did most of my informants, they used the idioms of race and class differences that exist in Latin America to sustain their own racial and class (dis)locations in their new home. They used their alleged whiteness (that was part of their *mestizo* background) as a marker of superiority toward any nonwhite racial and ethnic minorities in the city. Lourdes and Pedro, for example, asserted their white *mestizo* background rather than their indigenous one when talking about themselves. Even though in the eyes of other Bolivians they looked indigenous and were more *morenos* (dark skin) than *blancos* (white), they did not ascribe themselves an indigenous background or identity. Furthermore, they even considered their legal status different from the status of others because of their "middle-class" backgrounds and, more important, because they had entered the country legally.

It helped that, in London, my informants' ethnic and racial markers were not identified with or particularly targeted as being those of an illegal migrant, as with Latin American migrants in the United States. It was relatively easy to blend in. This aspect sharply contrasts with the experiences of Mexican migrants in the United States studied by De Genova (2004, 2005) in which deportability is constructed around legal frameworks, surveillance, and, more important, race. By saying this, I am not suggesting that the United Kingdom does not apply or design immigration policies (or other policies) filtered by race; the historical treatment of Afro Caribbean migrants in the United Kingdom proves otherwise (see Gilroy 1987). More recently, the United Kingdom has disclosed an open policy against migration by launching campaigns such as the "Illegal, go home campaign," which, without being explicit, has a strong racial component. However, *latinos* in the United Kingdom have not been defined as racialized subjects as other groups have (i.e., those from India, Pakistan, Bangladesh, and the West Indies). This might be a result of the size of the community, their lack of official recognition as a racial or ethnic group in the United Kingdom, and the weaker historic and colonial connections with the region. Nonetheless, the state in recent years has been catching up with the problem associated with the growing population of Latin Americans in London and continuously places legal restrictions on these migrants to access the United Kingdom and visas or citizenship while here.

Clandestine Occupations

People perceived and enacted illegality in several ways according to their own life histories, social expectations, and opportunities. In this regard, Cecilia and her partner Antonio (whom she met in London) found themselves carrying out unlawful actions that went beyond the use of fake documents. The first time I visited their flat, I saw a strange narrow door with a big padlock leading to a third room in what I thought was a two-bedroom flat. When I asked Cecilia what was behind the locked door, she said it was Antonio's dental practice.[15] "I was a successful dentist until people could not pay anymore for my services. When things were fine, I had my own car and enjoyed going out with friends who were like me. I had a good life," he told me once. By stepping into illegality and committing a serious criminal offense by working without a proper permit, he was nonetheless reclaiming part of his middle-class personhood. Having his dental practice at home meant that he could work in his profession instead of as a cleaner and assert his role as the main breadwinner. Still, there were important contradictions at play because by working at home he became the main carer for their baby daughter while Cecilia worked as a domestic worker during the day. This, in his view, was a problematic reversal of traditional gender roles within the household that did not correlate with his ideas of a proper family life.[16] "Cecilia should be caring for my daughter instead of working; as the man of the family I should be able to provide for my family, but life in London makes it impossible," he told me.

Unable to get Cecilia out of work and achieve his ideal traditional family life, practicing dentistry provided him with some sense of self-respect and pride. He maintained his clandestine practice for several years. In May 2012, however, they were visited by the Metropolitan Police, who wanted to see a former flatmate suspected of selling drugs. Antonio had nothing to do with this, but a few weeks later the police returned with a search warrant to inspect his dental practice and detained him. During the criminal case that unfolded, Antonio and Cecilia's illegal status was revealed. Antonio was not deported immediately because of a pending criminal case, but had to report to the immigration offices once a week. Having migrants return to the immigration offices on a weekly basis is a way in which the state executes power—both physical and psychological—over migrants. In addition to demanding their presence once a week, immigrations officers retain the information and knowledge about migrants' cases and deportation orders, leaving people like Antonio and Cecilia in an anxious and uncertain limbo. For them, the weekly encounters with the UK Border Agency authorities exposed them as deportable subjects who were uncertain about their future. Despite this, they refused to think of themselves as criminals who had carried out an unlawful act. As Cecilia remarked,

> Antonio is not a criminal, he is a good partner and a good father, he is just trying to provide for our family and for his two daughters back in Bolivia. He does not have the permit to work as a dentist in London, therefore he has to do it clandestinely. But he studied odontology, it is not fair for him to clean offices or houses, to do work that is beneath him.

At the beginning of this section, I referred to migrants engaging in clandestine occupations to make a living a London. My analysis would not be complete without taking into account the most clandestine occupation of all, that is, sex work. As I will show, matters were more complicated among sex workers whose illegal statuses were an issue of concern within their already-illegal profession. In Britain it is against the law to loiter or solicit on the street, to solicit clients by advertisement, to run a house of ill repute (brothel), or to financially or materially benefit from immoral earnings (this includes living expenses and financially supporting family or partners). In sharp contrast, workers *do* comply with the law if they sell sex in the privacy of their homes. Services sold in private flats resemble domestic environments where sex is exchanged between partners. "I sometimes feel more like a mistress or even a therapist at this job than a prostitute. Men come to the flat not because of sex, but because we offer comfort and a very unique form of intimacy," Sabrina said. Nevertheless, the same sex transaction is criminalized when more than one person works in the same place because it is automatically considered a brothel under the law.[17] Because of the financial investment involved, working in private flats is not a straightforward decision. Despite that, it was considered the best form of work within the sex industry. For women in my research it represented a way to become entrepreneurs running their own businesses, having total control over their finances, and meeting regular clients who could provide long-term benefits.

Amanda and Sabrina shared a flat in one of the financial districts in London for five months until they were caught by the police and were accused of, but not prosecuted for, working in a brothel. It all started when Amanda received a client who was a police officer in disguise. Two days prior to this, I was at the flat with them when a client sent a text saying that he had just been intercepted in the lift by another sex worker and was therefore leaving. Amanda was furious.

> "Why would she do that? There is enough work for everyone in London, we should not be stealing each other's clients. It is already difficult to deal with neighbors, now we have to deal with women trying to steal our clients," she said.

After the incident, I went downstairs and became a gatekeeper to make sure that the "rivals" would not intercept their new clients. As Sabrina said, however, it was just a matter of time before they faced more problems. Indeed, two days after the incident Amanda received a visit from five female police officers and one male officer. They were looking for evidence of a brothel, trafficking victims, and drugs. Because Amanda had signed the tenancy agreement, she was liable to be accused of pimping Sabrina and administering the "brothel."[18] It was very hard for her to prove that she was not a madam and to argue (untruthfully) that she was unaware that working with a friend in the same flat was indeed a crime.

During the raid, Sabrina's undocumented status was revealed. She was asked to give evidence that she was in fact returning to Brazil. Luckily, she dealt with a sympathetic police officer who decided not to call the Home Office to deport her. Because officers could not find any traces of drugs or trafficking, they only gave them a warning and told them to move to separate locations. They, like many other women working in the area, were tolerated as long as they kept their work private and unseen from the public so as not to disturb the moral order. After moving to separate flats, Sabrina's concerns centered on the threat of deportation, something that she said had not crossed her mind before. Getting deported would frustrate her financial goals and future plans back in Brazil.

The experiences of my informants show that in situations of structural precariousness and lack of opportunities, entering the realm of illegality is inescapable and inexorable. Using false NINs or documents or engaging in clandestine occupations represented the means to guarantee a steady income. For people like Sabrina, Amanda, and Antonio, it also became a way to mitigate and resist some of the class and status dislocations that migration produced. On a day-to-day basis, migrants' illegality is irrelevant;

it only becomes an issue in certain situations, such as facing immigration authorities. As a result, as Susan Coutin explains, undocumented individuals move in and out of existence. These spaces of illegality or undocumentedness are permeable and blurred. It is only "when legal reality is superimposed on daily life, they are once more in a space of nonexistence" (Coutin 2000, 40),[19] a space that is characterized by the threat and the possibility of deportation, hence the dissolution of their dreams and aspirations.

Narratives of Everyday Anxiety

Migrants experienced varying degrees of unease while working illegally. However, the anxiety produced by their undocumented statuses was also experienced while people commuted in the city and therefore faced the possibility of encountering authorities. Ultimately, they wanted to become as invisible as they could to remain unseen by the police and by other people who might be able to perceive their illegality. During my fieldwork I had the opportunity to witness authorities moving back and forth between the different bus stops in front of the shopping center of Elephant and Castle. It is a place where migrants buy Latin American food and clothes and get a *latino* haircut or manicure without having to struggle with the language.[20] Because of the strong presence of migrants, Elephant and Castle is one of the places that the Border Agency keeps under surveillance and targets for random immigration checks and deportations. On some occasions officers do no more than walk around the bus stops, scaring people by their mere presence. It is relatively easy to distinguish those who are afraid of having an encounter with Border Agency authorities or the police because they immediately change their route or hide. My informants had similar reactions the moment they detected the presence of any authority. Instead of walking down the sidewalk next to the bus stops, we would leave the street and venture into the Shopping Centre for a "shortcut." People also hid from the police and informed their friends about the presence of authorities by sending warning text messages. The policing of public spaces conspicuously exacerbates what Nicholas De Genova describes as migrants' sense of deportability. As he puts it, "illegality is lived through a palpable sense of deportability—the possibility of deportation, which is to say, the possibility of being removed from the space of the [US nation-state]"—or any nation state, in this case (De Genova 2004, 161). Deportability is then a strategy used by the authorities to render illegal migrants a distinctly disposable community. Because of the anxiety surrounding public transportation, Lourdes's husband, Pedro, decided to cycle instead of taking the bus to save money and avoid the raids that were taking place in south London. He had an accident while riding his bicycle and, as a result, entered the system and was deported to Bolivia.

> At 9 am I was riding my bicycle and crashed into another bicycle. The accident caught the attention of several people including police officers who came to see what had happened. The police asked for ID and as I did not have any documents with my photo on it, they started asking me more and more questions. I guess I started getting nervous and they arrested me under suspicion of being illegal in this country. They took me to the police station, [and] before I knew it, a week later, I was back in Bolivia.

When the police caught him, he was able to briefly contact his wife Lourdes and warn her that the immigration authorities might come to the flat and detain the whole family; as a result, Lourdes and her two sons temporarily moved to a friend's house.

Pedro's deportation unleashed a wave of anxiety in Lourdes that affected her mental and physical well-being. While waiting to hear from Pedro, Lourdes's anxiety grew considerably—not only when she was on the street, but also especially when she was at home.[21] Even when the door was locked and she had the company of flatmates, Lourdes was unable to feel safe. Pedro's deportation enhanced the "temporality of everyday risk" (Willen 2007, 22) as she was waiting to be caught by the police. The threat of deportation loomed even in her sleep and gave her nightmares. As she told me,

> I keep dreaming about the police coming to the flat. They are looking for our passports, turning all our clothes inside out, looking under the bed to see if there is anyone hiding. I am there with my two kids, under the bed hiding; suddenly the officer finds us and grabs my children from under the bed away from me. This is where I wake up, sweating and nervous, almost feeling that I am about to cry.

Pedro's deportation not only exacerbated Lourdes's liminality in London, but also infused her home with a frightening sense of penetrability, porousness, and danger. The terror of being caught by the police reinforced her personhood as deportable and created significant ruptures in the future of the family because she was forced to envisage a new unwanted present/future without Pedro.

In a similar vein, Angelica suffered episodes of anxiety for a long time after the police raided the place where she used to live. For some years she lived in west London and shared a flat with other Brazilian migrants, who she suspected were mostly undocumented. Immigration police officers came to the flat searching for illegal migrants in the middle of the day; most people were at work except for her, a Brazilian Portuguese man, and another Brazilian man who worked as a cleaner during night shifts. There was no place to hide, and she was asked to show her documents. She had none, but rapidly made up a story about how she was in the middle of her visa application and so the Home Office had her passport. She managed to show some papers from her local clinic in London, gave proof of holding a National Health Service number, and made up a story about how she had lost the letter from the Home Office. After being questioned for more than half an hour, the police decided not to arrest her. However, they arrested the Brazilian flatmate who was undocumented and was not able to evade the arrest by constructing a believable lie.

After this event, Angelica (who had been previously deported from Portugal) was unable to sleep for weeks; she was often reluctant to leave her room and started experiencing constant nightmares. Her dreams revolved around the moment when the police banged on the door and came into the house. "In my dream the police are standing outside my room. I am able to see the feet of the officer through the tiny gap between the door and the floor. The officer is there, without moving, just waiting for me to make a noise and enter my room," she told me. Her anxiety increased and for a couple of months she was convinced that the police were always waiting for her outside the flat.

When walking down the street with Angelica to return to her flat, she would ask me to walk ahead and check to see whether there was some-one at the door, or nearby, who looked like an immigration officer. In the meantime, she would stay hidden around the corner, waiting for me to return and let her know that the street was clear. "Home" felt unsafe and the people she lived with seemed untrustworthy. It took a while to feel normal again and she regained that feeling only when she moved to a new place, with strangers who did not know anything about her life or her legal status. Although the new place provided a respite, a temporary space of existence, the risk of being discovered by other people or reported to the authorities remained a latent threat.

The everyday illegality as a way of-being-in-the-world reveals the power of legal categories. My informants found themselves trapped and embodying a way of being-in-the-world that was, most of the time, alienating. They existed in a liminal space in which legal vulnerability and the terror of being caught by the police, each mutually reinforcing the other, emphasize migrants' personhood as deportable, thus creating further uncertainties. Despite these uncertainties, keeping the family together and providing a better future were recurrent reasons for people to remain in the country and engage in further illegality that then increased their deportability. What kept them going was knowing that if they were able to withstand the burden of being undocumented, they might, at some point in the future, gain the opportunity to become legal, to become citizens and thus take a significant step toward realizing their middle-class ambitions and migration dreams.

The Long Way to Legality

Current restrictions on migrants have made it almost impossible for them to retain their initial legal status and/or achieve a different one. Recent changes to student visas have affected both prospective and current students who were previously allowed to work part-time and whose partners were allowed to work full-time under the terms of their visas. To extend a visa, migrants are now required to complete a higher-level English test and prove that they are actually studying. Earlier, many were able to retain the fiction of being students while working full-time and attending classes infrequently or not at all. Many of the people I met had paid student fees to private colleges (£2,000–£3,000 a year) for several years to maintain their legal status, but this has now become much more difficult because the government has clamped down on bogus colleges that charge fees without offering courses.

When Jovanna arrived in London, she started working using the NIN of a woman from Bolivia. Her income was deposited into the account of the possessor of the NIN, who started stealing the money. To avoid further problems, Jovanna decided to enroll in an English course to get a student visa and thus gain access to a part-time work permit. At the time (2001) and until 2011, it was possible for tourists to change the status of their visa while in the United Kingdom, a practice that many migrants used to prove that they had some legal footing there.[22] Like many migrants, Jovanna took advantage of her student visa and managed to work over forty hours a week for different cleaning companies and in private homes for more than seven years. This was common practice among many of my informants even though they were, according to the law, engaging in illicit practices by breaching their visa restrictions (Menjívar 2006). Nowadays it is not possible to work on a student visa (i.e., while studying English). The current and growing impositions and legal restrictions on low-skilled migrants are increasingly defining distinct types of persons, drawing a stark divide between the "desirable" and the "deportable" person. For those who do not fit the desirable category (such as professional migrants and investors, among others), the constantly changing regulations force them to become and remain semilegal or undocumented for longer periods of time, hoping that at some point they would be able to regularize their legal status. In the United Kingdom it is still the case that migrants' perseverance and endurance of the anxiety produced by being illegal can help them acquire temporary or permanent resident visas.

For instance, retaining one's student visa allows migrants to accumulate years of residency so they can eventually apply for a residence visa.[23] Under current UK immigration law, those who enter the United Kingdom and remain there legally for ten years continuously—either as students or in possession of some other category of visa—are permitted to apply for permanent residence or, in legal parlance, Indefinite Leave to Remain (ILR). For those who become undocumented, either by overstaying their temporary visas or by becoming semilegal, gaining legal status is an arduous process because it requires them to navigate tightening and changing immigration rules.[24] One route to legality—at least until July 9, 2012—was to remain in the United Kingdom undetected for fourteen years and then prove that one had done so. People could then apply for permanent residence. In 2012, however, the state amended the law, lengthening the period from fourteen to twenty years.

Among my informants, one of the most common ways of legalizing status was to apply to the Home Office based on article 8 of the European Convention for the Protection of Human Rights. This article establishes that "everyone has the right to respect his private and family life, his home and his correspondence." The second part of the article establishes that the state should not interfere in an individual's enjoyment of his or her family or private life except "as . . . is necessary in a democratic society in the interests of national security, public safety or the economic well-being of the country, for the prevention of disorder or crime, for the protection of health or morals, or for the protection of the rights and freedoms of others." In the context of immigration law, and much to the chagrin of the signatory states, article 8 has been interpreted liberally by the courts as conferring rights on migrants who accumulate time in and ties to the host country even though they have been there illegally—the stronger the established ties or "family life" or "private life," the stronger a migrant's claim to legalizing his or her status. Children's lengthy and sustained ties to the host country have been given enhanced protection; as a rule of thumb, seven years' residence in the case of a child was often enough to provide the basis for a successful application for the child and, by extension, his or her family.[25]

The success of these applications often depends on how much evidence lawyers are able to gather to prove that migrants indeed have an established life in the United Kingdom. Lawyers are in charge of reconfiguring the undocumented person by piecing together a suitable, desirable, family-oriented migrant who has integrated. They can prove it by showing that they speak English, take part actively in the community (e.g., as church members or volunteers), or have English friends and ties in London (see James and Killick 2012). By proving that they have acculturated themselves, applicants argue that deportation or removal from the United Kingdom would be a traumatic experience for them and, more specifically, for their children. The use of supporting evidence such as letters from friends (especially British people), employers, church members, or teachers is fundamental in proving that they are rooted in the United Kingdom.

This type of application was not always successful because the Home Office argues that children could easily return to their countries of origin and readapt. Notwithstanding, I witnessed several successful cases during my fieldwork. The outcome of a successful application resulted in a Discretionary Leave to Remain visa that was granted for a period of three to five years. After this period, applicants must renew their Discretionary Leave to Remain for an extra three to five years and eventually apply for an ILR.[26] The Discretionary Leave to Remain speaks of yet another form of managing temporal legal statuses that places people in a legal but still uncertain situation because the state has the power to decide whether— but, more important, when—citizenship will be granted.

This onerous road to citizenship has effectively been designed to make a new category of people: residents with fewer rights than those possessed by citizens. At the same time, the law forces undesirable/low-skilled migrants to remain undocumented for long periods of time and wait for years to obtain legal documents. This draconian system of temporary visas and permits constructs a particular person who is positioned in a state of limbo and endures long periods of waiting (although people possessing an ILR can still live in the United Kingdom permanently). However, it has become increasingly difficult for people to get an ILR because the rules change constantly. Migrants must remain invisible or semi-invisible or prove that they have a pending application at the Home Office. Fundamentally, they must prove over a long period of time that they are worthy of becoming permanent residents and eventually citizens. Uncertainty remains, however, because immigration status, legality, and citizenship are not predictable.

Conclusion

A nuanced ethnographic account of the everyday lives of migrants shows that undocumented statuses and illegality painfully affect the external structure of migrants' worlds as well as their subjectivities. These alterations begin even before migration because illegality is imagined and anxiously lived before people's journeys. Once they become undocumented and therefore embody a new way of being-in-the-world, they inhabit the world in anxious ways that affect their bodies and minds. Their status, that of being unwanted, becomes a crude reality the moment they encounter state authorities and are reminded of their vulnerability; it is at this point when the threat of deportation creeps into their homes, dreams, and hopes for the future.

Entering the realm of illegality is ineludible; it is a consequence of wider forms of state control that are designed to maintain certain people deprived of citizenship rights and therefore guarantee a continuous flow and surplus of cheap labor. Illegality represents an overwhelming experience amounting, in some cases, to a state of invisibility. Its embodiment affects migrants' personhood because they are required to learn new skills and dispositions, new modes of being-in-the-world, to endure the liminality of the new legal status. Hopes and expectations for the future are hindered by this new status, and the future becomes more uncertain that it already is. However, regardless of the effects of illegality, people create tactics to temporarily overcome the anxieties and make efforts to normalize their lives and create opportunities for themselves. Migrants' everyday tactics shed light on the mechanisms that people use to take advantage of the opportunities they have in their everyday lives, to resist the liminality that they must endure on a daily basis.

In the next two chapters I continue my analysis of women's subjectivities as migrants. Both chapters show how intimate labor, because of its caring and emotional implications, produces a series of personal dislocations and moral conflicts that women need to resolve. They do this while finding themselves trapped in a global market that—although it is sustained by women's reproductive labor—promotes exploitation and inequality as yet another postcolonial practice of domination.

PART II

....

Dislocations at Work

CHAPTER 3

....

Domestic Work
and the Commodification
of Care

W hile in previous chapters I explained women's identification as migrants (documented or undocumented) and the contradictory frameworks that such identity produced in terms of race, class, and status, this chapter is more directly concerned with the exploration of personal negotiations—including moral considerations and ethical choices—of such contradictions within domestic work. As Rhacel Salazar Parreñas (2001, 150) and Pei Chia Lan (2006) have suggested, the main paradox and central dislocation that defines the experiences of middle-class migrant domestic workers is the juxtaposition between economic emancipation and a decline in social status. This dislocation is a concrete effect of larger structural forces of globalization that include a lack of recognition of educational qualifications and work experience of women from the Third World in developed countries, combined with restrictions on social mobility in Latin America. Acknowledging that this dislocation is pivotal in women's lives, I explore additional dislocations that women experience while dealing with and negotiating the conundrums that accompany the commodification of intimacy within domestic work. Following Nicole Constable, in this chapter I explore the commodification of intimacy within intimate labor as a way "to illuminate power relations inherent in a variety of intimate relations" without losing sight of the "power and the potentially liberating and transformative aspects of intimate subjectivities" (2009, 59). In this regard, my intention is to illuminate

how even in situations of precarious intimate labor, women assert themselves as ethical actors making choices, resisting power, and reconstructing
aspects of their migrant subjectivities.

My analysis contributes to the literature on domestic work—particularly
migrant domestic work that has acknowledged the increasingly significant
role that the occupation plays in transnational global markets. By privileg-
ing the historical, local, and contextual analysis of domestic work within a
capitalist world system, scholars have shown myriad patterns, practices, and
social dynamics that constitute domestic work in different regions of the
world.[1] There has been a particular emphasis on the intersections that exist
between gender, race, and labor among domestic migrant workers to explain
the racialization of particular ethnic groups associated with specific traits
related to womanhood and reproductive labor.[2]

In recent years, many studies have focused on the well-oiled transnational export industry of care workers—including those from the middle
classes—from different countries in the Global South to either the Global
North or the new rich economies in the south.[3] Within Europe several studies have considered and explored the particularities of domestic migrant
workers in different countries, thereby raising vital questions about the
diverse composition of new forms of social reproduction.[4] Although there
are important contrasts between these studies, there is tacit agreement that
first, domestic work reproduces and sustains economic, social, and racial
inequalities between women, and second, because of its caring nature, it
can produce significant personal conundrums and fractures in women's
lives. My own work has been significantly enabled by these earlier studies
and is partly motivated by them. I further the debate by critically assessing
women's understandings and experiences of the commodified intimacy
that results from domestic work. I do it by exploring domestic work as a
class and racial dislocation in women's lives, but in contrast to other studies, I enter the realm of morality to explore women's moral estrangements
and its accompanying ethical choices while caring at work.

Degrading Contradictions

Following Parreñas's notion of domestic work as a form of dislocation—
especially among middle-class women—my informants defined domestic work as a profound and significant personal dislocation in their lives
in London. As I have explained in the introduction of this book, women
explained their dislocations as feeling "out of place" or "feeling not like
themselves." This assertion partly referred to their decline in social status

resulting from the perception of domestic work as a demeaning job. In Latin America it is widely assumed among the middle and upper classes that domestic workers will do the manual work that they are not supposed to do. Employing a domestic worker is not only perceived as a necessity; it is also a fundamental part of their class identity and social privilege. In London, middle-class migrant women were deprived of their privileged position as employers of domestic help. Within their own national contexts, similar to their middle- or upper-class employers in London, my informants hired poor and, in most cases, racially different women to help with the housework and children. They talked about their subjective experiences in similar ways according to kindred understandings of the occupation. Their narratives included subtle and not so subtle forms of social and racial inequalities and prejudices that persist in Latin America, where they had been the bosses and not the maids.

Among my informants from Ecuador, Bolivia, and Peru, hiring poor uneducated or indigenous women (*inditas* or *cholitas*) was commonplace. Lesley Gill (1994), for example, elucidates how domestic work has been a persisting and expanding form of employment for indigenous women in Bolivia structured around historical processes of class formation, gender, and ethnicity.[5] Similar explanations can be argued for the rest of Latin America where the racial construction of the indigenous person has placed them at the bottom end of society vis-à-vis whites or *mestizos*. In connection, women from Brazil (and sometimes from Venezuela and Honduras) talked about the predominance of black women doing domestic work. These social dynamics have their roots in the history of slavery and racial relations in Brazil, where domestic servants were the slaves of their masters.[6] These tensions persist among middle- and upper-class Brazilians and domestic workers, regardless of discourses of love and appreciation, especially for those who devote their lives to serving the family (Goldstein 2003, 85–88). Nonetheless, employers maintain their class privileges by virtue of different forms of patronage and the designations of others— not white—as inferior.[7] In significant ways, domestic work exposes the systematic class and racial inequalities as well as the racialized oppression that is woven into the historic constructions of national identities.

Perhaps unsurprisingly for most of my informants, the racial and class hierarchies that persist in Latin America masked and somehow normalized the problematic connections between class, race, and domestic work. So, when women talked about their own dislocating experiences regarding the job, they referred to poverty and a lack of education as two of the underlying reasons for the existence and persistence of domestic work in their own countries. The meanings and consequences of racial difference (except for some of my Brazilian informants) were barely considered. In their new fragile and contradictory reality in London, they were often the low-class women who were hired by white middle- and upper-class people. Consequently, their personal conflicts were structured around having to painfully endure the obligation to take on these demeaning jobs. Notably, their new roles as domestic workers, along with their experiences of class and racial contradictions, contributed to the set of personal dislocations that women talked about during my fieldwork.

Freelancers: Freedom versus Alienation

I begin my examination of women's dislocations by identifying and describing the two types of domestic work performed by my informants. Domestic work exists in many varied forms. Women worked as free-lance domestic workers, as nannies/domestic workers, or as live-in domestic workers. Those who worked as freelance domestic workers were paid by the hour, could work in several households, and were not in charge of caring (directly) for family members. Because of the relative informality and flex-ibility involved, this form of work represented the most important source of employment for undocumented migrants.

Access to work greatly depended on social networks and women's personal abilities. For instance, Juliana firmly believed that if you could manage to establish a solid relationship with one of your employers, even if you did not have much contact with him or her, this could guarantee you better access to more sources of employment. Word-of-mouth rec-ommendations were based on trust and sympathy between the employer and the employee; accordingly, trusting the recommendation of a friend or acquaintance (or a previous domestic worker) was enough for employ-ers to share their private space and the keys to their homes with a stranger. Employers who hired freelance domestic workers never asked for docu-mentation or visas, thus significantly facilitating women's opportunities to make a living in London. For someone like Juliana, this meant being able to send money back to Brazil for the construction of her house in Minas. After working approximately eight hours a day (including some Saturdays), she managed to earn between £150 and £250 a week and sent, on average, up to £300 in monthly remittances back home. Although she admitted that being a *faxineira* (domestic worker) was difficult for her, she was earning more money than she had as a switchboard operator in Brazil and was enjoying greater flexibility with her time. Despite these seeming advantages, she had to endure the hustle and bustle of running from one job to the next and the tedious, endless repetition of the same types of activities during the day.

Juliana's day starts at six o'clock in the morning when she wakes up to get from her flat in southwest London to Victoria, where she cleans the house of a British family for three hours. I arranged to meet her at Victoria Station at eleven o'clock in the morning to spend the day with her. By noon we got to south London to clean the house of a British Portuguese family for two hours. After this, we went to northeast London to clean the house of a woman from Puerto Rico for two hours and then to a house in northwest London that belonged to an elderly Portuguese lady for the last two hours of her working day. Every other day includes the cleaning of a flat in central London for two hours for a couple from France, followed by five different houses scattered across two boroughs in southwest London. Juliana spent her days cleaning houses and commuting. She ate on buses and did not return home to her shared room until eight or nine o'clock at night. Every fortnight on Saturdays she cleaned the house of an English couple. Sunday was her day off, a day she usually dedicated to going to the Catholic Church in south London (which held services in Portuguese) and spending time with her sister and her son.

Juliana was entrusted with the keys of her employers' houses and had the freedom to manage her own schedule during the day as she pleased. In this respect, she did indeed enjoy greater flexibility and autonomy than other workers. Despite this, the perks of freelance domestic work did not compensate for the loneliness and isolation she felt while cleaning the houses (except on Saturdays, when the English couple was at home). "It gets really lonely, very quiet. Sometimes I turned on the radio or put my music on my phone, so I can feel less lonely," she told me. The presence of the inhabitants of the homes was evident in the piles of dirty laundry, dishes, unmade beds, and messy bathrooms. Sometimes employers left notes with instructions for Juliana to follow; sometimes they left food for her lunch and sometimes "gifts." They always left money on the table to pay for her services. Even though she managed to cope with the everyday cleaning tasks and claimed not to be particularly bothered by them, she suffered from the silence and isolation that characterized her work. One of the ways in which she coped with such ongoing alienation was to promote contact with her employers—to connect with them on a personal level— despite only brief encounters with them.

Sarita from Honduras also suffered from the isolation of being a freelance domestic worker. Sarita's workday started at five o'clock in the morning cleaning offices—a job she secured with the help of a fake Spanish passport—and was followed by cleaning several houses. Like Juliana, she spent most of her day alone and in silence. "I feel like a ghost, getting in and out of people's homes. I do not talk to anyone, I have no interaction with anyone until I go back home every night to my family," she told me. The invisibility that Sarita encountered every day at work was aggravated by her anxiety about her undocumented status. Although the isolation protected her from the deportation she constantly dreaded, it was also the result of broader structural economic forces that sustain precarious working conditions for domestic workers, particularly for those migrants who were undocumented and had very limited employment opportunities beyond cleaning empty houses. In retrospect, she longed for her life in Honduras and the poorly paid job at the food stand. "At least I felt like a human there, I spent the day talking to people. I never felt this lonely in my life," she said. For Sarita, going back home at night to her tiny studio flat to be with her family offered respite and reminded her she was not alone in London.

Sarita had been working for four years for the same employers, people she hardly ever saw, but who she claimed trusted her in their homes. In contrast to other domestic workers, she did not take advantage of her employers' absence to leave work early; it was "not correct" because it would be a betrayal of the trust her employers had granted her. Her work ethic forbade her from cheating them. This work ethic and the emphasis on honesty were used as ways to distinguish herself from other people:

> There are people like us [Sarita and her husband] who migrated because we want to work and advance in life. But there are other migrants who take advantage of their employers, do not work, and the moment they get documents they just abuse the system and stop working.

In this regard, Sarita and her husband were adamant about fashioning the image of hard-working migrants who had come to London to provide for their family and build a future for their daughter. Maintaining and nurturing the image of a hard-working migrant enabled her to deal with some of the dislocations that the occupation produced. This image could also bear fruit in the future because she knew that by the time they were ready to apply for a visa and needed proof that they were worthy candidates to stay in the country, she would be able to get good references from her employers that might help them with their immigration application.

Neither Juliana nor Sarita had ever worked as a domestic worker before going to London, and both claimed that they would not have done this kind of work in their home countries because of the occupation's low status and racial implications. However, they managed to mitigate their shame by contrasting the amount of money they were earning in London with their income back home. Juliana once explained this to me:

> If you were a *faxineira* in Brazil you would not be able to build a house like the one I am building right now in Minas. But if you come here and become a *faxineira*, you can earn enough money to build a house like mine.

Furthermore, she explained that in Brazil being a domestic worker was a prevalent job for *pretas* or mulattas (black or mixed race), because those who had lighter skin automatically had better opportunities in life. Juliana's explanation resonates with Peggy Lovell's (2000) argument regarding how the majority of Afro-Brazilians remain confined to domestic work because this occupation has the lowest wages within the Brazilian economy. Although Juliana (a self-identified mulatta) and I rarely talked about racial politics, she was aware of and explained to me the correlation that existed between race and poverty in some parts of Brazil. According to her, there was a sharp difference between being a domestic worker in London and in Brazil. In Brazil, the inequalities that persisted between whites and blacks were quite evident; they were reproduced everywhere, even in the media: "you see it all over, for example in the soap operas black women always play the role of the maid, they are never the protagonist," she told me. In contrast, London provided a less differentiated racial landscape because being a mulatta and a domestic worker was not inextricably linked as it was in Brazil. According to Juliana, race and class were not necessarily markers of one's job in London; it was mainly a result of being migrant.[8] Nonetheless, like Sarita, Juliana believed that there were several types of migrants:

> There are all these migrants with no education that have no other choice but to work in cleaning. For me this job is temporary, I am only doing this because I do not speak English and because I need to finish the construction of my house in Brazil. But once I get back to Brazil I will go back to my job and my life.

By distinguishing between the two countries and the racial politics that accompany domestic work, Juliana could place herself on one side of the spectrum, where she was not a mulatta working as a *faxineira*, but an educated migrant temporarily working as a domestic worker. It was not her African ancestry that determined her occupation in London, but her condition as a migrant with fewer opportunities.

As an illustration of what, in Juliana's words, could be referred to as a *racial democracy* in London, she told me that the English couple she worked for on Saturdays had invited her and her son to a birthday party. "They introduced me and my son as their friends. This would never happen in Brazil. No one invites the maid to the party, people from different social classes in Brazil do not mingle," she said. She was convinced that most of her employers in London did not think of her as inferior because of her job. This was proof to her that the social meanings of domestic work in Brazil and London were entirely different; in London she could be a *faxineira* and maintain a certain dignity that accompanied her education and middle-class identity.

Despite their different resources in terms of idioms of social inclusion or exclusion, freedom or alienation, women found ways to negotiate the personal estrangements that domestic work produced. In contrast to the alienation and loneliness that Juliana and Sarita tried to overcome, other women found working alone in empty houses appealing and liberating. For Cecilia and Jovanna, the loss of status and the shame accompanying the occupation characterized the way in which they maintained themselves as service providers who refused to develop any close intimacy with employers or accept jobs that would include child care. "I feel ashamed and do not want to see my employers. I would rather stay invisible and not have any contact with them. I know it is an honest job, but it makes me feel diminished," Jovanna told me. In Bolivia she had maids—they were generally poor indigenous women who worked at the houses of white people like her. Now she was not the boss, but the maid. Therefore, avoiding any contact with employers offered a sort of shelter and respite from personal embarrassment. Likewise, cleaning empty houses gave her a chance to do as she pleased and avoid the tribulations of care work—by *not* caring. Their choice of not caring was an active decision women used to exercise some sort of agency, some resistance against the menial labor they had to do in London.

> "It is not that I do not care, but I am a maid cleaning empty houses, picking up the shit from other people that I do not care about, therefore I clean as quick as I can. I really do not want to be bothered or spend more time than I have to. There are other things that I really need to care about in my life. This is just a shitty job," Jovanna told me.

Furthermore, by not caring, women like Jovanna and Cecilia could temporarily counteract their dislocated statuses as domestic workers and maintain a sense of self through the guardianship of their ideological middle-class and gendered identities. Unlike Sarita, Cecilia and Jovanna were convinced that as long as the houses were clean and the employers were satisfied, it was unimportant whether they finished the work in one hour instead of two. The liberty and invisibility that typified freelance domestic work were strategically used as a way to temporarily regain some control over, even reinstate, social hierarchies that had been practically (if not ideologically) reversed in their current lives.

One example of the quest for invisibility (related to the shame associated with the job) within the work space is the case of fifty-seven-year-old Luciana from Brazil. She worked every day as a cleaner for an architect's firm in west London and at an elderly people's home at the weekends. Luciana had come to London after living in Italy for many years. She said London was her final stop—her retirement plan—before returning to Brazil. The first time I met her, Luciana was very keen to tell me why and how she obtained the cleaning job at the firm. She had gone to the office after reading an ad for the position. She remembered waiting at the office with her curriculum vitae ready:

> There were so many women waiting, I was just there sitting feeling quite relaxed. I was not taking it too seriously, I was even dressed in my usual hippie/artistic way, when suddenly the boss passed by and glanced at us. At that moment I had the feeling that he had chosen me, yes, he had chosen me because he saw I was not a real cleaner but an artist like himself.

She defined herself as an artist who spent her days working on her art in her tiny room in west London. Working for only two hours every morning (from five to seven o'clock) allowed her to have the rest of the day free to work on her art. It was this very identity that caused her to feel humiliated by her job and that made her insist on the need to remain invisible as a cleaner at the firm. Paradoxically, her identity as an artist also pushed her to prove—while working—that she was not in fact a cleaner. Her attempts to bring about such complicated, everyday reversals were described as small actions that she thought were unique to someone who had never done this work before: "Yes, I clean but I also arrange papers, carpets, books, and notes for the architects in a way that a cleaner would never know how to do." These actions were signs of the fact that she was not a real cleaner.

Using the same logic, Luciana did extra work at her job on weekends. At the elderly peoples' home where she worked, she was only in charge of cleaning. However, because of the presence of other migrant workers, she felt the urge to demonstrate that she was different. Most people who worked at the retirement home as care workers were women from the

Proving Identity

Philippines. As the only Brazilian among the gang of Filipino women, as she called them, Luciana felt completely out of place and alienated (although she was of mixed race she self-identified as white). She felt she was nothing like them.

First, she was an artist and they were care workers who, according to her, mistreated and did not "really care" about the elderly people at the home. Second, they were uneducated, rude, and had no manners. Finally, the main difference stemmed from the fact that they were always hanging out with each other and were not interested in mingling or adapting to European culture, unlike Luciana. She was better than they were. As a way of contravening her ambiguous status in relation to the other care workers, she established close relationships with some of the elderly people at work. After finishing work, she usually spent extra hours brushing and doing the elderly ladies' hair, giving them manicures and grooming them. Engaging with and caring for elderly people were strategies she used to get close to people she regarded as similar to her—despite her racial difference and lack of English skills—and prove outwardly that she was different from other cleaners, thereby reasserting her idealized class location.

"I Am No Maid; Call Me Housekeeper/Nanny"

Protecting class and racial ideals were, for some women, only possible by entering into close proximity with rich people instead of viewing themselves as invisible workers. For some women, working as live-in domestic workers in wealthy and exclusive neighborhoods in London signified a radical difference from their counterparts elsewhere. Aside from earning a stable (and higher) monthly income compared to other domestic workers, they could claim to be living among the white upper classes of London, instead of sharing a flat with other migrants in less desirable areas of the city. For Amelia, working in a rich area of London was indispensable to her feeling less of a *cachifa* ("maid" in Venezuela); "It is not the same to be a *cachifa* in Holland Park [rich predominantly white neighborhood in west London] as it is to be a *cachifa* in the Elephant and Castle," Amelia told me on several occasions.

Despite the "advantages" that the proximity to the elite represented, the work of live-in domestic workers not only included the performance of similar types of activities around the house, but also overall proved to be more demanding, hostile, and alienating. This was because of the ambiguous proximity to employers, the absolute intertwining of work and private life (or lack thereof), and the incessant performance of emotional labor.

As a result, gaining access to live-in domestic work had to be done through relatively formalized routes. Although several recruitment agencies specialized in offering the services of live-in domestic workers, none of my informants used them; instead, women used the Catholic Church of St. Mary in Chelsea, west London, as a gateway to employment.[9] Similar to placement agencies, the church used the stereotype of the middle-class Latin American women who had recently arrived from Spain with European passports as a matching parameter for the needs of the upper-white-class congregation who needed domestic workers and/or nannies.[10]

At the church I was able to observe how women presented themselves in particular ways in front of the nuns, for example, by talking with a Spanish accent, dressing in fancy clothes, and helping with chores after the mass. "We have to play a role with the nuns, come to church and prove that we are well-educated and have experience in Europe. They know we need the jobs, especially old women like us, therefore they put us in the most complicated households, with the worst *jefas*," Cristina told me. While the nuns had recently started looking for younger candidates, they were still giving jobs to mature women who were mothers and who therefore would "naturally" be more patient with children and better able to work as live-in domestic workers and deal with the idiosyncratic behavior of their young, rich employers.

Live-in domestic workers generally followed a standard pattern of working—they all had similar schedules and carried out similar activities. They usually started working at seven o'clock in the morning and finished their shifts ten to twelve hours later, with an hour a day for lunch and rest. Their everyday tasks included cleaning the house, washing clothes, cooking, ironing, and caring for the children. Cristina worked in a three-story house that was—at least from my point of view and judging by her exhaustion—absurdly big for only one person to clean. There were glass windows and glass doors all over the house, as well as white marble floors and white walls that had to be kept pristine. There were hardly any decorative objects around the house, so she needed to keep the space immaculate because a speck of dirt or dust was easy to see. On Mondays she was in charge of vacuuming and mopping the second and third floors of the house. Tuesdays were dedicated to wiping the huge wall-to-wall glass windows in the rooms of the house. Wednesdays were reserved for deep cleaning the kitchen and the five bathrooms. On Thursdays she had to vacuum the main bedrooms and clean the playroom and the first floor. On Fridays she had to clean the rest of the house and wash and iron clothes. Her work was under the daily supervision of her employer, Paola, from Italy, who did not work and was at home most of the time. "It is impossible to do anything around the house without having Paola watching over my shoulder and giving me instructions about what to do. It is exhausting. I wish I could be alone in the house doing my own thing, working at my own pace," Cristina told me. On Saturdays Cristina had to be on call to respond to whatever demands Paola might make of her. She was finally set free at two in the afternoon, when her working week finished. Sunday was her day off. These daily routine activities were completed while helping Paola care for a six-month-old baby girl and two boys, ages six and four.

Following a similar routine to Cristina was Amelia, who, in addition to cleaning a four-story house (with the help of a freelance domestic worker), was a full-time nanny to a four-year-old boy. She was required to cook for the child, take him to the park, bathe him, and play with him every day. Without much notice, Amelia was often asked to babysit the boy at night while her employers (a Swedish woman and her English husband) went out. Like Cristina, Amelia also worked shifts of ten to twelve hours a day and only had one and a half days off. Both of them constantly found themselves multitasking between carrying a crying baby and vacuuming or mopping the floors. They were both under the surveillance of their female employers, and because they were live-in domestic workers, there seemed to be a tacit expectation regarding their full-time availability and readiness to help. By living in the house of their employers, they were close at hand. Amelia, for instance, lived in a studio flat in the basement of her employer's home, while Cristina lived in a detached flat above the garage of her employer's home. Accommodation was conveniently provided as part of the contract, but it was not free of charge; they had to pay a monthly rent that was deducted from their wages. They both had exclusive use of a kitchen, bathroom, and bedroom. Despite these benefits, they were not entitled to make any changes to the place in terms of redecoration, strategies that employers used to signal that these were not their homes.

Since these women lived where they worked, they all complained about not having a life outside work. Their lives unfolded within the homes of their employers' family spaces, spaces that were nonetheless unfamiliar and alienating to them. Live-in domestic work trespasses on the intimacy of home in a more complex way than the work done by freelance domestic workers. If domestic work in general is characterized by performing reproductive labor that women might have done at home for their families, then it is not difficult to imagine the psychic and emotional disconnect that they experience by doing these activities in someone else's home. Live-in domestic work magnifies these problems to an even greater degree because of the enforced physical intimacy and surveillance between employer and employee and the constant performance of emotional labor. The presence of a stranger in the intimate space of the home results in constant, difficult negotiations in constructing status boundaries between the worker and the boss. As Lan states, "female employers fearful of being usurped by their market surrogates, safeguard their womanhood by enforcing the maid–madam boundary" (2006, 14). This was achieved by, for example, assigning diminishing or difficult tasks, establishing food restrictions in the house, or using the language barrier as a symbol of class distinction and hierarchy.[11] "Gabriela speaks Spanish and knows how hard it is for me to understand English, yet, whenever she gets angry at me she gives me instructions only in English," Amelia told me about her boss. All in all, employers engaged in subtle but constant forms of exploitation and carved out rigid boundaries between themselves and domestic workers. By doing this, as Lan suggests, "they are simultaneously participating in the imagining of class and racial differences" (2006, 14).

Matters became complicated, however, the moment women were in charge of caring for others as part of their daily work. The boundaries or negotiations that took place in these situations were not always straightforward because they were cross-cut by women's ethical considerations of themselves as relational subjects immersed in fragile emotional relationships with strangers.

Moralities at Work

Eva tells me how hard it is not to get emotionally involved with Mateo, the little boy who lives at the house she recently started cleaning. He is sweet and tries to get Eva's attention, but she makes a huge effort not to pay much attention to him. "I would rather just come, clean, and leave," she says. She explains how her previous experiences as a live-in domestic worker and nanny in Spain have impacted the way she thinks about her work now: "they expect you to care for the child but with limits and then when they need you no more they fire you and you are left with nothing. It is such a waste," she explains.

A close look at domestic work brings to light the complex dynamics that characterize not only this, but also several other forms of intimate labor or care work.[12] Aside from its social construction as female, domestic work enhances the almost inseparable intertwining that exists between care as labor and care as an emotion. The work is "inherently relational, whether it consists in routine bodily care, such as bathing or feeding, or in emotional attachment, affiliation, and intimate knowledge" (Hondagneu-Sotelo 2002, 68). It cannot be reduced to cleaning the house, cooking, ironing, feeding, or taking care of children as automated activities. On the contrary, the activities performed by domestic workers are highly intimate and gendered. "The sense that caring labor, both paid and unpaid, is different from other sorts of labor stems from a variety of factors: its association with women and the family, the isolation of those who do this work, its intimacy in the sense of caring for the emotional and physical needs of others, and its affective nature" (Barker 2012, 576). In contrast to other forms of care work (such as nursing or counseling), the intimate knowledge that results from domestic work takes place inside the home, a space of subject formation that carries out connotations of heteronormative gendered intimacy and that separates internal household relations from other types of social relationships.[13] However, as feminist scholars have argued, home is not only a space of subject formation but also a space where various forms of inequalities (age, race, ethnicity, and class) are produced and reproduced. More important, it is the place where household labor has been naturalized as women's work.[14] As I have explained, this ideology has been used to keep women doing the work they "innately" ought to do, undermining labor rights and exploiting migrant women from the Global South.

So far, I have presented the various kinds of domestic work that women engaged with and the impact that they have in their everyday lives. In the next section, I hope to link this background to the ways in which women experienced the commodification of intimacy and the impact that it had on their labor relationships. I will discuss situations where women were in charge of caring for other people as part of their jobs. Although much of their work included the performance of emotional labor, women described their care work as juxtaposing moments when they were acting as if they cared and moments when they genuinely cared. In other words, real emotions were muddled by acting emotions while working. Much of the literature on care work addresses the tricky but inevitable intertwinement that exists between money and care; "their mixing, goes the argument introduces contaminating, self-interest calculation into the world of sentiment, but it also introduces non rational action into a world in which efficiency should reign" (Zelizer 2011, 277). This rationale, however, ignores the fact that "people constantly mingle intimacy and all sorts of economic activity" (173) and, therefore, the boundaries between intimacy, emotions, and money are never clear-cut.

While talking about paid forms of care in intimate settings, Viviana Zelizer explains that people find themselves constantly having to negotiate definitions of their social relations and, most important, "distinguish those relations from others with which they might become confused: are you my mother, my sister, my daughter, my nurse, my maid or my best friend?" (2011, 284). To achieve this, Zelizer argues that people draw on available cultural models to negotiate unequal social relations and forms of compensation. While her argument emphasizes the distinctive array of economic interchanges that emerge from these social relations, I focus on women's moral frameworks and ethical choices as mechanisms to make sense of emotional intimacies that emerge while doing their work. I explore those moments where women ask themselves how the right thing should be done in the situation at hand and when they asked themselves how emotions and confusing relationships with strangers should be managed. Whenever women found themselves immersed in social relations that did not look like labor relations, but more resembled kinship relationships, I argue that women engaged in an ethics of care as a way to negotiate the new social relations. I look at care as choices that allowed women to sort out the class and emotional dislocations produced by the occupation, to regain some freedom and autonomy, and to resist the commodification of intimacy. By caring for children and elderly people at work, they were able to recover the kinship roles that were a fundamental part of their sense of their real selves and therefore could momentarily leave the maid role behind.

Let me disentangle my argument through the story of Felipa. She came to London from Mexico twenty years prior on a domestic worker visa and was a live-in domestic worker for several families before she became a mother. I enjoyed sitting at Felipa's kitchen table and listening to her life story while eating handmade tortillas that reminded me of Mexico. Her stories of life as a domestic worker were diverse: they ranged from suffering ill treatment and various forms of exploitation while working for the rich Mexican family that brought her to London to caring and family-like relationships with other employers. For six years Felipa worked as a live-in domestic worker for a British family, until she became pregnant. She was the cleaner of the house and was also in charge of taking care of three girls. The eldest girl was six, the second was four, and the third was only three months old. "I basically raised them. Fiona was working all day and I had to do everything with the girls, especially with the baby girl. It was not hard for me to naturally care for them, after all I was the one looking after them every day," she said. Felipa's relationship with this family was indeed a caring one that, as I will show, was strengthened by the exchange of gifts between them. As a family, this was a relationship that had survived through the years.

By the time I met her she was no longer a live-in domestic worker since, as she said, she had her own daughter to take care of and no one to help her. She was still working as a domestic worker but doing it part-time. Over the past three years she had been working twice a week for an elderly British woman. Besides cleaning the house, she attended to her needs for five hours a day.

> As Felipa told me, "She is hard work. She is demanding, unkind, and abusive. She often shouts at me and tells me to go back to my country, accuses me of stealing things whenever she tries to find something in the house that she has misplaced. Her daughter is nice to me and she has apologized on many occasions. I know that she needs my help with her mother. "

It was a challenging situation that caused Felipa anger, guilt, and pity at the same time. Nonetheless, she could not envisage mistreating her employer: "I cannot mistreat her, it is against my principles, it would be like mistreating my own mother."

Felipa had a dilemma—she could not help but feel morally obliged to care for this woman. Her choice was not part of the contract or caused by virtue of her having developed an intimacy with her employer—it was more important and fundamental than that. She was not only *taking care* of this woman but also cared about her in a more personal way. Her elderly employer reminded Felipa of her own elderly mother, who was alone in Mexico. She explained that her mother too would age and that she would eventually require someone to care for her when that happened. Regardless of the lack of emotional intimacy with her employer and the emotional labor she had to perform, she made the decision to care based on a sense of moral duty toward another person. It was an overt decision that made her feel as though she was being true to herself—it was her attempt to bring her feelings in line with what was appropriate. Caring represented a way of working out the longing and the guilt she endured for not being able to care for her own mother. In many respects, while caring for her elderly employer, she was playing a social role very similar to her role as a daughter. Caring was the right thing to do. Felipa, like others, often found herself faced with what Robbins (2007) calls a value conflict. He explains that when conflict arises between values, a morality of freedom and choice comes into play and, as a result, people become aware of choosing their own fates: "it is because in such cases people become aware of choosing between values that they come to see their decision-making process as one engaged with moral issues" (2007, 300). Felipa's value conflicts made her acutely aware of her own moral values. More important, the choices emerged from her own experience and judgment regarding the good or ill treatment of an elderly person who reminded her of her own family.

Similar value conflicts emerged when women surpassed emotional labor and engaged in emotional intimacies with the people they worked for. For instance, Mariana, after working for an abusive Italian employer, started working as a freelance domestic worker for a British Brazilian woman. Besides basic housekeeping tasks that were shared with another domestic worker, Mariana's duties were mainly focused on caring for two children. Henrietta, her new employer, treated her with respect and appreciated the fact that Mariana was highly educated and thus wanted her to get involved in the education of her children. She wanted Mariana to teach them Portuguese and help them with their daily tasks. In contrast to other employers, she worked full-time, something that facilitated Mariana's work and the relationship between them. The lack of surveillance, the appreciation for her work, and the physical proximity that she had with the children permitted the development of an emotional intimacy. It was thus not hard for her to care for the two children (five and seven years old). "Ana, they remind me of my niece and nephew back in Brazil who recently lost their mother," she told me. In this respect, as for Felipa, Mariana's choice to care was structured around the longing to and current impossibility of being able to care for her own family. This transfer of kinship values to her caring labor eased her anxieties about the low status of the job while helping her to cope with the desire to see her family.

In a complex way, strangers functioned as links with the familiar, but, more important, as links with what some women regarded as their *real selves*. The emphasis the women placed on recovering their *previous selves* or locating themselves in familiar social roles through their caring labor was a recurrent theme among those who were mothers. Caring for children appealed to their social identities as mothers, which in turn facilitated their ethical choice to care. In their respective work among Mexican and Central American women and among Filipino women migrants, Pierrette Hondagneu-Sotelo (2001) and Rhacel Salazar Parreñas (2005) found that women who had left their children behind filled their absence with caring for and developing emotional attachments with other people's children. According to these scholars, these transnational mothers reconfigure cultural notions of what mothers should be in their own communities and develop new forms of care for their children at a distance. This suggests that women become involved in caring relationships with their employers' children as an opportunity to act as mothers. In contrast to these cases, my informants' motivations to work as domestic workers were not always driven by the need to provide for their children back home because their children were adults. Others had their children with them in London, and the rest were childless. Therefore, the ethical choice to care was not drawn directly from being transnational mothers, but rather from the social framework and values attached to wider roles within kinship relations, the emotional labor and notions of care.

For women like Cristina and Amelia, caring for the children was a "natural choice," as Cristina explained. Regardless of the complicated relationships that both women had with their employers, Amelia loved to spend time with the four-year-old boy she took care of. She considered the boy her grandchild. As I observed, when the boy was around—even on Sundays when he would come down to Amelia's flat to spend time with her—little Christopher was allowed to do as he wanted, but his behavior did not alter Amelia's affection for him. "Look at my little boy, he is so handsome, he has his mother's blond hair," she liked to emphasize. On one occasion I arrived at Amelia's flat while she was having an argument with Eva over Christopher. At the beginning I could not understand what was happening until I saw that one of the walls of Amelia's room had Christopher's scribblings all over it. Eva could not believe that Amelia had allowed the boy to behave in such a way, so she reprimanded Amelia for being too soft on him. In her defense, Amelia explained that she was not his mother—she could not correct the boy, much less reprimand him, because this would displease and create more conflict with the mother, Gabriela. "This is what happens when you have to take care of children. You become too attached but then you realize that you are not the mother, you have no right to educate them," Eva said. But Amelia thought about her relationship with the boy in a different way. The time she spent with Christopher offered her the respite and comfort she needed to endure the complex relationship she had with her employer. Within her general discomfort, dislocation, and depression, caring for the boy was the only meaningful aspect of her life in London: "He is the only reason I wake up every morning, the only reason I stay in this horrible job," she told me. "He is a sweet boy who reminds me of my own son when he was a child. He makes me feel cared for, he makes me feel like a grandmother instead of a maid."

For Cristina, likewise, it was impossible not to love the baby girl she took care of. "Look at her, Ana, she smiles when she sees me, she knows I love her, she could be my grandchild," she told me on one occasion. As the grandmother of two children, she explained to me how easy it was to transfer her role as grandmother. Caring for the baby girl, particularly, was one of the main reasons Cristina stayed in Paola's house for so long—she wanted to be close to the baby and take care of her. "She knows who I am because every time she hears my voice she turns around to see where I am. It is very hard not to get attached to her," she said. The relationship with the two boys was also a caring one, but it was combined with the need to educate them. This was not always possible, and she had to remain silent when Paola was around and mothered her children in ways Cristina thought were not proper. Yet in contrast to Amelia, when Cristina was alone playing with the boys and they misbehaved, she corrected them. On one occasion, I went to her work while Paola was out. While we were in the playroom with the children, one of them, in the middle of a tantrum, hit Cristina on the head with a toy. She reprimanded him and explained that it was not right to hit other people, that she loved him, and that if he kept behaving like this, she would not love him anymore. The child was ashamed of what he had done, asked her to forgive him, and promised not to do it again. She was patient and caring. She felt an obligation to discipline the children *and* love them.

Besides Cristina's ethical choice to care for the children of the family she worked for, there was an additional component that complicated her choices as well as her bargaining position within the labor arrangement. In her relationship with her employers, Cristina had been addressed as part of the family. Literature on domestic work widely acknowledges the kinship allusions that employers use toward domestic workers and the side effects of their use.[15] Bridget Anderson (2000, 2003), among other scholars, writes about how domestic workers become easily trapped in a web of emotional labor once they are branded as part of the family. *Being like family* is an ambiguous and politically charged term. Nonetheless, it is also an accurate way to express the work that these women do. After all, the women perform—through their care work—roles that are typically performed by family members in the household. Their work is characterized and mediated by the close proximity that exists between them and the families they work for. It is sustained by the full-time attention and emotional labor that they must perform as part of their job. My point is that the work invites an interaction between strangers that can generate a level of intimacy that somewhat mimics relationships that exist between family members. Although the kinship referent entailed unpaid work, paradoxically for Cristina, being part of the family made her feel less like a maid, as she once explained to me. It was this language of kinship that helped her make sense of her demeaning position as a domestic worker, while making her feel obliged to respond to more demands and assume additional roles at work (particularly when caring for the children).

Even so, any pretense that Cristina was on an equal footing with the family vanished the moment she asked Paola to formalize the labor relation through a written contract that would enable her to accumulate a pension and acquire further labor rights. This request was taken as importunate and as a sign of ingratitude on Cristina's part. Because she was like family, she should not need a formal contract for the work she provided. A few months after Cristina's request, the family dismissed her from her job, claiming that they were fetching Luca's (Paola's husband's) old nanny from Italy to take care of the children—because she was like family. Suddenly no longer like family herself, Cristina was given a month's notice to find another job without receiving any severance pay for the time she had worked there. The ambiguous labor relation that Cristina had with her employers was terminated, ironically enough, in accordance with the procedures of a formal job, but without any of the benefits. She could not help but feel that she had been estranged from the family, especially when she had been separated from the children, whom she genuinely cared for. While the term *like family* can be a genuine expression of affection, in this case it only enhanced the ambiguity of the labor relationship and was used as a way to exercise power, control, and exploitation.

After Cristina was dismissed from Paola's house, in moments of frustration and anger she promised me that she would never again take a job that involved caring for children because it was too painful to leave them behind. Nevertheless, after a few months working as a housekeeper, Cristina started working as a freelance nanny/housekeeper for an Austrian acquaintance of mine, Andrea, who had two children. I knew that Cristina was looking for a job and Andrea could at least guarantee fair treatment, a good salary, and a respectful environment overall. As I suspected, they immediately clicked. Andrea spoke Spanish and needed someone who could help with her four-year-old boy and six-month-old baby girl. I visited them a few times. I was not surprised at the way in which Cristina, once again, was genuinely becoming emotionally attached to the children. At Andrea's house she definitely enjoyed more freedom to work at her own pace and spend time with the family. Andrea told me that Cristina was like a grandmother to her children; she was thankful to know that she did not have to worry about leaving her children with a stranger. She felt that Cristina cared for the whole family as if it were her own. Here again, Cristina was like family. But this time that status involved the respect, dignity, and emotional intimacy that she never experienced at Paola's home. Unfortunately, after a few months of feeling at ease with her work, Andrea and her husband had to leave London. They were moving to Italy for

Andrea's husband's job. They wanted Cristina to come with them. Although the offer tempted Cristina, she did not want to work as a live-in domestic worker again and wanted to stay in London. Once again, she was forced to say goodbye to those she cared for. "It is like I get to be a grandmother over and over again," she said, a role she was unable to play for her own grandchildren because they were in Spain and Ecuador.

Conclusion

These stories of migrant domestic workers in London expose the inequalities of a labor market that sustains the performance of gendered female roles as the foundation of reproductive labor and the home and produces significant dislocations in women's subjectivities. For women whose racial and class identifications stand in contradiction to their current occupations, the need to locate themselves within their dislocated state becomes imperative. In light of women's contradictory racial and class positions within domestic work, I have shown that there are certain labor conditions that aggravate or ease these dislocations. Women's choices regarding different types of domestic work prove to have an important effect on the ways in which they sort out the frequent alienation and stigma of this labor market. While working as freelancers increases the overall vulnerability and feelings of invisibility for some, for others freelance work offers control, independence, and autonomy. By keeping themselves distanced from employers while cleaning empty houses, women avoid the shame of their decline in social status and circumvent the emotional demands of the occupation by not caring.

Matters are further complicated when women work and live in the same place. Live-in domestic workers find themselves performing emotional labor as part of their everyday lives. While emotional labor and intimacy can be detrimental to their working and personal lives, intimacy can also produce a familial attachment that domestic workers can take advantage of (Dill 1988). The attachments—or detachments—that women develop with the people they care for emerge from a conjunction of women's moral evaluations, notions of care, and their social locations within wider social relationships. Although the choice to care or not to care was used as a tactic to deal with the dislocations produced by their labor and reclaim certain identity markers, it was used in very different ways and with different effects. Those who chose to create emotional attachments in their labor relations were able to reclaim parts of their gendered subjectivities constructed around kinship. Nonetheless, they also risked more abuse, exploitation, and disappointment. Those who chose to deflect and not engage were able to protect themselves from disappointment and acquire more control in their transactions and social relations. Regardless of the differences between them, both choices marked their liminal position within the politics of care marked by exploitation, discrimination, inequality, and racism. Notwithstanding the liminality, through these ethical choices, women created selective moral universes that validated and reconstructed notions of self-worth necessary for the continuation and consolidation of bigger dreams and aspirations for the future. The following chapter continues to analyze the workings of intimate labor as it delves into the lives of those women who, after working in domestic work, made the decision to move into sex work. It explores similar conflicts and personal conundrums as well as the tactics that women use to deal with the everyday trials and tribulations of sex work.

CHAPTER 4

Managing Intimacies in Sex Work

"Was it a difficult choice? Yes it was," Denise tells me after I ask how she started doing sex work. She explains that she used to work for a Brazilian woman who ran a cleaning business. "We were like slaves. She picked us up at five in the morning and we worked until late, sometimes eight or nine in the evening. She drove us everywhere, surveilled our work, and did not give us time to rest. But I did not know anyone when I got here, it was a job, backbreaking, but a job," she said. After a few months Denise met a girl who had been offered a job in a strip club, and they were looking for new girls. She explains that the choice was difficult but the wages and the working hours compensated for the personal conflict. In Denise's case the personal conflict related to the fact that as a religious person, she believed that sex work was morally wrong; however, her faith and her continuous attendance at church alleviated some of the shame that was produced by her job. "I know it is wrong, but I do not have many choices as I do not speak good English. I was tired of cleaning houses and earning nothing, at least this job gives me a chance to earn good money and help my parents back in Brazil," she says. By engaging in sex work she thought she was being immoral in some sense; however, she also felt that, in her particular circumstances, it was acceptable for her to do so. That is, to do what she felt was right for the sake of her family, Denise found herself behaving immorally and ethically at the same time.

In this chapter, I present the lives of women who, after having worked in domestic work (nannies and cleaners), made the choice to move into sex work as a way to pursue dreams and aspirations that included securing financial security for themselves and their loved ones, gaining new experiences, or fulfilling desires of transnational love and romance. Their motivations and trajectories within sex work are as varied as the women are, yet they all found themselves having to deal with the often-delicate balance of sorting out the stigma of sex work, moral conflicts, and the consequences of sexual commodified intimacy with clients.

From Domestic to Sex Work

Sabrina started working as a domestic worker when she arrived in London, but after two years of struggling with the low income she was approached by a close friend who worked as a stripper in nightclubs and decided to start dancing as a way to supplement her income. As a domestic worker, Sabrina earned an average of £300 to £350 a week working eight hours a day, six to seven days a week. This gave her barely enough money to pay for her shared room, food, and transportation costs. Similarly, Amanda, who had been a schoolteacher in Brazil, was earning just a little bit more as a domestic worker in London than as a teacher. After covering her living expenses, she was left with very little—sometimes nothing at all—to send back to her children in Brazil. For both women, entry into sex work,[1] via strip dancing, was a solution to their economic problems. In only a few hours as strippers they could earn at least twice what they earned as domestic workers in more than a week.

The shift from domestic work to stripping, and from stripping to other forms of sex work, was neither seamless nor straightforward. On the contrary, it was gradual and piecemeal because women needed to take a series of incremental steps that included an occupational realignment and a personal adaptation. The first step was to diversify their sources of income, working two or more jobs daily. Sabrina, for instance, continued to work as a domestic worker as well as administering houses in north London, which included collecting the weekly rent of tenants plus overseeing the general maintenance of the flats. In exchange, she paid reduced rent and made a small commission. As she described,

> I was working during the day at the flats making sure that all the tenants paid the weekly rents on time and during the evenings I will go to the strip club while my flatmate took care of Ronaldo. After a few months it was too much work, I was exhausted, I was in a bad mood all the

time and did not spend any quality time with my son. I had seen other women getting into sex work and making more money than I was without the hassle of having two jobs. I made a decision, in order to earn the money I wanted to make, I had to become a prostitute, but I could not do it with Ronaldo in London. It was very painful for me, but I had to send him back to Brazil to my mom's, so I could start making real money that will benefit Ronaldo and our family back home.

Cultural beliefs that link women to specific female caring roles within their families were a strong motivation to get into sex work. Their income provided financial support not only for parents and children, but also, in many cases, to extended family. Although it is a highly stigmatized form of employment and often one of the last options among a restricted range of undesirable jobs, including domestic work, it was for many the only choice they had to make good money. It is no coincidence that all my informants initially worked as domestic workers or cleaners before moving into sex work. Under global neoliberalism there has been a flourishing of the service-sector economy in which occupations like child care, domestic labor, and sex work have been commercialized but maintained as low-income, and mostly precarious, occupations. It is within these conditions that sex work became a source of livelihood for my informants.

When writing about sex work, choice is a pivotal and contentious word. Among radical feminists the occupation is seen as a form of violence against and oppression of women, where the commodification of the female body becomes the ultimate symbol of patriarchal masculinity and violence.[2] For them, sex work always includes some degree of force or coercion. In sharp contrast, the liberal feminist approach sees sex work as a voluntary decision that, like any other occupation, can guarantee an income.[3] This approach focuses on the ways in which sex work qualifies as work, involves human agency, and may be potentially empowering for workers.[4]

As commonly represented, these positions do not fully explain the variations that exist in this occupation regarding entering and remaining in the job. When looking at the totality of women's lived experiences as sex workers (including those beyond their occupation itself) it becomes clear that commercial sex is far from homogenous and that the polarized debates within sex work cannot capture the totality of that experience. Therefore, following Ronald Weitzer, I agree on the need for an alternative perspective that includes the constellation of arrangements, power relations, and workers' experiences to fully understand "the structural conditions shaping the uneven distribution of agency, subordination and job satisfaction" (2009, 215).[5] As I will show, workers' stories reveal not only the diversity of this experience, but also the underlying structures involved in the process. For my informants, entry into sex work was a deliberate choice but was nonetheless made within a very limited range of options; this was particularly relevant for women who were undocumented, were not fluent in English, and lacked recognition for their former labor experience and education.[6]

For Money and Adventure

Women's descriptions of their entry into sex work often speak of their individual circumstances of emotional motivations and/or economic need. However, not all of them became sex workers because they had family and overall economic and care obligations to fulfill in their home countries. Although money remained an important reason to switch from domestic to sex work, there were other motivations, such as searching for adventure, gaining a middle-class lifestyle, and looking for potential romantic partners. Take Vanessa, from Colombia, who was single and came to London to study English and experience living abroad for a while. Like many English language students in London, she took an hourly paid job at a cleaning company to have extra cash to go out and enjoy the city. The work was hard and paid poorly, but after a few months she was approached by one of the security guards who worked at the building that she cleaned, who talked to her about opportunities to work as a stripper. He told Vanessa that she was too pretty to be working as a cleaner and that if she really wanted to make some money she should start dancing for men in bars. He told her that the job did not require any further contact with the clients "unless you wanted" and the payment was at least five times her salary (at the time of the study Vanessa was earning £5.80 per hour).

As a young, middle-class woman Vanessa believed that being a dancer/stripper would come to her more easily than working as a cleaner: "I do not know how to clean, I have never cleaned in my life—that is what my mom and our maid did, I am not cut out for this job," she told me. Vanessa grew up thinking that to get a husband she needed to be beautiful and pleasant; she was particularly obsessed with diets, fitness, and keeping herself slim and attractive for men. Becoming a stripper made more sense than being a cleaner because she would have the opportunity to show her body and gain attention from men while earning more money; it was an opportunity to experience something different in her life. She saw it as an empowering experience: "I literally have a gold mine with my body and my age, I must take advantage of it while it lasts," she said. The expectation of finding a partner while working at strip bars was remarkably common among the single women I met. Monica, whose migration plan included helping her siblings buy a house for her elderly parents in Brazil, also came to London with the expectation of falling in love and having a family. For her, becoming a stripper represented the possibility of having both love and money.

Others, like Sally, from Colombia, entered sex work via an escort agency. Sally worked for a few months as a live-in nanny, but the job was tiresome, paid poorly, and was too demanding. She missed the fun that the city offered, meeting handsome *monos* (blond white men), and enjoying the high life. In her English classes Sally met another young Colombian woman who had recently started working as an escort. Because she was young and pretty, the woman invited Sally for an initial photo session—organized by a madam—to test whether she had the looks, the class, and the disposition needed to work in such exclusive services. The agency specialized in young Latin American women who provided a variety of escort services for high-class clients. Sally, who had seen other young girls earning good money, traveling, receiving gifts, and even getting paid monthly allowances by clients, did not hesitate to become an escort herself. "I have seen friends getting their rent paid, their bills and also receiving all sorts of gifts like plane tickets, jewels, clothes, expensive shoes, clothes, anything really," she told me once while we were talking about her new job as an escort.

Nonetheless, for some women the adventure, excitement, and money did not counterbalance the stigma and the moral conflicts. "Sometimes I wonder if I am ever going to be able to have a real relationship with a man after being a prostitute. How can a decent man love someone who has been a *puta* (whore)?" Vanessa once told me when talking about her desire to marry and have a family, just like her mother did. Others, like Giselle, wondered about being able to cleanse herself of sex work: "maybe when I get back to Brazil, see my family and stay away from sex for a while, I will get rid of the stain and the guilt." However, once they established themselves in safe working environments that were conducive to achieving their personal dreams, some women like Sally and Vanessa enjoyed being on the game.

In her discussion about middle-class sex workers, Elizabeth Bernstein (2007b) argues that the conditions of possibility for middle-class women to get into sex work have been influenced by a postindustrial economy that has rapidly changed the cost of living in urban areas, while at the same creating a highly stratified occupational sector characterized by ample quantities of low-paid, temporary "junk" jobs. Compared to men with similar class and education backgrounds, women still find themselves occupying the lowest-paid jobs in the service and hospitality sectors or in other poorly remunerated part-time jobs. The amalgamation of these various conditions is reflected in the lives of my informants, whose migration projects were partly motivated by the lack of job opportunities that coincided with their educational backgrounds and expectations in their home countries. It also resonates with women's desires to travel to Europe and gain new experiences before settling down. When looking at the totality of women's lived experiences within sex work, it becomes clear that commercial sex is far from homogenous and that choice is underpinned by a complex set of overlapping social, cultural, economic, and personal factors that contribute to women's decisions.

Secrets and Stigma

Acknowledging the structural socioeconomic conditions that limit women's employment opportunities in London, my informants talked about migration and the distance from family and friends as factors that facilitated their choice to enter into sex work. As Patty Kelly (2008) and Tiantian Zheng (2009) have suggested, women who work as sex workers usually do so in a location far from family and friends because it provides them with the anonymity necessary to perform such stigmatized labor. For transnational mothers, the distance allowed them to protect their family role by keeping their work secret, given that the marginalization, stigma, and shame attached to sex work could potentially affect women's kinship and social identities. In Latin America, deeply rooted cultural beliefs tie women to their families even if economic changes and migration strain traditional family bonds and roles. Among my informants, daughters were compelled to support their parents and at the same time were expected to behave in ways that demonstrated a degree of respectability and good comportment. Likewise, mothers, as the main carers of the household, had to provide for children (and sometimes siblings) and be good role models. The combination of traditional cultural identities, kinship obligations, and guilt results in a volatile combination for sex workers that can create situations of conflicted moralities.

In his classic sociological work on stigma Erving Goffman states that stigma is an "attribute that is deeply discrediting and that reduces the bearer from a whole and usual person to a tainted, discounted one" (quoted in Link and Phelan 2001, 364). The stigma of the occupation circumscribes women's social relations; it causes fear and shame. "I do not agree that this job is like any other job. It is not right to sell your body. If it were the same as any other job we would not have to hide it, but you do not go out on the streets saying that you are a prostitute," Amanda told me. She liked to think of herself as a *pessoa com valores moraes* (person with moral values). As a result, she was deeply ashamed of being a prostitute and thought of herself as an immoral person, a person who was *infamada* (discredited). Amanda's main conflict arose whenever she was required to fulfill her role as a mother. She often talked about how she felt like a hypocrite (*hipocresia, falsidade*) every time she needed to reprimand her children for misbehaving. Her fourteen-year-old daughter, Thais, had been lying and secretly leaving home to meet up with friends. Amanda's parents were finding it very difficult to deal with Thais and her brother, who were rebelling against their authority.

Amanda talks to her daughter on Skype while we are sitting at the dining room table in the flat where she works with Sabrina. She reprimands her for having lied to her grandparents; although her voice is calm, she maintains a serious facial gesture on the web camera throughout the conversation while she talks to Thais. She does not leave any room for discussion but tells Thais that she must follow the rules and behave while Amanda is away. She tells her how much she misses her and how much she loves her. She hangs up the phone and turns to us, with an anxious look on her face. "How can I ask them, especially my fourteen-year-old-daughter, to behave, how can I be an example for her? How can I pretend to be a good a mother if I am a prostitute?"

It was relatively easy for the women to hide their real jobs from their families at a distance, but it required a great amount of effort and anxiety to maintain secrecy in the course of their everyday lives. Goffman states that stigmatized subjects must create different biographies and use concealment practices to survive among "normal people" (1968, 99). However, by doing this, stigmatized people experience a biographical discontinuity between their past and the shady parts of their present. As a result, women employed several strategies to separate their work and home identities. However, as I will show, the compartmentalization was never fully complete, and it was riven with difficulties.

When Amanda decided to start working at a brothel she was living in a house where her brother-in-law lived. He came to London after Amanda did to earn money to pay off some debts and eventually return to Brazil. Consequently, Amanda was forced to help him find accommodations and a job in London. She did not want her family to know what she was doing, so she decided to keep her brother-in-law close to control any possible gossip that could affect her life in Brazil. "I knew that it was a matter of time before he would find out because of the *fofoca* (gossip) within the Brazilian community. So, I decided to tell him part of the story and confessed that I was working as a stripper in a club at nights and that during the day I gave Portuguese lessons to children," she explained to me. In addition to lying, Amanda started helping her brother-in-law by giving him extra cash, saying that she was earning a good amount of money from tips at the bar. He never inquired any further, and according to her he was very discreet and never asked her whether she was selling sex as well. The tacit agreement of "ask me no questions and I'll tell you no lies" allowed her to sustain her social identity in Brazil.

The stigma of sex work forced women to keep their occupation secret, to hide it from their families and loved ones (Day 2007, 210). The elaboration of lies was a complicated endeavor that caused moral conundrums as they were intentionally opposing values that they believed were foundational to their personhood, such as telling the truth. Yet, because lying facilitated the possibility to care for their families, in a way it was an ethical thing to do. This reflects one of the main predicaments in sex work: to do what they felt was right in one way (caring and supporting their loved ones), women found themselves behaving in ways that they considered immoral. "I would never be able to confess the truth to my family. It will kill my mother to know that I am a prostitute. I know it is wrong to lie, but I do it because I care for them," Giselle told me. They hoped, however, that the moral dilemmas would disappear in the future when they were no longer sex workers. The present thus functioned as a temporary space that demanded ethical responses and the suspension of the meantime for the sake of a utopian future in which they would have realized their dreams and would be able to return to their previous lives, to "normality."

The Work in Sex Work

Having made the choice to move into sex work, women did not restrict themselves to one type of work. Throughout my fieldwork I witnessed how they moved from one type of erotic work to another to increase their income and their social and business connections. Upward mobility—when it came—depended on opportunity, business skills, dedication, and luck. All of them performed sexual labor; however, their accounts of that experience varied dramatically. The source of those differences may lie, as Wendy Chapkis argues, "less in the 'nature' of erotic labor than in the social location of the worker performing it and the conditions under which the work takes place" (1997, 98).

Women in my research entered sex work via strip dancing before moving into brothels, swing parties, private flats, or escort services.[7] This choice was underpinned by social and practical circumstances. First, strip dancing was not considered prostitution because it did not necessarily include the transaction of sexual intercourse. Second, it was considered exciting work that could offer more than money: it could offer the opportunity or the fantasy to meet potential romantic partners. Third, it was a job that women could combine with their normal day jobs without arousing suspicion among friends and family. And fourth, because it was based on social connections, it mattered very little that women did not have working visas. Within the diversity of the sex work market, strip dancing appeared to be the least morally problematic choice. It thus enabled women to accustom themselves gradually to the idea of becoming sex workers.

Among some of my Brazilian friends, working as strip dancers at a club administered by Paula (a former Brazilian sex worker) seemed to be a rite of passage. Giselle explained:

> Paula used to run a clandestine strip bar back in 2007, where many of us started working. She was also a good madam who had several connections in the sexual market and therefore gave us work at private parties and in several swing parties organized all over London. She knew everyone. On top of this, she also helped many women find men willing to get married for £3,000–£4,000 pounds, for visa purposes. Back in those days she helped a lot of us who were just starting to work as prostitutes.

Giselle and Sabrina met at Paula's in 2007 when they both started doing sex work. For Giselle, becoming a stripper gave her a sense of satisfaction from the power she realized she had over men. "I really enjoyed the attention that I got from men, it made me feel better about myself and I did not have to sleep with them," she explained. For Sabrina, being a stripper was acceptable for the time being because it enabled her to learn the skills of the trade, but she was uncomfortable with the idea of working for someone else. Furthermore, in contrast to Giselle, she found the job physically and emotionally exhausting and poorly remunerated. And she was skeptical of the long-term prospects: many girls working at strip bars, she explained, were fooling themselves by thinking that they would find a man who would fall in love with them.

Monica was one woman who underwent the typical rite of passage outlined above. After working for a year as a domestic worker, she moved into strip dancing as a way to meet a potential boyfriend. While working as a stripper, she established and developed intimate relationships with some of the men who frequented the bars. "I was always getting into relationships with the wrong men—Portuguese, Albanians, Romanians, once a Turk, you name them, all of them bastards who wanted to take advantage and did not respect me—because I was a stripper and worked in the clubs." The love stories ended to a greater or lesser degree in abuse and, on some occasions, attempts to pimp and exploit her. Although she initially enjoyed the attention, Monica's goal of finding a partner among her clients resulted in disappointment. As a result, she decided to enter prostitution and grew savvier about finances, hoping that by doing so she would regain the control she had lost over her emotional life. "To be honest it was easy to become a prostitute because I was already sleeping with some of the clients at the bar. The difference was that I was getting paid for the sex, for the company and the time," she told me.

Women sometimes were able to choose their own niche or move between the niches that provided varied incomes and ways of protecting their personal lives. For some, working at swing parties—events where women and clients interact in a collective space and engage in semianonymous sexual exchanges—offered them privacy and freedom to work a few hours a week and still earn more than in domestic work, without having to spend the day at a flat waiting for clients. Swing parties were organized through the internet and advertised an array of diverse groups of women according to ethnicity, age, or body type. The going rates oscillated between £100 and £200 for a shift of four to five hours with resting intervals. The work that women do depends on the number of clients attending the party, which, as many recalled, is usually far larger than the number of women working. Apart from being demanding work, "literally back-breaking" as Denise said, the organizers of the events exercise total control over the women's work, bodies, and payment. Although a few good swing parties procured a safe environment and respectful clients, for most women swing parties were exploitative and gruesome; they were the last resort that some would use when they needed money.[8]

Women's choices within sex work were constrained by the logic of supply and demand in the sex market and by their precarious status as undocumented workers and migrants. Women like Pamela, a fifty-five-year-old British sex worker who had been working in the industry for more than fifteen years, talked about the changes within the industry: "There are more services and more women arriving from all over the world to work in sex work. Many of them do not practice safe sex and offer their services at lower prices in order to get clients. They get easily exploited by pimps without knowing." For many women, it was becoming more difficult to make ends meet. For this reason, some of my informants had to increase their working hours or combine several types of sex work.

Furthermore, the competitiveness pushed women to reconfigure themselves as racially sexualized women from Latin America as strategies to promote their business within the different working spaces. For instance, Angelica once explained that she would usually be called on to take part in the Latin American swing parties because she fit the racial category of what clients imagined as an exotic Latina beauty: "they call me because I am *morena* with long brunette hair and brown eyes. I am neither white, nor black." Some, like Amanda, who had fair skin and considered herself a white Brazilian, talked about her *bunda* (buttocks) as a way to exacerbate her Brazilianness when she worked as a strip dancer and then while working in private flats.[9] "Clients love the big *bunda*, they think that all Brazilian women look like this." Sabrina, whose mother is a black Brazilian, considered herself not a mulatta,[10] but an exotic *morena* who had a complex mixture of different racial backgrounds: "I am *misturada* (mixed), I have black, white and indigenous blood. I take advantage of my "indigenous" looks in order to get clients; this is what Brazil really is, a *mistura*."[11] *Mistura* is a marker of mixed race, which is, according to Denise Da Silva, "one step on the road toward complete whitening" (1998, 218). In other words, emphasizing their Brazilianness through their bodies and skin color became an efficient way of advertising their services and competing in a racially varied and saturated sexual market, but it did not affect their racial identifications, which were located closer to the white spectrum, or at least including it: "any body is more or less black, more or less white, more or less both" (Da Silva 1998, 228).[12] This competitiveness, combined with the uncertainty of the market, also influenced the speed and extent to which some of my informants entered full-time sex work, whether working in brothels or, for those who could afford it, in private flats.

Risky Business

Sex work can be radically transformed when control passes from a third party (brothel owner, escort agency, manager, madam, or pimp) to the worker herself. Although strip clubs and swing parties demanded less emotional labor and were less time-consuming, it was in these places that women were more liable to be exploited by abusive pimps and managers and had very little control over clients and money. In brothels and private flats (or escort services) women had more control of their labor, clients, and income and hence were more satisfied with their work.

Notwithstanding, in private flats women were more susceptible to becoming targets of abuse and violent attacks because of the lack of security normally available in a brothel. As I explained in Chapter 2, the regulations around sex work in the United Kingdom are conveniently ambiguous when it comes to offering sexual services in the privacy of one's home. While it is not illegal to work by oneself, it is a crime to work in the same space as other people, because the space is then considered a brothel. This law (from the 1956 Sexual Offenses Act) pushes women to work under highly risky circumstances because they gamble every time they open their door to a new client. This regulation speaks not only of a prudish Victorian morality with respect to sexuality, but also of a patriarchal domination over women's work that excludes them from having a safe and fair working environment.

Although I spent a lot of time with Sabrina at the flat while she worked, she was alone the day she was attacked by a client who wanted his money back after claiming to be unsatisfied with the service. After he beat her up and tried to sexually assault her, Sabrina managed to escape. She opened the door of her flat and screamed for help, after which the attacker got scared and fled. She called me after the attack. It was late at night and she did not know what to do; she was feeling scared and completely vulnerable. It was the first time that Sabrina and I were forced to face the crude reality of sex work and its consequences. Sabrina's face was swollen and covered in bruises. She could not stop crying and was blaming herself for not having been able to see it coming. My friend had been deeply hurt and because of her undocumented status, she did not know whether she should report the attack to the police. Her precarious working and legal situation in the country became terrifyingly real in a matter of hours. She did not want to run the risk of getting deported and of being discriminated against by the police. However, after much deliberation, we called the police to press charges. A group of officers, including a female officer, arrived around two in the morning and set up the crime scene. They collected evidence (a strap-on that she had used with the client and a glove that he accidentally left) that led to the capture of the attacker, prosecution, trial, and imprisonment six months later. Sabrina moved in with me for a few days. When she went back to the flat I started staying with her more often, frightened by the possibility that another violent client might come to the flat.[13]

Women in sex work face risk and violence every day. Sabrina's story reflects patriarchal state regulations that negate women's rights and autonomy over their labor. But, as with most women in sex work, she did not have many choices. Working in private flats guarantees a steady, high, "legal" income that women must counterbalance with the daily risk of violence. In Sabrina's case, the risk of working in private flats was worth her future and the future of her family. During 2010 and 2011 she earned a total of £300,000, money that was used to buy not one, but three flats for herself and her family in Brazil.

Sex as Emotional Labor and Intimacy

Besides the risks and the economic advantages, in private flats women had to perform various services that included intense forms of emotional labor and intimacy—which could either complicate women's lives or offer new opportunities for the future. "Clients want to talk to you about their problems and they expect that you will offer emotional support," explained Giselle, who worked at a private flat with Sabrina. According to Elizabeth Bernstein, the relocation of sexual labor from the streets to indoor venues has affected both the setting and the quality of the occupation. In modern prostitution what was sold and bought was an expedient and emotionally contained exchange of cash for sexual release (2007a, 102). This led prostitutes to develop mechanisms to distance themselves from their labor so they could treat their sexual services as work. Several studies have shown that women in sex work talk about the need to maintain a division between their public and private selves.[14] Although workers of different kinds construct separation between their identities at work and their identities at home, Sophie Day (2007) argues that because the work site of sex work is the body, the work environment is not externally demarcated, and therefore the division between the two persons requires a further separation—that between the inner body and the outer body.

In my own research, women talked about this division in terms of a working person and a *real self*. I am not arguing that this dislocation was restricted to the sphere of work alone; they experienced personal disjunctures that were a result of their class, race, and status dissatisfactions as middle-class people. But for those who did sex work, the notion of the real self was particularly germane as a resource to differentiate who they were before becoming sex workers. Their experiences of sexual labor corroborate what many studies have found on the need to separate work from the self, including the techniques women use to detach themselves from their labor, such as mental distractions, psychological games, and physical barriers. "When I am having sex with a client, I just think about my children, shopping, the fact that I have not called my mother while I am with a client," Amanda explained to me. Besides these psychological mechanisms, I witnessed how she took several showers during the day and lit incense and candles that, according to her, would get rid of the odor of sex at the flat. I was able to see that she kept a strict distinction between the bed sheets, pillows, towels, and wine glasses used by her clients and those she used. She also had a strict rule about separating home from work. Whereas Sabrina felt that renting a room in a shared flat was a waste of money, Amanda felt the need to leave the place every day to "feel like herself again."[15]

Another way of separating the two worlds is by creating several masks, biographies, or identities.[16] One remarkable example of the construction of several biographies is illustrated by Denise and the use of various names. At the beginning of my fieldwork, when I was still learning about the complex ways in which women deal with the conundrums of sex work, I met Denise. She invited me to her home, which she thought was the safest place for us to talk. I knocked on the door and two men greeted me. When I asked for Denise, they looked at me, surprised, and asked, "Who are you looking for, Denise who?" In that moment, I realized I had made a huge mistake because I was using her working name. I then tried Gina, thinking that her second name was probably her real name, but their reaction was the same. It suddenly dawned on me that I did not know her real name. Feeling nervous, I apologized and said that maybe I had the wrong house number. Suddenly one of the men said, "The only Brazilian girl that lives here is Roberta." Mortified by my mistake, I replied, "Oh yes, Roberta, I forgot her name, I am an English teacher but because I have so many students I am constantly forgetting their names." At that moment, Denise phoned me to say that she was running late. When I finally met her, I explained to her that to rectify the mess I had unknowingly created, I had pretended that I was an English teacher meeting her for the first class and that I had confused the names of my students. Denise told me she had to be cautious in hiding and lying about her working identity because she worried that her friends and her boyfriend would find out about her real job. Later, once she had relaxed in the space of her room, she told me how tiring it was to work in an occupation that required such a complicated administration of different characters that, at particular moments, clash with each other and complicated her ability to have a normal life. "I am so many different persons that sometimes I even get confused and do not know anymore who I am," she said. This example not only demonstrates how the multiplicity of identities is a necessary mechanism that women use when trying to separate their private from their working lives, but also speaks of the conflicts that we can, though unwillingly, create while doing research.[17]

The creation of several masks or identities within work is also a form of emotional work in which women learn how to perform what is required by their occupation without necessarily getting involved or entangled in an emotional process with their clients. At the heart of the question of sex work is the task of understanding the limits of emotional labor. Perhaps more clearly put, how does emotional labor look in sex work? On the one hand, my informants talked about the surface acting that they had to perform as part of their services by wearing a fake smile, speaking in a sweet tone of voice, and demonstrating attention to their clients.[18] These displays of affection were easily performed with the regular hourly paid clients. As Amanda put it, they were selling a fantasy: "This is not real, the woman I pretend to be is not me, but they like it and pay for it. It is my job to make them feel that I am the woman of their dreams, the one who can make their dreams come true."

However, clients demanded more than sex. They wanted to create—or recreate—an intimacy beyond the sexual exchange. Amanda often mentioned that she was a feeble actress and could not feign for too long that she actually cared for clients. She could perform emotional labor and act only while she was working, rather than sustaining a long-term performance. However, there were women who—because of the intensity and intimacy of their physical involvement in sex work—did not experience the same partition of the person. Moreover, some did not necessarily find the distancing or the separation process easy or even desired. In other words, some women were not worried about maintaining a clear-cut boundary between *caring* and *not caring* at work. One of the reasons for this relies on the current sexual commerce that, according to Bernstein (2010), incorporates a great deal more emotional as well as physical labor within the commercial context. She states that the new variety of sexual commerce resides with the provision of "bounded intimacy—the sale and purchase of authentic emotional and physical connection" (2010, 154). Indeed, clients do not necessarily only look for sex; they want other types of services like affection, counseling, or other forms of attention.[19]

Sabrina's case is an illustration. After moving to a flat on her own, she began to build up a large portfolio of regular clients who purchased more than sex.[20] While talking about a client who had just left her flat, Sabrina looks at me and smiles at a thought that has crossed her mind:

> You know Ana, this client is a special one. He is one of my regulars, a very nice and well-educated man. I think he is in his mid-thirties, he is handsome and likes to be dominated in bed. Today, we spent quite a long time talking about his wife. He has not been married for long, but says that he does not share with his wife the sexual intimacy that he shares with me. He is afraid to ask to be dominated in bed. There I was, giving him advice on how to involve his wife in his private sexual desires. While spanking him for cheating on his wife, I told him the things he had to do tonight to satisfy himself and his wife. Then I said, now you go back and tell your wife that a prostitute, a professional in terms of the heart, is helping you both. At the end, I asked him to give me a backrub, it was the least he could do in exchange for the therapy.

For Sabrina, this client was more interested in the emotional intimacy that they had developed over time than in sex. She was a self-styled counselor who helped men achieve a better sexual life with their partners. She also thought of her relationship with this particular client as a form of friendship—albeit, as she said, a very strange one.

Similarly, Monica reserved one day a week for one of her most demanding regular clients who paid for five hours of her time and services. According to Monica, her services alternated between sex, massage, listening to music, and conversation: the latter was predominant. They spent hours talking about their lives: "He likes to ask me questions about my life and my plans for the future. It is as if he wants to pretend that we are lovers when we are together, sex is not really that important between us anymore," she said. Through recurrent contact he developed into someone she felt she cared for. While telling me the story, she explained to me how strange it was to accept that she actually enjoyed and felt satisfied by doing the work she did with regular clients. Sex work was different from what she had imagined. It was more complicated than she had expected because she was selling more than sex: she was selling care and intimacy. Some of her clients were considered friends, people she had fun with. However, because she had a romantic relationship with a man who did not know about her occupation, she did not pursue any closer relationships with regular clients, as some other women did.

Still, not all sex workers were willing to comply with these demands for emotional intimacy. Among my informants women often referred to some of their clients as "too chatty" and "needy" of attention. In such situations women commented that they felt more like psychotherapists than prostitutes. "They talk too much, they want to tell you about their lives and problems, they want to pretend that you are something else. It is exhausting," Amanda told me. She would rather just have sex and move on to the next client without having to listen or talk at all.

For others, however, offering bounded intimacy in the private spaces of their homes (or brothels) meant that they could develop long-term relationships with clients. Although regular clients could potentially become a burden by taking advantage of the personal connections and, as I will explain in the next chapter, could bargain over the payment for sex, they could also become long-term beneficial investments. The sexual services that women offered, particularly to regular clients, involved authentic emotional ties and a sense of desirability or even love. The extra skills that sex workers sometimes performed with regular clients provide evidence of the complexities and nuances of sex work. At the same time, analyzing these skills expose sex workers' main predicament, that of being in an occupation that oscillates between a market transaction, an intensive form of emotional labor, and a source of different forms of authentic intimacy.

Dilemmas of Care

During my fieldwork I encountered several stories of women who, although they were aware of the stigma of their occupation, were hoping to find love within work. The type of love that women were looking for generally fit into traditional heteronormative views of the nuclear family and romantic partners. Most of my friends wanted to get married (preferably to white European men) and have children and a home. These desires became particularly relevant when sex workers made the choice to develop close relationships with regular clients. I had the opportunity to witness how several clients became friends, boyfriends, and failed relationships in the lives of my informants. For some women, making the choice to move forward with a particular client was inextricably related to the possibilities it offered for their future in terms of love, romance, family, and overall respectability (Brennan 2004; Carrier-Moisan 2017).

Consider Giselle, who started working at Sabrina's flat by the end of my fieldwork research. After a period of working by herself, Sabrina decided— because of the presence of local groups coercing and sexually attacking women in the area—to accept Giselle as a "flatmate" and working partner. They were both working full-time at the flat and had a constant flow of regular clients buying their services.[21] One of Giselle's regulars was David.

Initially, he would go to the flat at least twice a week. Soon after, he started paying Giselle for the girlfriend experience type of services, including going out for dinner, concerts, movies, and short trips around London. After a while, as did many of my informants who started more intimate exchanges and relationships with regular clients, she stopped charging money for the company and eventually for the sex as well.

David was no longer only a client but was also considered a sort of friend who bestowed on Giselle comfort, care, and the company that she had not had in a long time. "We meet all these men everyday but at the end of the day we are alone with no one to share the hassles of the everyday with," she told me once. David was involved in Giselle's private life, knew about her family, and seemed not to care about her being a sex worker. Among Giselle's friends (other sex workers) he was considered a boyfriend and not a client. Still, for many women this distinction was not always that clear-cut because relationships with clients were shaky and could vanish in a blink of an eye. "Am I in love? Not really but he is a good man and he might be my last chance," she told me once after a party at the flat where I had met David and was able to see how close they were and how much he was involved in her life beyond work. He was learning Portuguese and was thinking about visiting Brazil with her. He had long-term plans for them both. Although Giselle cared for him and liked his company, she was not in love with him, and according to Sabrina, she was not interested in his money: "She is not doing it for the money, love or documents, as many women do. She is with David because she wants to have a family and have a husband who will take care of her," Sabrina told me. In her forties, Giselle was worried that maybe this was her last chance to fulfill that dream.

Like Giselle, Melissa's (Brazil) decision to start a relationship with Sam was deeply influenced by her desire to be a mother and have a part-ner. She had been working in sex work for over a year when she met Sam. It began as a casual relationship that was kept within the boundaries of her occupation. However, the more contact they had, the more emotion-ally involved they got. Although at the beginning he seemed to be able to deal with her being a sex worker, after a while he could not cope with the idea that she was sleeping with other men. She had to leave sex work if she wanted to continue her relationship with him. However, the decision was not that simple because whatever she chose would have significant repercussions on her future life. By choosing Sam she was choosing to love and the potential to have the relationship she was hoping for, to have a traditional family in which she would be a mother and a housewife;

more important, she would be married to a British man (something that automatically elevated her social status). However, if she left work she would lose her economic independence and purchasing power. Sex work had given her the possibility to have a lifestyle that corresponded to her class aspirations. The job had provided her with luxuries, entertainment, and commodities that appeal to her taste. Choosing love would mean the end of it.

These sorts of conundrums were fairly common when women talked about their romantic relationships. However, Melissa's case caused too much deliberation and gossip among some of my informants. While talking about her, Giselle mentioned that the problem with Melissa was that she was in love, that she really cared for him. Although she was a bit skeptical, she believed that if Melissa thought that love would erase her past as a sex worker, then she needed to risk it. For Carolina, also from Brazil, the problem was with Melissa's financial independence. By choosing love, she would be economically dependent on him and would lose all control and power over her life. For Sabrina, the main problem resided in a contradiction intrinsic to these relationships. She claimed that if a client, or a partner, really loved you, he or she should not let you continue to be a sex worker. At the same time, it was highly risky if the person you were falling in love with was a client and was asking you to stop working (and thus give up your independence). It was a gamble: not only would you lose your income, but also there was no way to guarantee that he would not continue sleeping with other sex workers. After all, for Sabrina, "a man once a client (*a punheteiro*, literally a wanker) would always be a wanker. *Os punheteiros não mudan Ana, não.*" Indeed, Sabrina's approach to her relationships with regular clients was deeply influenced by her cynicism toward love in sex work. For her, the best choice was to either enter a relationship with someone who was not a client or sustain close friendships with them without having to abandon her plans and dreams. Regular clients represented the access to an upward class and status mobility that she wanted to achieve while working in London.

I had the chance to meet Robert, one of Sabrina's regular clients. After her incident with the police while working with Amanda, Robert helped her by signing the tenancy agreement of the new flat where she installed her business. Although they were already close, helping Sabrina brought Robert closer to her. He was a friend who cared for her and attended to her everyday needs, such as buying groceries for her or fixing things around the flat. It was common for me to bump into Robert at Sabrina's flat while we were waiting for her to finish with work. We would usually have dinner together and talk about Robert's work and family and Sabrina's day before watching a film together. Their relationship was based on the exchange of gifts, company, and free sex, but more important, it was based on Sabrina's choice to transform their original commercial relation into a caring relationship. In other words, Robert could remain close to her if he respected her autonomy and independence.

Under these conditions Robert was slowly introduced to other aspects of Sabrina's life that had nothing to do with work, such as her son. Sabrina's son came to visit her before she returned to Brazil. During her son's visit, Robert acquired yet a further role. He was a friend introduced into her family life; by doing this, she was able to expose other parts of her identity that Robert had not seen before. I was surprised at her decision, especially considering her views on friendships or relationships with clients. "He will always be a client, but he also knows too much about my life. I want him to see me beyond my work, to see me as a mother," she told me. As a sex worker she had been a woman providing comfort and care for Robert; as a friend she needed to disclose who she really was. Somehow, by doing this, she was normalizing her new relationship with Robert and was being true to herself. This decision did not change her views on relationships with clients but helped to temporarily leave the sex worker role behind and embody more familiar roles, closer to her sense of self.

For women whose work consists of the creation and performance of various personas entwined with emotional labor, intimate dislocations are common. These dislocations are enhanced by the bounded intimacy that women offer as part of their services in which romantic love is purchased as a commodity. Although on a daily basis women impose very clear emotional boundaries on their customers by not kissing, not engaging in personal conversations, and spending less time with them, some relationships surpass the already blurred boundaries of sex work. Relationships with regular clients, although cherished by most, are filled with contradictions. They can create close—and real—intimacies that affect the original transaction or lead to further and closer relationships. The affective ties that women develop with regular clients and the decision to move forward or not is not a simple one because it is infused with moral conflicts. Amanda, for instance, felt particularly guilty about one of her regular clients with whom she had a good relationship and enjoyed spending time, because he was married, "I hope she does not find out, because I do not want to make his wife suffer, she does not deserve this. It is not right."

While women weigh their options, the choice to care or not to care appears to be trapped in the constraints and contradictions of their work, yet women carefully manage their emotional ties by enforcing or lowering the boundaries. In some cases, the choice to facilitate intimacy and care is a resource women use to normalize the commodified intimacies with clients, to deal with the moral conflicts, and to fulfill romantic desires and aspirations. Furthermore, in many cases pursuing permanent or romantic relationships with clients entails the promise of permanent residency status. Sex work proves to be more than a job—it is also a source of social connections that can potentially yield romance and further social and economic security. Attempting to separate love and pragmatics not only is artificial but also blurs the nuances involved in the intertwinement of money and intimacy. As Nicole Constable argues, "Underlying such a dichotomy is the idea that 'true love' is somehow selfless and 'pure' and not only incompatible with but also diametrically opposed to pragmatic or practical concerns" (2003, 128). The performance of authentic love and intimacy in sex work becomes particularly relevant when looking at people immersed in precarious socioeconomic conditions. Choosing to care, to love, legitimates women's migration journeys, notions of respectability, and, most important, as Carrier-Moisan argues, "feel something" and selling authentic intimacy is inextricably linked to women's own projects of self-making (2017, 134).

Conclusion

In the midst of a growing intimate economic regime that has diversified the commercialization of sexual services, migrant women are increasingly finding better opportunities in sex work to improve their chances in life. As I have discussed, the decision to become part of this market is constrained by wider structural conditions of inequality that reflect women's lack of opportunities to secure other forms of subsistence. For some women, sex work is the means to guarantee economic stability for themselves and their loved ones. For others, it represents an opportunity to advance their middle-class dreams of visas, love, and marriage. Their approach to selling intimacy in sex work is determined partly by women's migration projects and partly by the conditions imposed by the services they sell. However, regardless of their motivations, as most studies have demonstrated, women in sex work hardly escape the dilemmas that are inherent to the stigma of the occupation, the moral conflicts, and the contradictions that the commodification of intimacy and desire encompass.

As a result, women find themselves having to reconfigure the meanings of their labor and the social relations within on an everyday basis. As I have explained, the choice to care (or not) involves a recognition of women as moral subjects with agency taking control of their own labor and managing the overall precarity in which they live.

This chapter and the previous one examined the satisfactions, dissatisfactions, and negotiations of middle-class women working in domestic and sex work. Both chapters show how these occupations deeply affected women's subjectivities as they were placed in contradictory racial and class identities that stood in opposition to their idealized notions of themselves before migration. As a result, I analyzed the tactics women used to tackle their various dislocations, as well as the tactics used to negotiate the everyday commodification of intimacy. In placing the chapters next to each other, my aim was to demonstrate how both occupations are part of a continuum in a neoliberal global economy of care that has promoted the growth of a precarious intimate economic market sustained by millions of women and their caring labor. This market reproduces global inequalities that persist between the Global North and the Global South and it extracts physical labor and emotional resources from women who are already struggling to subsist and maintain their own physical and emotional worlds. The following chapters examine further struggles women engaged with to locate their fractured migrants' subjectivities. The attempts are difficult and filled with contradictions; however, they demonstrate that not everything is lost and that there are possibilities for the future.

PART III

Impossible Locations

CHAPTER 5

The Intimacy of the Gift

Having argued that the complex nature of intimate labor produces familial bonds, emotional intimacies, and durable relationships with employers and clients, I question the ways in which women negotiate and define their new relationships. I have already discussed the ethical choices that women made and how they were used as resources to solve the dilemmas presented by the commodification of intimacy. In this chapter I pay close attention to the ways in which employers, clients, and women used gifts (and other exchanges) as mechanisms to manage unequal social relations and to negotiate the emotional intimacies that emerge from selling care. What did these exchanges look like? From the beginning of my fieldwork I noticed that both domestic and sex workers received a miscellaneous combination of things, most of which were given and branded as gifts. The exchanges included all sorts of objects, services, and favors and various monetary transactions. They were genuine displays of affection and gratitude or, to paraphrase Pierre Bourdieu (1977), a pretense of generosity—or something that looked like aid.

Following Marcel Mauss ([1950] 1990), anthropologists have long been interested in gift giving as a way in which enduring social relations are established and maintained.[1] Gifts create social relations (Laidlaw 2000; Godelier [1996] 1999), develop alliances between groups (Humphrey and Hugh-Jones 1992), or generate obligations and debts between individuals who might otherwise have nothing to do with one another (Graeber 2001, 27) because of their capacity to produce an almost immanent obligation to pay back, to reciprocate. Reciprocity, understood as an equivalent or balanced exchange, is one of the most salient aspects of gift giving since Bronislaw Malinowski's model (1922). This model has had a long history and influence in Western thought because of its economic rationality, since it implies that sociality is dependent on the principle of give and take. In other words, one gives because of the expectation of return and one returns because of the threat that the other part might stop giving. The cycle of reciprocity means that rights and obligations are "arranged into well-balanced chains of reciprocal services" (Malinowski [1926] 1962, 46) and therefore it maintains a social equilibrium. With regard to reciprocity, Marcel Mauss ([1950] 1990) continues to be the most important referent and the most discussed among anthropologists. To explain reciprocity, he developed the notion of the spirit of the gift based on the concept of the *hau* (the soul) in Maori philosophy. According to Mauss, gifts contained part of the giver's soul and it is the desire of this fragment of the soul to return to its native lands and former owner that obliges the recipient to offer something in return, to reciprocate (Graeber 2001, 179).

The obligation to reciprocate—as an inherent and almost universal characteristic of gift exchanges—has been criticized extensively because not only has it been used uncritically (Parry 1986, 466) but also it easily "leads to an obscuring of significant differences between them [gift exchanges]" (MacCormack 1976, 101). Critics of the reciprocity model have questioned the impact that this notion has had on the dichotomous view that we sustain in the West, which counterposes the gift as either a self-interested exchange or a disinterested free or *pure* gift. The notion of a pure gift is, according to Jonathan Parry, related to belief systems (in all of the major world religions) that place great stress on the merit of gifts and alms, ideally given without any expectation of return (1986, 467).[2] It also derives from the fact that "our ideology of the gift has been constructed in antithesis to market exchange. The idea of a purely altruistic gift is the other side of the coin from the idea of the purely interested utilitarian exchange (Bloch and Parry 1989, 9). Recognizing this tendency to view gifts as either interested exchanges or disinterested free gifts, I take into account gift exchanges that move between the two extremes, often blurring the boundaries. This perspective offers an opportunity to see that "people are not always the independent, calculating beings of Malinowskian individualism; they are made and experienced that way in some transactions but not in others" (Carrier 1991, 121). In this chapter, I do not focus on the reciprocity that may or may not develop from gift exchanges; instead,

I take Mauss's broader point, which explains that the bonds between individuals or groups can be created through the association between persons and things. Following Yan, I analyze "what people think about the message conveyed by the gift: love, friendship, caring, obligation or a supernatural spirit" (2005, 283) and the effects that these various messages have on intimate labor relationships.

My exploration departs from the analysis of gift exchanges within intimate labor relations characterized by unequal, but at the same time, caring and emotional relationships. These exchanges take place between transactors who are constrained by the economic, social, and power relations that exist in domestic and sex work (Gouldner 1960; Gregory 1982, 47–51). Following literature on the gift, I show that gifts produce a myriad of social relations either of debt and unequal social obligations or of further emotional and social links between workers and employers or clients. Acknowledging the complex intertwinement of work and emotional intimacy in both occupations, I argue that gifts are strategies that are also used by clients, employers, and workers to reembed and to normalize relationships and the emotional dependencies that could emerge from these labor relations. Gifts, however, can also be used as mechanisms to take advantage of intimacy and enhance the inequalities between workers, clients, and employers. I do not reduce gift exchanges to one dimension: to manipulative calculative instruments, to strategies based on self-interest with the aim of getting as much as possible for oneself (Bourdieu 1977, 1994, 180), or to notions of gifts as friendship contracts (Derrida 1992). Doing this would only confirm the impossible dichotomy between having interested exchanges and disinterested free gifts. In this chapter I will show how these boundaries are not clear-cut because gifts can be "at once free and constraining, self-interested and disinterested and are motivated by both generosity and calculation of expectation of return" (Yunxiang 2005, 258).

To explore gifts and other exchanges between workers, employers, and clients, I follow women's perceptions and understandings of the exchanges based on their material, social, and economic value. I analyze the ways in which they sort out the ambiguous meanings of these exchanges and of the relationships in which they are exchanged. I therefore pay attention to the role that gifts play in either enhancing the social, gender, and class inequalities within intimate labor or producing new social arrangements that might benefit women's aspirations and migration dreams. In this regard, I consider that exchanges within domestic and sex work have social and emotional value that women might use to transcend some of the status and class contradictions these occupations generate. My analysis takes into account how gifts are embedded in the structural conditions of intimate market transactions that problematize not only notions of love and intimacy, but also notions of payments and labor.

Gifts, Regular Clients, and Sugar Daddies

I can vividly recall my conversation with Vanessa when she told me that she had been working in a flat where she was not only making good money but also meeting clients on a regular basis. So far, she had already met two regular clients. Giorgio was young and single and had come from Europe in pursuit of new experiences. By contrast, Mark was much older than Vanessa and already married. She told me that Mark was visiting two or three times a week and would pay extra money to spend more time with her that did not necessarily involve the transaction of sex. More important, every time, without exception, he would bring a gift for her. "I think he is really rich, he is always bringing me gifts," she told me. Mark's gifts started with things like flowers, chocolates, and wine. After a while, he gave her an expensive bag, a trendy jacket, and a pair of leather boots, expensive gifts that very much appealed to Vanessa's taste. "He brought me a Juicy Couture heart-shape necklace, just like that," she said. Vanessa perceived these gifts as tips and tokens of appreciation for the services and the emotional labor she was providing. This was the first time in Vanessa's experience as a sex worker in which a client wanted to talk, to be pampered and cared for in an intimate way. The continuous visits along with the gifts were bringing Mark closer to Vanessa on a personal level. He was slowly becoming different from other clients. After a while he became what she and other women referred to as a sugar daddy.[3]

Parallel to her relationship with Mark, Vanessa started making the acquaintance of Giorgio, the young Italian, who also spoke Spanish. She described him as fun, caring, interesting, and open-minded about her being a prostitute. Similar to her relationship with Mark, the relationship with Giorgio was evolving into something that felt different from work—whatever it was, it was also moving out of the brothel. In a few months, their relationship evolved into what she thought of and described as a boyfriend/girlfriend-like relationship in which—in contrast to her relationship with Mark—she no longer charged for sex. By virtue of these changes she began to develop feelings for Giorgio She was falling in love with someone who could actualize her desire of finding a white European husband. Intimacy—both sexual and emotional—was growing between them on the grounds of sharing more time together as well as sharing personal information that was not widely available and that would be damaging to Vanessa if offered to third parties (see Zelizer 2009, 162).[4] First, Mark knew about her occupation (which was hidden from family and friends back home) and second, he knew about the impending expiration of her student visa. "I want to stay in London and the easiest way for me to do it is to get married. Giorgio has offered to marry me for £5,000," she explained.

The transaction, however, was not as straightforward as it appeared. Vanessa was unable to cover the cost of the marriage. However, because he wanted her to stay in London and become his official mistress, Mark was willing to make the payment to Giorgio. On the one hand, this complicated three-way relationship fueled her hopes and expectations for the future, yet, on the other hand, it could potentially become an ongoing source of speculation and debt repayable in that future. At the same time, Mark's "gift" was imbued with potential benefits because it represented the possibility of staying in London and starting a relationship with Giorgio, in addition to securing (even if temporarily) the upward mobility she was looking for. In addition to the £5,000, Mark also provided her with a flat where she lived with Giorgio to fulfill the marriage requisites for the Home Office. In exchange for his help, Mark demanded fidelity from Vanessa. In other words, he wanted her to stop working for other clients.

In parallel, Giorgio, who was prepared to countenance her relationship with Mark—in addition to other mature, rich clients—requested that Vanessa stop seeing younger clients. "She should take care of Mark and treat him well, otherwise he will stop paying the rent. I am sharing her with him, therefore he needs to pay the price," Giorgio told me on one occasion while we were having lunch together. These arrangements speak of the sexual inequality that existed among the three of them. However, the same arrangements speak of certain ideals that women associate with romantic love and reveal Vanessa's economic and personal calculations within these relationships. Despite these demands, she found a way to take advantage of the new terms in both relationships. Thanks to her sugar daddy, she was living in an upper-class area of the city without spending any money on rent and was covertly using the flat—whenever she could—for working purposes to get cash. Sex work had acquired a completely different meaning as she continued working and providing emotional and bounded intimacy but was no longer receiving cash from Mark and Giorgio.

In her discussion of payments, intimacy, and social ties, Zelizer (2011) explains that the matching of payments to intimate ties has important consequences for participants in erotically tinged relations because different forms of payment define different ties. She distinguishes three possible ways of organizing monetary payments: "Money as compensation implies an equal exchange of values, certain distance, and accountability among the parties. Money as entitlement implies strong claims to power and autonomy by the recipient. Money as a gift implies subordination and arbitrariness" (2011, 137). She further explains that people care deeply about making such distinctions because the wrong transfers can confuse the definition of particular social relations. In Vanessa's relationship with Mark, money had an ambiguous meaning: it stopped being a form of compensation and became an exchange that sometimes looked like a gift and sometimes looked like an exchange between a breadwinner and his partner used to pay for rent, groceries, bills, and overall household expenses. Money was used as way to cement more durable social relations between them, but also as a mechanism to enhance Vanessa's economic dependency on Mark.

The ambiguity of money was also present in her relationship with Giorgio. While the £5,000 was a gift Mark gave to Vanessa to prolong their relationship, the same money was compensation for Giorgio and the visa, money that could affect the development of a romantic relationship with Vanessa. Aware of this possibility and to prevent it from happening, Vanessa initiated an exchange of gifts with Giorgio. "I tried to make him feel special, like my boyfriend. The other day I bought him a very nice jacket that he wanted. I cook for him, do his laundry, pick up his clothes, and give him gifts. But he still behaves as if he does not trust me, he does not treat me like a girlfriend," she said.

In his work among transgendered prostitutes in Brazil, Don Kulick (1998) maps out the ways in which men differentiate their various relationships with clients by way of different modes of payments and other exchanges. Relationships with clients are characterized by payment for sexual services, whereas in relationships with boyfriends or *maridos*, transvestites provide money, meals, gifts of all kinds, and drugs; according to Kulick, this marks a relationship and signals to others that a relationship is under way (1998, 109). In similar ways, by giving gifts (clothes, dinner invitations, trips) Vanessa attempted to normalize her relationship with Giorgio or, more precisely, to signal that theirs was indeed a romantic relationship, in contrast to her relationship with Mark. The gifts had symbolic and emotional relevance because they were linked to the emotional investment that she put into the relationship. But Giorgio's approach to the relationship was different; he was not interested in developing a loving relationship with Vanessa because he believed he could not trust her. On one occasion while I was at the flat with Vanessa and Giorgio, Vanessa received a phone call and left the room. I was having coffee with Giorgio; I could see that his expression had changed and he was uncomfortable. "Did you see how she left the room as soon as she got that phone call? She is doing it again, she is lying to me. I am sure that she is seeing other men, or even women. Who knows?" he told me.[5] Although Giorgio had accepted the fact that Vanessa would see other men to earn money, his jealousy and constant insecurity prevented him from having a romantic relationship with her.

Bargaining with Gifts

Not all money transactions "as gifts" created this sort of arbitrariness and inequality. Let me elaborate my point using Sabrina and her relationship with Robert. They became closer when Robert helped Sabrina by signing the tenancy agreement of the new flat where she installed her business after her incident with the police (explained in Chapter 2). Later, during fieldwork, I realized that Robert had not only signed the agreement but also paid the rent and the bills for the flat for a few months until Sabrina got her business running. Their relationship was indeed a close one. After a few months of going to Sabrina's, I started to recognize when Robert called because her voice changed to a sweet but relaxed tone, in contrast to the tone she used with other clients. "Hello my love, how are you? How was your day? . . . Yes, precious, you can come, of course, you can come anytime you want, you know that, you are my delicious," she would tell Robert over the phone.

On one occasion I asked her if she saw Robert every time he wanted, to which she replied, "Yes, Ana, I have to. He helped me with the flat. I owe him so much, so if he wants to come I let him come." She thought of him as a decent man and a good friend who helped her when she most needed it. However, despite Robert's good intentions and favors, she could not help but think that nothing was for free—"*ay amiga, nada é grátis.*" She said that she knew she would eventually need to repay Robert for his help by sustaining their relationship, which had already surpassed the working space and the payment for sex. Although Robert did not explicitly demand special services from her, there was a tacit agreement that she would spend more time with him. Time was an expensive commodity for

Sabrina because she habitually worked eight to ten hours a day, seven days a week. The fact that she dedicated most of her days off (which were very few) to Robert was a sign of her willingness to engage in reciprocity and to continue the friendship that existed between them, which might help her with her plans.

Besides spending time at home having dinner or watching a film, Sabrina and Robert also spent time together on the weekends. On one occasion we went on a day trip to Stratford-upon-Avon because Sabrina wanted to visit Shakespeare's birthplace before returning to Brazil. She treated Robert kindly—they looked like a couple in love who held hands, kissed each other, and enjoyed each other's company. Although she was not fluent in English, they managed to communicate with each other quite well and knew about each other's lives. We spent the entire day in Stratford-upon-Avon, walking along the river, visiting the tourist sites, and having lunch at a pub where Sabrina wanted to eat. Just before we entered the pub she approached me and said in Portuguese, "Ana, we are not paying for anything, Robert is going to pay for everything. We will not spend a penny on this trip." That is exactly what happened, and this pattern was repeated every time I went out with the two of them.

Sabrina was fully aware of her debt to Robert; however, she was unable to see how their relationship could surpass the bounds of their original transaction. "I do not know if he is seeing other sex workers, that is why he needs to pay for my time, even if it is with a pack of cigarettes or groceries. I am not in this job to get a boyfriend." Having a boyfriend was trifling and was not in her plans; her strict calculations and boundaries were the only resources she had to locate the new intimacy between them without jeopardizing what she came for.

Sabrina's relationship with Robert, although it resembled the relationship between Vanessa and Mark, evolved in a quite different way and there were important differences between them. For instance, in contrast to Vanessa, Sabrina never lost control of her labor and finances. Although she wanted to have a close relationship with Robert because he had helped her and because she believed that he was a good friend, she never let Robert and his favors get in the way of achieving her financial goal. In contrast, Vanessa became immersed in a series of gifts and other exchanges with Mark and Giorgio that left her emotionally vulnerable and with very little income. More important, Vanessa's future was in the hands of both men. Her livelihood was in the hands of Mark, who could withdraw his help and gifts any time he wanted, and her legal status was in the hands of Giorgio, who could do the same.

The different approaches to exchanges and outcomes of these relationships were somewhat a result of women's personal aspirations and migration projects. In Sabrina's case, migration represented a temporary experience that would help her achieve her financial goal to obtain the lifestyle she wanted in Brazil with her son; thus, she was not interested in developing a romantic relationship with a client that could jeopardize her dream. Vanessa, however, wanted to stay permanently in the United Kingdom, marry a European man, and have a family, hence her need to establish more permanent relationships with clients. As these examples show, women's desires and aspirations led them to engage in specific ways with regular clients and to respond to the gifts they received from those clients. This process was far from straightforward and, as I have shown, was filled with contradictions.

Differentiating Gifts

The new relationships that Sabrina and Vanessa developed with their clients created new arrangements in which cash as payment for a service turned into gifts, and gifts—according to both women—turned into payment for their ongoing services. However, gifts—because of their ambiguity—in contrast to cash, acquired different meanings that depended on the value of the objects and the person who gave the gift. For instance, before Sabrina returned to Brazil in December 2010, Robert bought several gifts for her son; these were things that he knew Ronaldo wanted, such as games for the Nintendo XL, a Nike jacket, and a pair of trainers. Robert brought the gifts over one night while we were having dinner at Sabrina's; it was his contribution to the ongoing purchase of gifts that she bought before going back to Brazil. When Robert gave her the items, her face completely transformed—she was pleasantly surprised by Robert's gesture. It was not the first time she had received gifts from him, but it was the first time she had received such a personal thing. These gifts reflected the intimacy that they shared and the relationship that Robert was trying to create with her, one that entailed a familiar, almost kinlike relationship. Although there were several exchanges between them—both monetary and nonmonetary—these objects held emotional value. They were not a form of payment; these were real gifts because they were intended to please the most important person in her life, her son.

For Vanessa, however, a proper gift meant an expensive item. But getting expensive gifts that correlated with her taste involved time and effort. For example, although there were occasions when Vanessa did not want to see Mark, she knew that at least once a week she had his entire attention. At these times, she was able to ask for things she wanted or needed, but to gain those benefits she was required to perform a particular emotional labor that involved playing out the fantasy of the girlfriend. "I can actually get the things I want when we go to the hotel on Thursdays. We eat, dance, and when he is half drunk I ask him for special things. That is how I got a plane ticket to go to Colombia," she explained.

Though it might appear that these gifts were purely calculative and instrumental, they became personal over time and were deeply embedded in the intimacy of the new relationship. As an example of this shift, in November 2010, I attended the marriage of Vanessa and Giorgio, and a few weeks before the wedding I participated in the enterprise of buying a wedding dress, sponsored by Mark. Initially I thought that Vanessa would buy a normal party dress for the wedding because we were not visiting any wedding shops. But as the day progressed she became excited by the idea of a white dress because of what it represented in her life: marrying a white European man was fulfilling her middle-class aspirations and desire to stay in London and form a family. In addition to the dress, Mark bought the wedding ring that Giorgio needed to give to Vanessa during the ceremony. The ring was engraved with the words "I love you forever, Mark." "If I am paying for the whole wedding—including the groom—at least I want to be present on her finger during the ceremony," Mark told me sarcastically. However, the ring, in opposition to other gifts, was problematic; it made Vanessa feel conflicted because it was "charged" with Mark's person. "Wearing the ring is like being attached to Mark beyond our relationship. I cannot do that. I feel like I am carrying him with me," she said. When I told her that she could sell it after the wedding, she said that she could not do that and could not even give it back to Mark because it was such a personal object. In other words, this ring was unambiguously a symbol of their intimate relationship beyond the commercial exchange, an exchange that Vanessa was not willing to sustain forever.

In the midst of this complicated set of transactions, both economic and emotional, the question is, Were the clients maximizing their profits with their gifts, or were Vanessa and Sabrina maximizing their stakes with the exchanges? The answer is far from simple because both the clients and the women were maximizing their original investments and future aspirations while becoming entangled in relationships that were unsustainable in the future. As a result, the women became acutely conscious about blurring or maintaining the boundaries at work in the presence of gifts and therefore disengaged or engaged in further intimate relationships with their clients.

The Sweetness of Cash

Perfection was the word Sally, from Colombia, used to describe the sugar daddy who was fulfilling her aspirational middle-class dreams of having access to expensive things, traveling, participating in London's nightlife, and overall experiencing the lifestyle she wanted. "Apart from the possibility of getting the bills paid, you can always get all sorts of gifts such as plane tickets, jewels, clothes, expensive shoes, bags, manicures, lingerie—anything, really," she said. Sugar daddies, according to Sally, could function as a form of insurance. Nonetheless, it was necessary to learn how to set boundaries and thus prevent them from taking too many liberties. The secret, according to her, was to keep herself at a *safe distance*; in other words, even though she would provide emotional services and create the romantic intimacy that he was paying for, she would not become emotionally involved with him—she was just playing a role. I then asked Sally how she managed to draw her boundaries. Her answer was simple: with cash. It did not matter whether she received gifts from her clients; business was business and if they wanted her services they needed to pay for them. The constant presence and flow of cash as compensation kept the transactions within the sphere of economic relationships. It also helped to maintain a certain distance and accountability between Sally and her clients (Zelizer 2011, 136–37). This is not to simplify the complexity of the sexual commercial transaction or to pretend that the presence of money as compensation automatically empties the social relations that are created by that money. On the contrary, in the face of commodified intimacy, women like Sally really cared about making distinctions between the diverse types of payments and exchanges that occurred within her relationship with her sugar daddy. By doing this, she retained control and autonomy over her life and emotions.

With this in mind, I turn to cases in which women adamantly rejected the idea of having a sugar daddy or developing personal relationships with regular clients. Consider Amanda, who was convinced that clients were looking for experiences that they were unable or ashamed to ask for from their sexual partners. As prostitutes, their role was to fulfill clients' fantasies, nothing more. Men were not really looking for a girlfriend: "We are only whores (*somos putas*) to them; they already have their girlfriends or wives waiting for them at home after they have fucked us. They would never want to marry us and have children with us," she said. Sex work was a pretense, a simulation of intimacy that was sold at a price. Amanda believed that the gifts that she received from clients were part of the charade of attempting to normalize something that was nothing more but business and, more important, strategies clients used to obtain free sex. "When they give you gifts all they want really is a free ride, it is not that they really care about you. I am not here to have a relationship. It is not possible to have a real relationship with a client," she told me. She would not provide any extra time, sex, massages, or blow-jobs as a gift. For instance, whenever clients brought something to drink with her (like a bottle of wine or champagne) she would make up excuses, such as having a headache, so she did not have to open it and share it with them. The less contact and information they both shared, the better it was for her.

In *The Gift*, Mauss argued that to refuse to give, just as to refuse to accept, is tantamount to declaring war: "it is to reject the bond of alliance and commonality" ([1950] 1990, 13). Amanda's choice to refuse further exchanges with clients or to reciprocate their gifts was an explicit effort to separate her personal life from her working life. This decision was influenced by her moral conflict regarding prostitution and the weight of its stigma. It was also intertwined with a relationship that she maintained with her boyfriend in Brazil, who was unaware of her job. She held her romantic relationship as a model of emotional intimacy and assured me that she would never have that type of relationship with a client. In other words, the active obliteration of other forms of relationships with clients was a reflection of Amanda's values and views on intimacy. By increasing the distance between herself and her clients, Amanda attempted to keep some control over her life and plans.

That said, over the two years that she had been working in London as a sex worker Amanda inevitably developed personal relationships with regular clients. They were neither friends nor boyfriends; they were regular clients who paid well and did not take advantage of the familiarity that existed between them. They always paid and were under no illusions of being anything other than clients. With them she did not feel that she had to pretend that she cared. Paradoxically, at some level, it was those clients for whom she genuinely had some respect and did care for in a way. Relationships with them were always kept within the bounds of the job: she was exchanging sex for money. The empathy, comfort, and care appeared because of time spent together and the success of the arrangement.

So far in this chapter I have uncovered the complexities and new arrangements that emerged from the exchange of gifts within labor relationships that encompassed significant degrees of sexual intimacy. Studies on the role of gifts within sex work show that, "like other forms of monetary exchange, [gifts] serve multiple purposes in signifying the type of relationship and the level of commitment" (Cabezas 2009, 123). As I have shown, gifts can solidify and strengthen affective connections between sex workers and clients and at the same time serve as a way to exercise more control and create more inequality within the labor relationship. I have taken into consideration women's agency, choices, and perceptions while dealing with gift exchanges, but we must not lose sight of the socioeconomic and legal conditions under which women work and must weigh difficult decisions. Given that many of my informants were undocumented, they were embedded in wider structures of power that can place women in an economically and emotionally precarious position.

The Emotional World of Secondhand Gifts

The exchange of gifts was not unique to the relationships between sex workers and clients. Gifts were also part of the labor relations between domestic workers and employers. Although sex and domestic work are radically different forms of services, they both entail emotional labor. For both sex and domestic workers, the idiom of care was an intrinsic part of their daily work. The outcomes of their work, as I have explained, provoked moral dilemmas regarding the type of care they should be providing within their labor relations. The dilemmas that emanated from the commodification of intimacy were complicated and sometimes mediated by the presence of gifts. Whereas gifts within sex work reflected the sexualized and gendered relations that existed between clients and sex workers, gifts in the realm of domestic work mirrored the class, racial, and social differences that existed between employers and domestic workers in sometimes drastic ways.

Acknowledging the low status of domestic work, it is unsurprising that most of the gifts domestic workers received were secondhand items.[6] They resembled things that might be exchanged or given to family members: an unwanted coat to a sister or a pair of shoes to a daughter. At the same time, they were things that someone might want to dispose of: a used sofa, an old table, or shoes given to the maid. Overall, gifts given to domestic workers were commodities handed to people who were assumed to accept them out of need or obligation; they signal—and confirm—the class differences that are intrinsic to the occupation. The practice of giving gifts within domestic work has been criticized as a strategy used to underline the deep class inequalities between employers and employees. Pierrette Hondagneu-Sotelo refers to this widespread practice as *maternalism*, "a one-way relationship, defined primarily by the employer's gestures of charity, unsolicited advice, assistance, and gifts. The domestic employee is obligated to respond with extra hours of service, personal loyalty, and job commitment" (2001, 208). As I explain below, some exchanges augmented the class and status inequalities within the labor relationship. However, some gifts were tokens of appreciation and care that reflected the emotional intimacy that existed in the labor relationship.[7] In her work among domestic workers in Bolivia, Lesley Gill (1994) suggests that secondhand gifts can create close relationships that nonetheless remain unequal at the same time. These gifts have effects that seem to be contradictory. In other words, secondhand gifts can express the familiarity of the relationship and therefore cement social relations; at the same time, however, their secondhand nature guarantees the maintenance of inequalities between employer and worker.

The first time I visited Felipa's house I was impressed by the sheer number of things, in particular the many pieces of furniture, scattered throughout the house. It was difficult to find a clear hallway or corner in the flat. One room, which appeared to have been the living room, Felipa had made into her bedroom. This room was quite unusual because it held her bed and a chest of drawers for her clothes, right next to a big wooden dining room table and six matching chairs. There was something odd about this arrangement that made me think about the random presence of furniture around the house. When I asked her about the table and chairs as well as the rest of the furniture, she told me that they were all gifts. Gifts from whom?, I wondered. They were from her former employer, Fiona.

Whenever I asked Felipa about her favorite employers in London, she never hesitated to talk about Fiona and her girls. After six years working at Fiona's house and ten years struggling with the Home Office, a pregnant Felipa gained her British citizenship and with it was able to access some of the social benefits offered by the state, most important a council flat for her and her baby. It was at this point that Fiona gave her the furniture for the new flat. These objects, as she told me, were part of a continuous flow of gifts (including clothes, shoes, bags, and toys) that her employer gave over the years.

In her discussion about gifts within domestic work, Rhacel Salazar Parreñas found that gift giving not only is a deliberate form of exploitation on the employer's side but also can be a sincere display of affection and can have real advantages for employees (2001, 187–88). Furthermore, in addition to the material benefits she received from Fiona's gifts, the family helped her by paying for an immigration lawyer to sort out her citizenship application and provided her with reference letters. "I'm in their debt forever," she told me. She did not experience this debt as overwhelming or burdensome, however; rather, it was an outcome of the caring relationship that she had with her former employer. Consequently, Felipa talked about being morally indebted to Fiona's family. Every time Fiona called her to babysit her girls for a few hours, Felipa would do it without any economic retribution. Fiona always wanted to pay her, but Felipa never accepted the money. In her view, the exchange of money would have affected the ongoing relationship. As a friend, she could not charge for her services: in her mind, she was not working, but rather doing a favor. Thus, Fiona would then "pay" with more gifts whenever Felipa needed her help.

For Felipa these gifts, despite being secondhand, were a result of the emotional intimacy that she and Fiona's family developed throughout years of exchanging care. Their significance resided in the fact that they once belonged to people she considered her family: they were personal. According to Jonathan Parry, the general principle of the gift is "the absence of any absolute disjunction between persons and things" (1986, 457). This, he argues, is what creates enduring bonds between persons. Furthermore, he explains that gifts are reciprocated because of the social contract they contain. For Felipa, the secondhand things that she received from Fiona were somewhat considered gifts that held the relationship that she had with the family, and hence they contained emotional value that helped in cementing strong, kinlike relationships between her and her employer. In other words, "what makes a gift is the relationship within which the transaction occurs" (Carrier 1991, 122).

"Because You Are Part of the Family"

The material presented so far lends itself to thinking that secondhand gift exchanges in domestic work allowed for the development of meaningful relationships and feelings of care between employers and workers. However, in some cases gifts were strategically used to extract free labor from women. Take Cristina, who had been called "part of the family" because of her caring work. In Chapter 3 I explained that this denomination can be a double-edged sword because it may be a genuine kinship idiom and a sign of respect, but may also function to disguise exploitative practices within the labor relationship. This was especially so for Cristina because when the family bestowed on her the sobriquet "part of the family" and gave her gifts, her tasks in the house increased considerably, with no extra payment.

I used to go to Cristina's house on Wednesday evenings around eight thirty to help her with her English homework after her work shift ended. However, we were constantly interrupted by her employers asking for favors.

She was usually asked to help with ironing, help with a crying child, find things around the house, or babysit the children in the evenings without compensation for the extra hours. Although this was clearly free additional labor, Cristina talked about these services as assistance to the family. As family, she received secondhand gifts from her employers that included used clothes, shoes, shirts, bags, and baby clothes intended for Cristina's granddaughter. In addition to the secondhand gifts, she was allowed to attend English classes twice a week, time that was granted by Paola with the caveat that Cristina had to pay back the hour she missed of work (one hour of ten working hours per day) by doing extra work around the house on Saturdays.

As Mary Romero states, "When employers grant favors, make promises and give gifts, the employee becomes ensnared in a web of debt and obligation that masks considerations of the employee's rights. . . . Gift-giving is simply another employer tactic of keeping wages low and for extracting additional unpaid labor" (Romero 1992, 131). Hence, for Cristina, vacating the flat to accommodate family guests or doing other favors appeared to be a normal aspect of her work. The more gifts or favors she received from her employers, the more unpaid labor she had to perform. In contrast to the exchanges between Felipa and Fiona, the exchanges of gifts in Cristina's work only exacerbated the inequalities between her and her employer and placed Cristina in a precarious situation in which both care and exploitation were embedded in the logic of gifts.

Gifts or Charity

Not all women were trapped in the inequality created by calculative gifts. More important, not all women perceived these exchanges—secondhand items—as gifts. For instance, when Juliana received secondhand gifts from her employers, she did not feel that these exchanges were real gifts. "They hardly know you, but they leave bags with old clothes, shoes, coats, you name it," Juliana said. As a freelance domestic worker, she did not experience the same physical and emotional intimacy as a live-in worker, nor was she required to perform the same kind of emotional labor. The work of freelancers was bounded by the limited contact they had with the families they worked for. Still, they also received secondhand items. Are these gifts? I once asked Juliana this question when she showed me a big bag full of clothes, and she responded, "Not really, they are just things."

When is an object considered a thing or a gift? It has been argued within anthropology that gifts, as opposed to commodities, establish relationships between subjects.[8] In his classic discussion of gift versus commodity, Chris Gregory argues that gift exchanges produce a personal relationship between the subjects transacting, while commodity exchanges establish objective relationships between the objects transacted (1982, 41).[9] For Marshall Sahlins (1972), gifts and commodities are extreme points of a continuum. He explains that the movement from one extreme to the other is kinship distance: gift exchanges tend to occur between people who are relatives and commodity exchanges occur between strangers (1972, 196). Several anthropologists have argued that these distinctions are not definite because gifts and commodities coexist in certain circumstances (Carrier 1991; Godelier 1999; Bloch and Parry 1989). In some cases, commodities can be appropriated into gifts; gift wrapping, for example, can transform an impersonal commodity into a personal gift (Carrier 1995). In line with this argument, rather than making radical distinctions between gifts and commodities, I show how gifts and commodities "are instances of the many shapes that 'things' assume in social exchanges, such as 'commodity,' 'gift' and 'trash'" (Sleeboom-Faulkner 2014, 326). These shapes take form because of the social meanings of the exchanges as well as the ideological constructions, distinctions, and values that women attach to the objects.

Therefore, for Juliana the clothes, shoes, and bags packed in plastic bags that she received from employers she barely knew could never be gifts. A real gift, she explained, was something that had meaning. "For example, Ana, I once received a birthday gift from one of my employers. It was a wool sweater, very cozy, warm and exactly my size. It was the perfect gift, as she knew how much I suffer with the cold weather in London. That to me is a real gift," Juliana told me. This confirms what Braudillard notes regarding the significance of the object given as a gift: that it "is insepa-rable from the concrete relation in which it is exchanged [. . .] The gift is unique, specified by the people exchanging and the unique moment of exchange" (Braudillard, quoted in Carrier 1990, 20). As I have previously explained, my informants' perceptions of exchanges were inextricably linked to the relationships they had with the givers and the moments in which these gifts were given.

In Juliana's view, the gifting of secondhand items was essentially a matter of disposal—just part of the excessive consumption that Londoners engaged in. "People in London have many things. They buy too many things they do not need. Therefore, when they want to get rid of these things, they give them to us or send them to a charity shop," she said. She was part of a larger flow of extra commodities; she was helping them get rid of things they no longer wanted. However, even when these secondhand objects were understood as discarded commodities, they could still contain symbolic capital that women could use to counteract their dislocated social position as menial laborers. The possibility of finding good-quality things for her or her family and friends was enough of a reason for Juliana to always accept the gifts. When she received a bag of goodies, she carefully selected and distributed the items accordingly. After keeping the best items for herself and her family, she would send some items to Brazil and then bring the rest to a charity shop. "There is always a good pair of shoes, a coat, or trousers," Juliana explained.

Similarly, when Cristina started working as a freelance domestic worker (after being dismissed from Paola's house) she also received secondhand things from her new employer. Like Juliana, Cristina accepted the bags because they could contain valued items. On one occasion she called me because she wanted me to pick out some items for myself. I must admit that I was surprised by the number of things in the bag. There were perfumes, leather bags, nightgowns, trousers, shirts, boots, and four pairs of shoes. Cristina wanted me to choose a perfume and take a leather bag and a pair of shoes. In her view, these were sophisticated items because of the economic position—and therefore good taste—that her current employer held. She wanted to thank me for the English classes by giving me these items, and at the same time she used this opportunity to display her knowledge of expensive brands and middle-class taste. I felt obligated to take the gifts, bizarrely entering the cycle of secondhand gifts myself.

As my own experience demonstrates, the disposal or flow of commodities extended to third parties, to people who were part of the social universe of the domestic workers receiving the gifts. Consider Rosa, from Peru, who lived and worked at her employer's home. Besides lacking privacy, she had limited space in her room to keep gifts from the family she worked for, except for clothes. But when her employer wanted to refurbish the living room, she asked whether Rosa knew someone who might be interested in the old furniture. Eva, Rosa's friend, was about to move to a council flat with her daughter and was looking for furniture. The deal was perfect for Eva—she would save money and furnish her house. Aside from the economic advantage that these items represented, Eva's sense of taste correlated with Rosa's employer's taste. Eva had very particular preferences when it came to buying things, especially for her house. So it did not matter that the furniture was secondhand, only that it was expensive and had belonged to a rich family. The gifted items contributed to her symbolic capital, sense of distinction, and the middle-class position that she cultivated.

The flow and recycling of secondhand gifts featured prominently in the relationships between domestic workers and employers. The materiality of these gifts bears a cultural meaning that is embedded in the logic of the job; they are evidence of the social dynamics that are played out within domestic work. More important, they are indicators of the gender and class differences that characterize the work arrangement. Yet, as I have shown, women used their own social capital and emotional investments to make sense of these ambiguous transactions. Women's class and social aspirations also played an important role in valuing the various things, as they reconstruct their employers' cast-off clothing into desirable commodities. These commodities are not static; they circulate among strangers, kinship, and friends and, as a result, their meanings as well as the outcome of the exchanges are not fixed, but fluid and constantly changing.

Conclusion

In this chapter I have demonstrated how gifts given within intimate labor relations can be spontaneous acts of generosity in which care and love are involved but can also be used as strategies to gain economic or moral profit. Gifts can be both sincere and exploitative. The calculative features of these exchanges become relevant when the exchange hovers ambiguously between payment and gift, something that inevitably disrupts previous commercial arrangements and the social relations underlying the transactions (Bourdieu 1994, 180). Zelizer suggests that people differentiate among various economic transactions—especially gift giving—in intimate relations as a way of making sense of the economic activity taking place (2009, 99). Indeed, as I have shown, the subjective understanding of the meanings that women attach to the various transactions is a key aspect in defining new social ties and the power dynamics therein.

By following the trajectories of gift exchanges within intimate labor, I have shown how gifts have the potential to be instrumental, particularly when the conditions of exchange (i.e., the nature and value of the gift) determined and manipulated status within the relationship. This instrumentality sharply marked the class, racial, and gender inequalities that persist in these forms of intimate labor. Overall, gift exchanges created further inequalities and debts that were difficult to sustain. Yet the instrumentality of gifts proved to work both ways because women were able to weigh the social and emotional value of gifts to speculate on potential material or emotional profits from their relationships. The exchanges—and their possible outcomes—depended on the intimacy developed within the work relationship: the personal and cultural expectations of the services and the potential for reciprocity.

Gift exchanges within domestic and sex work confirm the complex nature of caring labor and the challenging work that women must perform to maintain safe boundaries between themselves and their clients and employers. While gifts can be used to contain the excess of intimacy and care, they can also enhance it, leaving women trapped in unequal emotional relationships. At the same time, they can function as mechanisms to advance utopian aspirations, fantasies, and desires. Approaching gifts as exchanges that (on some occasions) helped women, clients, and employers to normalize the complicated outcomes of selling care lays the groundwork for the following chapter. The final chapter expands on the analysis of the practices women used to reconstruct what they called the *normal* and to deal with their class, racial, and social dissatisfactions in London. The women, dislocated in multiple ways, tried to locate themselves in their new lives as different ethical persons. Although these (re)locations prove ultimately to be impossible, I want to show, as Sherry Ortner does, how "the ability of social beings to weave alternative, and sometimes brilliantly creative, forms of coherence across the damage is one of the heartening aspects of human subjectivity" (1995, 186).

CHAPTER 6

Utopian Selves

"Who We Really Are"

Throughout this book I have presented a complex picture of a group of middle-class women who found themselves experiencing and dealing with deep personal ruptures and dislocations provoked by their migration enterprises and their lives in London. I have explained how these estrangements were interconnected with the downward status mobility the women experienced because of their occupations as domestic and sex workers, insecure legal status, alien home arrangements in the city, new racial (dis)identifications, and ethical considerations. These dislocations left my respondents with a sense of nostalgia for the normal, which they explained as those aspects they wanted to regain from their previous lives. Kathleen Stewart has argued that nostalgia is "a cultural practice, not a given content. . . . In positing a 'once was' in relation to a 'now' creates a frame for meaning, a means of dramatizing aspects of an increasingly fluid and unnamed social life" (1988, 227). Nostalgia is about the production of a present rather than the reproduction of a past (Berdahl 1999, 202). For my informants, it entailed dealing with present estrangements by way of idealized versions of the past in which they claimed to feel normal or *like themselves.*

The scope of normality ranged from education credentials to access to material goods and leisure time, but, most important, home ownership, which they had all enjoyed at some point in their own countries. It also entailed an understanding and relocation of women's gendered identities involved in caring roles within their families. When referring to the normal, women pointed to a middle-class lifestyle before migrating, without considering that in many cases, it was precisely this lifestyle that influenced their migration journeys. The nostalgia for normality in my informants' accounts confirms what Rachel Heiman, Carla Freeman, and Mark Liechty have referred to as "longing to secure," which is "central to the ontology of middle-class subjects across cultural and national boundaries" (2012, 20).[1] This suggests that the idea of normality is more an ideological construction than a real reflection of their pasts. Listening to these women talk about the normal reveals the dissonances that prevail in the narratives of their pasts, which are incongruous with their present lives and their dreams for the future. In what appears to be a disjuncture, women maintained the illusion that they could recover some of that normality in London. If this is the case, what were the strategies that women used to create, or recreate, the normal on an everyday basis?

In this chapter, I investigate practices of consumption and sociality as constitutive of women's middle-class, racial, and gendered subjectivities. I focus on the tension that exists between the idea of trying to reestablish the normal on the one hand and migration as a process of radical change on the other. I explore this tension by examining the various emotional, economic, and material investments that my informants directed at the reparation of their idealized class identities, social statuses (along with notions of taste and distinction), and the idea of feeling like their real selves. I chart the competing conceptualizations of the transnational aspirational middle class by attending to the ways it is both imagined and realized in specific material and social settings. *Middle-class* is intimately linked to a sense of normality and becomes meaningful materially and affectively when my informants imagined and materially constructed *home* at a distance, when they enacted an ethics of care through reembodying kinship roles and relationships with loved ones through shopping, and when they used sociality as a strategy to perform and reaffirm class distinctions between themselves and others (Heiman 2009).

Remembering and Imagining a Normal Home

Early in my fieldwork, I was invited to the places where my informants lived. In most cases, women only experienced privacy and intimacy within their bedrooms. The lack of a space that women could call home, a space where they could live, either alone or with their families, instead of having to share it with strangers, was an important source of personal anxiety, insecurity, and social decline. Room doors were the entrances to their "homes" and were kept locked at all times to protect both their belongings and their privacy. The women, who generally worked eight to ten hours a day, did not spend much time at home. Therefore, they generally did not interact with the other inhabitants of the flats and houses where they lived, unless they shared a bedroom with a stranger or met their flatmates in common areas such as the kitchen or the bathroom.[2] In most cases they lived among other Latin American migrants because they tended to look for flats where people would at least speak the same language or have a similar cultural background.

Women were eager to explain to me that this place was not their real home and that they did not enjoy their current living arrangements, because they knew "what home really was." What did home mean to them? Whenever I asked this question, women would usually explain that home—a real home—was not supposed to be shared with strangers. "Back in Bolivia no one lives with strangers, everyone lives with their family. Everyone, even poor people, has a home. It may be small and humble or big and fancy, but we all have a house," Lourdes told me. Home was described as a site for the reproduction of family, and homeownership was considered not only a marker of social status but also constitutive of their middle-class identities. Many of my informants had lost their homes back in their own countries because of structural conditions of unemployment, which in turn provoked situations of indebtedness, mortgages, and foreclosures. Now, they all wished for a home in which they could cultivate family relations and feel secure, comfortable, and rooted.

Such notions of home echo those discussed in social science literature, which, despite some disagreement, continues to see home as a place of respite and tranquility. Home has been described and understood as a space where people can rest, withdraw from the world outside, and have some control over what happens in their lives (Seamon, quoted in Cresswell 2005, 24) or as the center of meaning and a field of care (Tuan 1977). While my informants' descriptions and meanings of home resonated with these quintessential and traditional notions of home, the reality of their lives in London contradicted them. As de Lauretis (1986) and Martin and Mohanty (1997) have discussed, home is not necessarily experienced as a place of care and rootedness. Not all groups experience home in the same way; on the contrary, gender, race, and age are conditions that deeply affect the way in which home is perceived and lived. Furthermore, for those who live under the uncertainty of an insecure legal status, low-income jobs, and precarious housing conditions, home can become a site of uneasiness, anxiety, discomfort, and potential conflict.

These conditions pushed women like Eva to do everything they could to construct a home in London. Eva had come to London with the belief that people could more easily obtain housing through social benefits in England than in other countries in Europe. After the many evenings that we spent together filling out the necessary forms for housing benefits, Eva's belief was confirmed: within just three months of submitting the paperwork she was able to move into a one-bedroom flat in south London with her daughter, Maria. The need to have a proper home was grounded in Eva's idea of developing and securing what she called a normal family life in London and had taken shape well before she applied for the housing benefit. "I came to London for good. I do not want to go back to Spain or Peru—I want to construct a home here in London. This is the place where I can actually achieve that dream," Eva told me.

When I first visited Eva's house, she showed me some of the things she had bought for her future home. In her room in south London there were two single beds, a wardrobe, an old desk, a small table, and an old-fashioned chair. The beds had matching duvets, cushions, and pillows coordinated with the purple and pink motifs decorating the room. Eva was meticulous about the decoration of her room because she wanted to create a pretty space for herself and her daughter, even though, as she often lamented, it was "only a room."[3] Eva's room also contained two antique tables and a chair, clashing with the purple and pink theme. She had bought these pieces of furniture for the living room of her future home. "They only cost me £20 each. Look how beautiful they are, they look really refined and expensive, they are antiques," she said.

Eva's imaginative construction of her future home took place during the weekends when we visited car boot sales, shopped at TK Maxx, or went window shopping around London. Every time we went to TK Maxx, Eva sighed with melancholy as she looked at the decorations she wanted but could not afford. She developed narratives and detailed descriptions of her future home through the different objects that we saw in the aisles of the shop. A lamp, vase, or teapot was a reminder of the things that she left behind in Madrid. These objects were simultaneously remembrances of things past and signs of a future in which she thought she would be able to achieve her dream of having a home for herself and her daughter. She believed that, in addition to obtaining the housing benefits, in the future she might be able to be allocated a council flat in London.

In a similar vein, Mariana was constantly haunted by the things she had left behind in Perugia, Italy, to come to London. "I had a home there. I bought all these things when I got married, I had an espresso machine, duvet covers, plates, glasses, everything; it was a real home with my husband," she told me. These things provided a source of comfort and a sense of belonging[4]; they represented Mariana's appropriation of the world outside and at the same time were a reflection of her ideas and aspirations toward her future as a married woman. Although the flat in Perugia had been a temporary home, it had been constructed through her relationship with Ricardo and the gendered roles they shared in the production of the space, where she was the carer in the household and Ricardo was the breadwinner. Mariana had left Brazil broken-hearted and feeling like a spinster because most of her friends were getting married; therefore, her married life in Italy enabled her to gain some transnational status. In contrast to London, in Italy she had been a successful migrant who had a home, carried an Italian passport (by claiming ancestry), spoke the language, and, more important, did not have to work in a menial job.

Mariana's desire to have a home in London was temporarily appeased by skimming through the pages of the IKEA catalog and constructing narratives of the future. "I need to have a house with my husband just like I had in Italy. I need to feel that I have something more than just this humiliating work and this lonely life. I need to feel normal again," she constantly told me. Mariana's parameters of normality coveted the idea of having a place she could come to every night after work, talk about her day with her husband, cook for him, watch television, and relax instead of having to cohabit in a house with strangers.

Sabrina, too, withdrew from the present by planning and imagining her future home, particularly when she flipped through the pages of the Argos catalog and described to me the things that she liked, the things she wanted for her loved ones, and why they were such excellent value. Sabrina set herself the goal of saving 1 million *Reales* (approximately £300,000), and every evening she assiduously recorded her daily income and expenditures in her diary. Each page of her diary bore witness to her life as a sex worker in London. More important, the process of writing down her daily finances provided her with the opportunity to imagine the near future, a future that included the purchase of a home for her loved ones.

Making a Caring Home

The imagination of home was followed by its material and symbolic construction. This entailed a careful assemblage of cultural capital and a particular taste that would reflect women's desired class membership and lifestyle. Like Silvia Fehérváry's (2002, 2011) informants in postsocialist

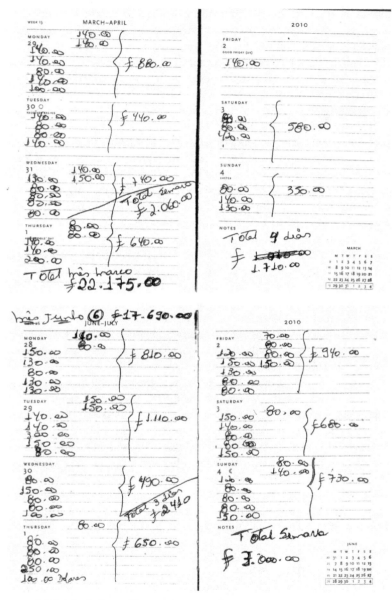

FIGURE 6.1 Sabrina's diary with everyday accounts.

Hungary, my informants' ideal lifestyles were grounded in what they described as symbols of modernity, middle-class respectability, and normality, such as western European homes and appliances. "Look at the things you can buy in IKEA, everything looks so modern and well-designed. It is possible to have home with nice modern things. Back in Bolivia you would never be able to access things like these," Jovanna told me.[5] Furthermore, the desire to acquire a modern middle-class lifestyle turned women into thoughtful consumers who tried to find a balance between recreating a sense of distinction and fulfilling obligations to family.

Anthropology has long recognized the importance that consumption and material goods have in the construction and maintenance of social relations and the reproduction of meaningful differences between social groups. Marshall Sahlins started the debate by explaining how people make symbolic statements through consumption (1976). He explained that the symbolic differences between objects produce and reproduce "the meaningful differences between" social groups (1976, 181). Mary Douglas and Baron Isherwood (1978) were also interested in the symbolic meaning of objects but were more concerned about the relationship between the meaning of commodities and people's active engagements with them through different social practices. Later, Pierre Bourdieu (1984) moved beyond the individual and understood consumption and taste as social practices embedded in structural class relations. Following these approaches, Daniel Miller, among others, has given detailed ethnographic attention to the lives and practices of consumers and the ways in which people appropriate market goods and imbue them with meaning (1995a, 1995b, 1998).

In this chapter, I adopt an approach to consumption and material culture that, like Bourdieu's, highlights the class orientation of individuals through notions of taste. I explore the meanings and values that people give to objects to make sense of their social worlds. Such value, as Bourdieu explains, is rooted in people's social and cultural capitals and indexed by a sense of taste that inevitably produces social distinctions in society (1984, 174).[6] For Bourdieu, the different choices that people make are all distinctions, that is, choices made in opposition to those made by other classes. These choices reflect the position within a class system and create a system of power relations in which minute distinctions of taste become the basis for social judgment. Rather than limiting the analysis to status-seeking goals or seeing consumption as only an expression of identity and lifestyle,[7] I locate women's practices within a wider context of migration and analyze how these practices are linked to women's personhood and social relationships. Consumption becomes a process whereby women imbue objects with meanings that help them to (re)construct social relationships, signaling social statuses and (re)configuring aspects of their migrants' subjectivities. Although the objects themselves are an important part of the analysis, my specific interest is in consumption as a process whereby women realized—or (re)invented—themselves as middle-class people. These matters bear witness to Miller's observation that "consumption has become the main arena in which and through which people have to struggle towards control over the definition of themselves and their values" (1995a, 277).

Taking into account these theoretical underpinnings, let me go back to the moment Eva received the news from the Council Office about the successful outcome of her housing benefit application. Once she got the approval, she immediately started planning the construction of her home. The enterprise of choosing things for the new house, albeit constrained by her limited economic resources, was nonetheless carefully crafted. Her plan included a careful appreciation of used and secondhand goods that signified and could project her middle-class taste. She considered the Battersea car boot sale on the South Bank one of the best places to find secondhand objects because it was where better-off people, that is, white British people, sold their things.

During our visit to Battersea, Eva would classify the sellers, as well as the goods for sale, using her own criteria for what she considered good porcelain, ceramics, antiques, and clothes. It would take hours for her to decide what she wanted to buy because she first needed to calculate very carefully the amount of money she wanted to spend. Usually, the things she ended up buying were not only things that she needed, but also things that she considered sophisticated enough for her taste. After a few weeks of visiting the market together, she managed to buy a complete set of silverware cutlery and a set of old English porcelain dishware for four people. With pride, she showed me the old plates and the forks that had old insignias and emblems, a feature that automatically granted these objects a sense of distinction. They were signs of what she idealized as a middle-class, white, European taste—a taste she had cultivated after years of working in a rich household in Madrid.

While Eva's desires for material respectability were prominent in her deliberations over purchasing secondhand things that had belonged to rich, white, British people, for Sabrina objects contained value if they were brand new. By buying new commodities for the household, she was appropriating symbols of distinction and status that would be displayed in the near future back in Brazil. Therefore, in November 2011, a month before she returned to Brazil and to her son, Ronaldo, Sabrina began her shopping. Over the course of just one day, she bought eight different satin sheets and duvet covers for her own future bed and for those of her mother and her aunt, plus four goose feather pillows and one Norwegian cotton duvet for her son. Sabrina also bought appliances for her kitchen at Argos. "I have already bought a flat in Sao Paulo. Now I want my kitchen to have domestic appliances of the same color and design," she said. She opened the box that we had recently brought from the shop, which held a red toaster with a matching red kettle and red coffee machine. We went to the kitchen and placed them next to each other; she wanted to see them in their "natural environment." As Miller suggests, "material culture within our homes appears as both our appropriation of the larger world and often as the representation of that world within our private domain" (2001, 1). Through these objects Sabrina was not only communicating her success as a migrant but also performing care based on the idea that gifts would help her restore family ties.

Before Sabrina returned to Brazil we spent all day shopping, buying gifts for the entire family. We walked along the aisles of JD Sports to find a pair of tennis shoes for her son. She was not sure which color he would prefer, so she got him one black and one red pair; she was convinced that he would love the fact that they were Nike shoes. Once we got to Primark she picked clothes for her nieces—miniskirts, t-shirts, jackets—items that she said were fashionable and, more important, different from the clothes that they would buy in Brazil. For Ronaldo, she carefully picked out jeans, shirts, pants, t-shirts, hoodies, and shorts. "It is quite hard for me to buy clothes for Ronaldo as I have not seen him in a long time. I do not know what his taste is and I am not really sure about his actual size, but I hope that he would like the gifts I am bringing. It is very important to me to get close to him after all this time." After the shopping trip, I spent three days at her flat helping her pack nine suitcases. The packing turned into a ritual sustained on a narrative of care and the momentary reconfiguration of kinship. I say momentary because her daily life and work imposed itself on the time she had to prepare for the trip. The packing alternated with receiving clients and seeing Robert, who, during this shopping extravaganza, could not help but think that Sabrina's shopping practices were flashy and irrational.

For Sabrina, however, the purchase of these items was evidence of her financial wisdom and thriftiness because most of these things were cheaper in London than in Brazil; for her, it was without doubt the best economic choice. Was Sabrina making a free choice in buying these gifts, or were these shopping practices, as is often asserted about excessive consumerism, a form of *false consciousness*?[8] On the one hand, we could argue that she was (as Robert thought) deluded and dazzled by the cheap commodities that London offered. She was trapped in the consumer society that, according to Henri Lefebvre, manufactures goods along with consumers—in which there is a transfer from need to desire (2014, 304). And yet, Sabrina's attraction to transnational commodities allowed her to demonstrate her new status both materially and symbolically—as a successful migrant and mother.[9]

These conspicuous consumption practices were recurrent among many of my informants, who accumulated a great amount of stuff—particularly clothes, which were packed in plastic bags waiting to be sent back to their home countries. For Angelica, the accumulation of things represented the future possibility of reconnecting with her daughter, even though her unstable working life in London did not allow her to go back to Brazil. Yet, within her precarious living conditions, Angelica's extravagance mitigated some of the discomforts that she experienced resulting from a previous deportation from Portugal and her current undocumented status. These experiences had important repercussions for the ways in which she perceived her present and future life. Accordingly, she had an immediate, *seize the day* approach to life and to consumption. Accumulation seemed to mean more to her than just ownership of things; it was a way to deal with the alienation and liminality she experienced on an everyday basis. In her ethnographic study on prostitution in Mexico, Patty Kelly explains that although women in sex work lose the worth ascribed to "respectable" women by ascending the economic ladder, they experience a new kind of worth associated not with gender, but with class (2008, 190). Women like Angelica and Sabrina were able to use shopping as a way to perform middle-class taste and, in the process, partially mitigate the stigma and anxieties produced by selling sex. There were two dimensions to Angelica's consumption practices. The first was the personal dimension, which responded to her desire to obtain things for herself and for her family. The second dimension was of conspicuous shopping for the sake of accumulation. This inclination to accumulate was intimately linked to the need to make place—although temporarily—in London. Both dimensions were directed at the creation of normality and also eased Angelica's deep-seated anxiety about her uncertain future.

The room in west London where Angelica lived until June 2010 was packed with things, including televisions, videos, shoes, clothes, and beauty products. Angelica's world (her room) was filled with items she had acquired over the three years that she had spent in London. Her shopping practices were mapped around secondhand shops located in affluent neighborhoods of the city, which she preferred because they offered better-quality items. She was thrilled every time she found clothes that were of good quality and sophisticated while also being cheap, especially if these were intended as gifts for her daughter and family.

However, in contrast to Sabrina, the dream of bringing or sending the items back to Brazil was not currently possible for Angelica. In the meantime, she used things to construct a sense of permanence in the face of her nomadic lifestyle. The more she bought, the better she felt about her living space. In addition to accruing more and more things, she enjoyed organizing and reorganizing them in the room. Rearranging the room triggered memories of the things she was forced to leave behind in Portugal because of her deportation. Those things were lost forever; they were ghosts that resurfaced through the new things she bought in London. In the event of future deportation, she did not want to lose what she had accumulated in London, so this time she had a plan. "Everything is packed in air-sealed plastic bags with a list attached to it. In case something happens to me, my friend Romina will send them to Brazil. I have already saved a little bit of money for that," she explained to me while showing me the bags. Through these place-making practices she reconstructed the narrative of her life as a migrant. She seemed to be trapped between the past (memories of things), the present (accumulation of things), and the future (when she would finally be able to send those things back to Brazil).

The imaginative and physical processes that shaped the women's homemaking practices were intertwined with their middle-class subjectivities and social aspirations. They not only allowed the women to accumulate and articulate their cultural capital, but also reflected their ambitions and projections of ideal social relations. The things that they acquired had a value beyond the material one: they will (re)construct home, the vital site for the performance of gender roles and the maintenance of kinship relationships. In this regard, there was something meaning-making about the very process of shopping. They were performing care—they were contributing to the family and asserting kinship roles and female obligations that they had not properly performed in recent years and, as a result, were reconstructing a sense of self. The salience of home as a utopian space where women would recuperate what they had lost confirms that, even at a distance, women are regarded as responsible for erecting it through their caring labor and for signifying the social identity of the family.

Relocating the Real Self through Idioms of Distinction

The need to recreate a sense of permanence and normality was, for some women, appeased through plans to construct a home. However, for those women whose plans did not include a home, the recreation of a sense of normality took different forms and meanings. Instead of buying things for the family, these women used consumption, as well as idioms of fashion, to invest in themselves, prove their class identities, and distinguish themselves from other migrants. Luciana thought that people who, for example, bought fake branded items had bad taste. "Since I have been in London I have never bought shoes other than the MBT fitness shoes, I do not care if I spend more than £100 on a pair." She claimed that MBT were the original fitness shoes and that she could never buy a cheap knock-off. For her, buying expensive, "genuine" shoes was part of the definition of herself as different from the cleaners she worked with; she was not a real cleaner, but an artist who was temporarily engaging in menial labor to have more time for her art.

I saw Luciana's fixation with such shoes when I visited her tiny studio flat, where she had several pairs of MBT shoes stored in various boxes. The flat was full of things—there was hardly any space to move—but she was proud to have a place that she did not have to share with other people, especially other migrants. Despite the lack of space, Luciana had inhabited the place in an extraordinary way with shoes and clothes and with her art, what she called her *nonpaintings*. These nonpaintings were collages composed of scraps from magazines and books that she glued together to compose scenes or landscapes. She pasted these scraps using the logic of perspective, creating fantastic scenes where the various images overlapped each other. Her art was influenced by different Renaissance, Baroque, and Romantic painters; while we looked at her art pieces, she enjoyed explaining the technique to me and the different artistic influences. Such conversations displayed Luciana's cultural and symbolic capital and sense of taste. Her taste for shoes and her artistic sophistication built up her cultural capital, providing evidence of the contrast that existed between herself and others.

In a similar vein, as an entrepreneur who had worked in real estate back in Venezuela and Madrid, Amelia (discussed in Chapters 1 and 3) was deeply humiliated and resentful about being a domestic worker in London. As was the case for most of my informants, her middle-class identity was based on her position within the labor market in her country of origin. Having lost this position, she found a way to ameliorate some of these tensions by spending most of her free time shopping at TK Maxx, secondhand shops in South Kensington in west London, and car boot sales with her friend Eva. Although she was €25,000 in debt, she was forever telling me that spending £10 or £50 would not make any real difference to her financial situation (for indebted consumers, see Lehtonen 1999). "It does not make a difference if I buy a coffee, or get fancy organic bread at Whole Foods Market, or if occasionally I buy a nice shirt at TK Maxx. Spending a few pounds here and there will not make me poorer, but they do make me feel less of a maid," she told me.

During our visits to TK Maxx, Amelia created narratives of taste and distinction through branded items. She usually focused her attention on signature accessories that held a special significance because of the social status that these things exemplified in Venezuela. Shopping at the brand discount store TK Maxx represented for most of my informants the paradise of the democratization of fashion. Bourdieu (1984) claims that the price devaluation of fashion diminishes its power of distinction for middle-class people like my informants. However, price devaluation allowed partial access to a world of distinction that otherwise only belonged to the rich. Although the women were aware that these were discounted items, the value resided in the brands that they considered sophisticated enough for their taste. "Here in London I can buy things that would have taken me years to buy back in Brazil," said Juliana. Cheap but signature items were the best possible combination to match their middle-class aspirational taste.

While walking through the aisles, Amelia often stopped in front of the sunglass section and tried on at least twenty pairs. "Look Ana, I look like a posh woman from South Kensington, not like a cachifa (maid) from London," she said. She liked to explain to Eva and me that people made the mistake of buying sunglasses just for the sake of showing off the brand, although the glasses often did not fit the shape of their faces. According to Amelia, the need to show off branded goods, without taking into account the intangible aspects of fashion, was irrefutable evidence of bad taste, a lack of distinction and class. As Mark Liechty explains in the case of middle-class taste and fashion in Nepal, "the notion of fashion 'suitability' is a characteristically middle-class sensibility," so the fact that Amelia wanted to display her fashion knowledge, as an acquired and embodied knowledge, "helps to naturalize middle-class privilege and ensures that fashion is not only the province of the rich" (2003, 110). Through the idiom of fashion as a form of symbolic capital, Amelia was performing a social class she felt she rightly belonged to, regardless of her current precarious situation in London.

Bad taste and lack of distinction were also linked to people's racial and ethnic identities. Many of my informants relentlessly and persistently classified other people by judging their fashion styles interweaved with their skin color. While standing on the second floor of a shopping center in south London (regarded as a Latin American enclave), Vanessa and Barbara (both from Colombia) often enjoyed guessing people's nationalities by way of analyzing their style of dress and "lack of taste." Yet this lack of taste correlated with their prejudices and ideas of race/ethnicity and beauty. People with indigenous looks, "those *cholitas*," for instance (as Barbara called women from Bolivia who looked indigenous), were simply not able to look good in jeans. "It does not really matter what they wear, they cannot get rid of their indigenous look," she told me while pointing at a woman passing by. "I think it comes down to the anatomy, the type of body—with ample hips, flat bottoms and prominent bellies it is difficult to look good in tight jeans," Vanessa reiterated. The whiter people were, the better they could pull off clothes and style. Using phrases like "they just cannot help it," their racial judgments spoke of wider cultural notions around inferior, fixed racial traits that stand in opposition to the mainstream white, "superior" traits. These notions confirm what Peter Wade explains as the key to race in Latin America, that is, "that racism and mixture coexist and interweave," (2008, 179) creating societies in which categories such as black and indigenous exist and are part of the national imaginary. Yet, because modernity, development, and high status are often associated with whiteness or at least mixedness, people with lighter skin automatically place themselves at the top of the racial pyramid. People like Vanessa and Barbara, who self-identified as white, did not find it problematic to judge people's taste based on racial traits. After all, they might have been Latin Americans, but according to their own national and racial classifications they were whiter than other Latin Americans.

Locating the Normal through Sociality

Fashion and the display of cultural capital was not the only medium that women used to recompose their sense of self and class location. Social events and gatherings were also situations in which they could embark on a battle for distinction. In November 2009, I was invited to have lunch at Amelia's flat. She opened the door of the basement flat where she lived and worked in west London, receiving me with a big smile and a hug. *"Bienvenida a mi humilde hogar"* (Welcome to my humble home), she told me while laughing at the irony of welcoming me to the mansion of her rich employers. She asked me to come in and introduced me to a nicely dressed group of women who were sitting together around the kitchen bar table where there were wine, olives, cheese, chips, and other nibbles. "This is Ana, my friend from Mexico, she is an anthropologist and is doing a PhD in London. She is doing a study on women like us, *cachifas* (maids)." Amelia and Eva knew each other from Madrid and had met Rosa and Cristina at the church in South Kensington where they were all looking for jobs. This was the first time I had met Cristina and Rosa. After I had explained what anthropologists do, the women told me where they came from and what they did in London. In the meantime, Amelia was cooking Venezuelan *arepas* (thick corn flour tortillas) and passing them around for us to eat. I sat next to Eva, who passed me a plate with an *arepa* that Amelia had just prepared for me. While eating the *arepas*, the women began talk about their own national foods and how much they missed them.

This was the first time I had spent time with the women as a group. The encounter gave me the opportunity to see them outside their everyday working activities and in interaction with each other. Getting together for lunch at Amelia's house felt, for Rosa, "as if I were back in Peru or even Spain with my friends having coffee." The place was not Amelia's, but on this specific Sunday she had the permission of the *jefa* (female employer) to invite some friends over on her day off. As I explained in Chapter 3, Amelia lived at her employer's house in a basement flat where she had a tiny kitchen, bathroom, one bed, and a sofa. Despite her employer's restrictions and rules concerning the use of the space, Amelia had added some personal touches to the room by setting out photographs of her family and rearranging the furniture.[10] The space, the food, and the company created a sense of normality that women longed for while working as live-in domestic workers.

Conversation soon turned to their families back home, including matters such as the recent death of Cristina's brother in Ecuador. When the tone of the conversation turned sad and nostalgic, Amelia decided to elevate the mood of the party and put on some music for us to dance and forget our sorrows. She explained that she had a marvelous party music mix from her son's wedding in Spain that would definitely lift the spirits of the gathering. To the rhythms of *reggaeton*, Cristina stood up and showed us her "sexy *reggaeton* moves," as she called them, to encourage the others to join her on the dance floor. Dancing reminded Cristina of her youth in Ecuador where she would spend all night in disco bars. With the music at full volume, Rosa and Amelia joined Cristina.

Amid the dancing and laughing, Amelia told us about her son's wedding, claiming that it had been a very elegant event for which no expense had been spared. Later I became aware that she had gone further into debt because of the wedding, hindering her plans of going back to Venezuela to her normal life. When the song was over, she appeared at the table with a big fancy box containing the photo album and DVD of the wedding. The velvet box contained a plastic leather album with a sepia cover photo of the couple. Amelia's son was in coattails, while her daughter-in-law wore a white wedding dress with a long train and was crowned with a tiara. Amelia's outfit, which was approved by her guests, featured a long red satin dress complemented by a traditional Spanish *peineta* (decorative headdress) and a long, embroidered mantle. "This dress is a traditional outfit from Spain that women use for special occasions," she told us. In addition to showing the photos, she played the DVD for us so we could understand and appreciate the event in all its splendor. During the video Amelia talked about her life and about the people who composed her earlier life in Venezuela. By sharing these aspects of herself with other women she was actively reconstituting her affected status and temporarily regaining some respectability in the eyes of others who experienced similar dislocations and longed for the reconstruction of normality.

Events like the one described above were few and far between because of the limited free time that live-in domestic workers had. It was even more unusual for me to meet women's relatives because of the distance that separated them from their families. However, in March 2011, after a year of developing close relationships with my informants, Cristina invited me to the wedding of her daughter Ivonne in Madrid. Ivonne's wedding offered me the chance to meet Cristina's nuclear and extended family in the place where she had had a different life, a better life. Apart from she and I having become close friends, she wanted me to understand where she had come from, who she really was, as she expressed it to me. The invitation was extended to Felipa (and her daughter) and myself. We all flew to Madrid and for four days we became part of Cristina's family, who had come all the way from Ecuador to attend the wedding. The occasion had brought together *la abuela* (grandmother) and her four daughters, who had not seen each other in years because two of them had migrated to Spain.

Wedding preparations were in place, many of which Cristina had contributed to financially. The whole event had been carefully organized by Ivonne with the help of her family and her in-laws. Even at a distance, Cristina had been attentively following the organization and thereby performing care and fulfilling her kinship role with her daughter. She talked about the event for months ahead of time, telling me that it would be a break from the harsh reality of her life in London. The wedding, though an extraordinary event, became an occasion to temporarily retrieve and recreate what she referred to as normality. However, the recuperation of this normality necessitated additional work. To achieve it, we both spent a morning at the beauty salon, where she dyed and styled her hair and had a pedicure, manicure, and facial that would help her get rid of what she referred to as the *mucama* (maid) look; she needed to look *decente* (decent) for her daughter's wedding. "This reminds me of my life back home where I had the time to spend on these unnecessary but pleasant luxuries," she explained.

The wedding ceremony took place in a church in downtown Madrid. After the ceremony, 150 people headed to the reception venue where a troupe of waiters with sparkling wine and canapés were waiting for the wedding guests. We were entertained for a few hours by a quartet playing classical music before the meal. Dinner was a feast, a sophisticated array of Spanish food and wine. Overall, it was a night of sumptuousness and overindulgence. It was a night in which Cristina could prove her success as a migrant. Despite her life in London, she had raised a daughter who was marrying a white Spanish man and had a second daughter who was dating a young, white British man (who was also invited to the wedding). "I know that my daughters can marry whoever they like, but I am glad that they are with European men rather than the Latin American *machos* that would only take advantage of them." In contrast with other young women from her family, Cristina's daughters were not marrying Ecuadorians or Dominicans in Madrid, something that I learned was considered a sign of failure, as well as a racial concern, among Cristina's family. In the eyes of her family and friends, she had succeeded as a mother and as a migrant. "Cristina has done a lot for the family. She has raised two beautiful girls who are hard-working and are in good relationships with decent men. She also brought two of her sisters to Spain and helped them finding jobs. She is a good example for the family, but most importantly, for her daughters," *la abuela* (grandmother) told me. It was during these occasions that women needed to prove that they had gained economic stability, as well as preserve a level of respectability through fostering traditional family values among their children. Among my informants, respectability encompassed a range of different things. Values around femininity regarding sexuality and ways to behave and treat men were regarded as important aspects of being a good, respectable woman. Respectability was also circumscribed to modes of comportment in front of others. For instance, Eva insisted that women who cursed or talked loud in public were vulgar; she constantly reprimanded Amelia for raising her voice when using public transportation. Dress code according to age and manners at the table were also signs of being respectable, according to some of my informants. Respectability, as Carla Freeman explains, is a characteristic that seems to encompass the middle classes across time and space (2012, 86); it continues to be "one of the most ubiquitous signifiers of class" (Skeggs 1997, 1). For Cristina, her daughter's wedding was the only way to prove that she had not lost everything, that although she was a domestic worker she had raised good daughters who were making the right choices in life.

Social gatherings were particularly important for women who, besides experiencing class estrangements, were undocumented. Although in this book I do not use my informants' legal statuses as reified categories to define them, being undocumented certainly affected their notions of normality as well as their place-making practices. As I have explained, being undocumented meant that people were forced to engage in illicit practices and to live clandestinely in a constant state of anxiety because of the threat of deportation. It is mainly in contrast to these aspects of women's lives, along with the fragility that illegality represented, that the aim for normality must be analyzed. For instance, birthday parties, christenings, and *churrascos* (barbecues) after church on Sundays were occasions in which migrants momentarily put their dislocated London lives to one side, felt at ease, and escaped the negative aspects of their occupations. They were not domestic workers or illegal migrants; they were just people enjoying their social lives in London. These events were reproductions of social events back home. They functioned as transnational social spaces where migrants socially and materially reconstructed distinct aspects of their personhood and the establishment of links between their countries of origin and the new location.

The baptism of Lourdes's grandchild was a festive occasion. One-year-old Camila's baptism—in which I was asked to be the godmother—was a day to celebrate. Following the ritual at a Catholic church, which introduced Camila into the faith, the celebration was a day of lavish consumption— and a performance of status and class. As the godmother, there were certain responsibilities that I was required to fulfill. One included overseeing the purchase of Camila's christening gown. After viewing various options, I decided to buy a simple christening gown that I thought would be proper for the occasion. When I showed the dress to Patricia (Camila's mother) and Lourdes, they looked quite disappointed with my choice. Saying that it was the incorrect size, they told me that I needed to change it. In search of advice, I turned to Jovanna and showed her the dress that I had selected. "Ay Ana, you do not understand, this dress is way too plain for *their* 'taste.' These are low-class people that like flashy things and want to make in impression at this type of event. You need to buy a big, garish dress for Camila," she told me. I was surprised by Jovanna's remarks about Lourdes's family social class, especially the condescending tone she used.

Her explanation was simple: they belonged to a different class. It was not only their taste, but also the fact that Lourdes's family came from an indigenous background that gave Jovanna the authority to signal them as lower class. For Jovanna, as a self-defined white person, race was intrinsically linked to a sense of taste that was not properly white but aspirational. This aspirational taste, which according to Jovanna did not fit a middle-class esthetic, revealed Pedro's and Lourdes's background. This belief, however, stood in sharp opposition to the way in which Pedro and Lourdes defined themselves as middle-class people, particularly in relation to their levels of education. Whenever we talked about Bolivia or when I asked them about their own class identifications, Pedro and Lourdes explained that they could not identify themselves as poor people.

> "The poor people in my country are really poor and have no real oppor-
> tunities to improve. My mother was poor, she was an indigenous women
> who spoke *quechua*, but she did not want us to learn the language and
> made huge efforts to send us to school in order to have better oppor-
> tunities in life. If I have to choose, I would probably say I am middle
> class because I am educated," Lourdes told me.

She was also very keen about reminding me that Pedro had a master's degree, a clear sign of their middle class.

Despite their social and racial backgrounds in Bolivia, events such as the baptism allowed people to make sense of their new homes, to find themselves in their new realities. On the one hand, in the making of new places they were able to reinvent their social class and race, partly because the United Kingdom does not recognize Latin Americans as an ethnic category as a racial group; on the other hand, they remained trapped by the social class, ethnic, and racial stereotypes that prevailed in their countries. In this regard, for Pedro and the baby's father, the baptism was an opportunity to display their new status by splurging on the event, trying to make people feel at home, and at the same time displaying their own sense of distinction and taste.[11] In this case, they were not interested in displaying European/Western symbols of sophistication and taste as a sign of success, but showed their success by being able to recreate "home" in London. They had both spent more than £1,000 on the party: renting the venue, food, music, entertainment for the children, alcohol for the adults, sweets, gifts for the children, birthday cake, and a Bolivian *piñata*.

There was a feast of Bolivian food: potatoes, rice, chicken, pork, tomato salad, yam, *chuño* (dehydrated potatoes), and *mani* soup (peanut soup), in addition to sandwiches, hot dogs, and crisps for the children. As Pedro said, "This party is as good as it gets back in Bolivia. It is even better because we are in London." These sorts of events reproduced secure familiar spaces where, apart from enjoying food from their country, they could reclaim some parts of their everyday, dislocated selves. As Cecilia said, "Today I do not look like a domestic worker, I look like myself," to which Karina jokingly replied, "Yes, you might not look like a domestic worker but you still have the hands of one." Though the remark was meant as a joke, it hints at the tension that existed between women's realities and their (re)imaginings of previous notions of the self. It refers to their embodied experience of a class dislocation through the physical evidence of dried hands, calluses, and ruined manicures.

These get-togethers also provided opportunities for the women to spend time with their children and partners, to perform their roles as mothers in front of others. While the men were drinking and talking among themselves on one side of the room, the women were attending to their children's needs and helping Lourdes with the food and drinks for the guests. The sharp gender division within the party was enhanced by the women's comments on their ideals for married life: "If it were up to me, I wouldn't work. I will spend the whole time with my child and taking care of my home. I would really like to be a normal housewife, like my friends back home," Cecilia told me. Several women expressed their agreement: they wanted to have time to raise their children and support family life. These gender roles were linked to what they traditionally thought of as women's work and men's work within the family. However, women's occupations, living arrangements, and gender roles within the household in London contradicted their idealized notions of motherhood and marriage. The ordinary family life they longed for was substantially removed from their reality. They could only hope that in the future, they would be able to live the way they really wanted.

Conclusion

Women's everyday efforts were channeled into the artificial reconstruction of what they called the normal, which was in constant contradiction with their lives in London. The struggle to recuperate a sense of normality must be understood in relation to the aspirations women placed on the migration project and the future; it should not be understood as an exact or real reflection of their past lives. Who they really were was a constant self-definition women performed and constructed on an everyday basis to differentiate themselves from others. In his analysis of aspiration among the middle classes in Egypt, Samuli Schielke (2012) examines the role that the temporality of the future had in people's sense of aspiration, frustration, migration, and consumption. He explains how among those whose resources are limited, "daily life becomes a breathless race to keep up with the demands of the future" (2012, 53). Among my informants the present was never good enough; it was a temporary trap with money yet to be made, houses to be bought or built, children to be educated, and debts to be paid. Living in the future and constructing their present lives as an attempt to achieve their dreams provided women with a perpetual aspiration for a better life.

The stories presented in this chapter described the efforts women made to reconstitute their class, status, and disrupted subjectivities, while at the same generating new ones. The attention to workers' consumption practices and sociality points to the cultural conflicts involved in migrant labor, but as Mary Beth Mills has argued, it is also "an important arena wherein women can mobilize dominant symbols and meanings to serve their own interests and to stretch, if only temporarily, the limits of their subordination within the wider society" (1997, 54). In this regard, the practices of consumption and sociality that I have described might appear as detached from the political. However, women were not only trying to make home nice—because of their lack of entitlements and rights—but also trying to insert themselves in new class locations. Through various normalizing practices such as acquiring commodities and displaying a sense of distinction and taste, women were able to reconstruct themselves as caring mothers reasserting their sense of real selves. Although a self appears to be a seemingly private, contained thing, it proves to be always in flux and influenced by internal and external factors.

CONCLUSION

....

It was the beginning of June 2016, just a few days before the United Kingdom's European Union membership referendum was going to take place. The atmosphere in London was strained by the unfolding of these events; the referendum, despite our incredulity, was going to happen. The UK Independence Party and the pro-Brexit politicians in the United Kingdom actually stood a chance of winning a vote that had been carefully crafted under the rhetoric of anti-immigration, xenophobia, islamophobia, economic precarity, and national sovereignty. As with Trump's presidential campaign in the United States, right-wing UK conservative reformists were slowly gaining ground and the trust of the people who had been left behind by the liberal agendas of previous administrations that they believed had undermined the well-being of British people for the sake of the global economy.

I was talking to a friend about it and—assuming that he was voting "in" (i.e., to stay in the European Union)—jokingly asked whether he was voting in or out. To my surprise, he said out, just like that. I was astonished, frozen by his response. It took me a few seconds to process what I just I heard, as images of Trump, Le Pen, and Farage crossed my mind and clouded my thoughts. I could feel the blood running through my veins and turning my face red. He was the first person I knew who had said that he was voting out. Instead of reacting negatively, I decided to take the opportunity to try to understand what was behind his choice. I asked why.

His answer, as I feared, went straight to blaming migrants. "There are too many migrants and not enough jobs," he said. He explained how unfair it was for people in Britain to have to paid for a health-care system that was used and abused by migrants who were "not paying" taxes. He said that as a teacher, he could see firsthand how British children were being left behind because of the increasing presence of migrant children who did not speak English and did not share the same cultural values. Migrants were taking advantage of a welfare system by claiming housing benefits, child tax credit, and free health care and were not giving anything back. "So, this is about migrants," I said. He said that unfortunately there were too many, too many. "What about me? I am a migrant, I am taking up a job that a British person could have. Is it my fault as well?" I asked. Of course, he remained silent. His silence, though, encompassed the deep class and racial underpinnings that discourses like Brexit's have as part of their agenda to recover white supremacy in the West.

Unsurprisingly, this conversation with my friend led me to think about my informants and their role in the whole Brexit anti-immigration mess. Which migrants was he talking about? For those who—like some of my informants—do not have documents and live their lives as illegal migrants in London, Brexit or no Brexit does not make a difference because they remain invisible and hard to pinpoint. They have increasingly become expendable, worthless, and forced to navigate lengthy draconian legal systems that fracture their inner selves and exploit them in new ways. While the conservative pro-Brexit rhetoric stigmatizes low-skilled European migrants for taking advantage of the state institutions and the welfare system, there is a parallel anti–illegal migrant discourse that includes thousands of undocumented non-European migrants. Under these agendas, both groups appear to be on the same boat, and both debates echo neoliberal ideologies of deservingness that have enormous impact and resonance in times of austerity and economic crisis. They are a dreadful and alarming reflection of the current state of the world ruled by intolerance, racism, discrimination, and new forms of postcolonial exploitation. If a state like the United Kingdom is now deporting and blatantly denying citizenship rights to people who were brought from the ex-colonies to work on the jobs that white people did not want, grew up in the United Kingdom, and have their families in the country, like the current case of the Windrush generation migrants, then the future for undocumented migrants like the ones I worked with is nothing but dire. While this book is being revised and edited, a new anti-immigration scandal is erupting in the United States. In the course of June 2018, Trump has reinforced his political agenda and is not only separating immigrant families (and old anti-immigration policy in the country), but is keeping children in detention centers, effectively in cages. "It looks like a zoo", I heard on the Radio while the senator from Texas was being interviewed. This expression made me wonder about Nazi officers visiting concentration camps, probably thinking the same. On top of the horror behind this scene, as a Mexican I cannot help to feel deep anger, frustration and an overwhelming sadness for those people from Mexico and Central America who are now suffering the consequences of right-wing, nationalist and what looks like neo fascist, white supremacist governments in the West.

Migrants now more than ever are trifled by liberal states that need their cheap labor, but at the same time have the power to exercise the sovereign right to deport those without documents and, probably in the near post-Brexit future, those who are Europeans as well. Now European Union nationals fear for their legal residence. They will no longer be favored by the system to occupy low-skilled vacancies. Maybe British people will now occupy those positions that, as my friend believed, rightly belong to them. Fair enough. Yet these explanations about rights, citizenship, and sovereignty do not address the role that neoliberalism, as a form of postcolonial power, has had in the creation of millions of informal, flexible, low-paid jobs that exploit millions of people around the world, such as those described in this book.

Using the stories of a group of middle-class women from various countries in Latin America, I have brought to light how women's trajectories are deeply intertwined with the functioning of the neoliberal apparatus and its creation of new socioeconomic boundaries for those who migrate. I have demonstrated that this global economic system perpetuates the growth of a global chain of female care labor that remains cheap, informal, and hidden in plain sight. Despite the current global rhetoric that places migrants as the scapegoats for the failure of states, the intimate labor that women migrants supply both contributes to and remains necessary for the functioning of the system.

The lives and experiences of migrant intimate laborers expose how class inequalities—within neoliberalism—cannot be understood without paying attention to other structures of power, including those at work in the most intimate relations. The focus on intimate labor provides an opportunity to observe these subtle forms of power exercised on the ground. It can be seen in the everyday activities of my informants while they cleaned the houses of strangers, washed dirty laundry, and vacuumed accumulated dust. It can be seen in the upkeep of homes, as well as in the upkeep of people, in the interactions while caring for children or the elderly or while offering love and sexual pleasure to men. Their caring activities at work confirm and reproduce wider structures and relations of power across nations, households, and people.

The stories I have presented confirm the failures of states around the world in their obligation to care for their own people. The social contract has been broken. Global capitalism has produced nothing but an increase in labor market vulnerability and insecurity for a considerable proportion of the world's population. The creation and reproduction of what some people have addressed as the *precariat* is expanding rapidly. Its membership includes my informants, along with many other workers surviving under precarious conditions and little to no social protection. The irony, though, is that through their labor women gain some degree of personal and financial independence that justifies their participation in this market regardless of the psychological and physical consequences. This "economic" empowerment only masks the subtle ways in which the system keeps producing and reproducing inequalities, as women continue to live within a larger framework of dependency that cross-cuts their existence and produces ruptures in their selfhood.

This book's point of departure was how these women forged a new sense of self as they struggled with difficult circumstances in London while remembering—and mourning the loss of—their former middle-class statuses. If migration represented the initial rupture, entering the occupations of sex and domestic work resulted in a second one. The focus on dislocations prompted me to explore the creation of new forms of personhood composed by new racial, class, gender, and legal identifications. While women's work appeared to have had a crucial role in their dislocations because it circumscribed their lives in many ways, it was not all-encompassing. There were other places, situations, and moments in which the fractured person existed. Drawing on women's experiences while navigating the city of London, I revealed the power that illegality had in their lives. For many, having an undocumented status not only encroached on their morality but also deeply affected their everyday practices, relationships with others, and engagements with the city. Likewise, women's notions of racial and ethnic identities were problematized or worsened once they faced the racially diverse and divided landscape of London. Amid such radical change, I presented the efforts that women put into recuperating a sense of normality, of what they called their real self.

Is there a resolution for such ruptures? This book questioned the possibility and suggested that these dislocations—experienced as temporal—compelled women to adapt to the new location, but in the process recognized themselves as ethical subjects in a way that had not characterized their previous lives. They framed some of their ethical thinking in terms of care as a way to make sense of their labor, various social relationships, and their uncertain futures. Through these choices women were not changing the structure that oppressed them, but they found better ways to negotiate with clients, employers, and family. These ethical decisions also framed their economic calculations when they actively—through shopping—constructed home and recomposed ruptures in their kinship networks. The choices that I referred to were highly constrained by the system in which migrants exist. And yet, their choosing opened possibilities for agency or action. These ethical decisions speak to the capacity of social beings to "interpret and morally evaluate their situation and to formulate projects and try to enact them" (Ortner 1995, 185). A focus on ethics and morality brings to light how these women, caught in the global commodification of intimacy, tried to mediate, take advantage of, and sort out their everyday life estrangements. In showing this, the book reveals the creation of new complex ethical subjects longing to recuperate an ideological notion of who they once or really were, while interlacing creative alternatives across ruptures for the sake of the future.

The Future

Is there a happy ending? Is the future (now the present) as bright as the women wanted it to be? Are they now enjoying the world they hoped for and imagined back in 2009? The future, which can sometimes present itself as a time of hope and aspiration and at other times as a time of doubt and uncertainty, is an intrinsic part of the migrant experience. To offer some closure for the life histories that I have presented, I will give a brief sketch of what happened to these women after the period depicted here.

After I finished fieldwork, I remained in contact with my friends. Although I made efforts to establish a new form of relationship that would entail some distance between us, living in London made that difficult. Their lives continued to develop parallel to mine and they wanted to see me as often as they had before. Some women changed their lives radically, while others did not. Some disappeared from my life, but many remained and kept me as part of their families. Many of them achieved what they had planned to, while others continued to defer the realization of their ambitions. All kept dreaming of a better future. This imaginative practice was a key feature of their lives in the present; it was not a fantasy, but represented the possibility of reconstructing the life and the person they felt they had lost as part of the migration process.

The Hope for Documents

One of the main aspirations for the future was to be able to secure legal status in the United Kingdom. In 2012 Lourdes and Pedro, after being in the United Kingdom for eight years, gained their residence permit by claiming the right to family life under article 8 of the Human Rights European Convention. The news was celebrated as the grounds for beginning a new life. As Pedro said, he was no longer invisible because he had now been given the opportunity to be who he really was. With this remark, Pedro referred to his earlier undocumented status and to the possibilities that the residency afforded in terms of his profession. For Lourdes it meant that she would be able to ask for benefits for herself and her children that would guarantee some income for the family. Of the benefits she obtained, the housing benefit was the most significant because it allowed the family to move into a separate residence rather than sharing their accommodation with others. Although they now have legal residence in London, Pedro has not been able to go back to his profession and still works as a cleaner. For the past few years, he and Lourdes have been trying to become entrepreneurs via a pyramid-scheme business in London. Thanks to her participation in the business, Lourdes has managed to save money for a family trip to visit Bolivia.

Sarita struggled for several years to have her application accepted. The wait was long and painful. She feared that she would be deported back to a country that did not offer anything but endemic violence, unemployment, and increased inequality. She has always believed that she and her family are good migrants, hardworking people who deserve to stay in London. By the end of 2015 Sarita, her daughter, and her husband, after several failed applications and appeals, obtained their legal residence under article 8 of the Human Rights European Convention. For Sarita, obtaining documents meant the possibility of going to Spain to visit her daughter and son. They still live in the same flat, but Jesus is now receiving more carpentry jobs. Sarita still works as a domestic worker but she is now able to relax while commuting in London and is sleeping at night.

Cecilia and Antonio's situation began to change when Antonio was acquitted in the criminal case over the illicit dental practice in his home. They are still undocumented but over the years they have kept a pending visa application in the Home Office. This involves investing a significant amount of money, but also provides them with a sort of security such that, if caught by immigration, they would not be easily deported. According to Cecilia's lawyer they might have a good chance with their next application because of her daughter's age. Cecilia still works as a cleaner but has more time now to be with her daughter because Antonio has taken a full-time job in a cleaning company.

Returning Home

For others, the future involved going back home. For Sonia the present and the future both look promising. After winning a substantial lawsuit against the taxi driver who hit her in 2009, she earned £70,000 and returned to Bolivia. The money, she said, would be used first to pay the debts she still had in Bolivia, and the rest would go toward buying a house. After four years of not being able to repay the money to loan sharks and family, Sonia felt that she was finally in a position to clear her name and to mend her own and her family's dignity, which she had lost by becoming indebted. Few people in London knew about the money—she had chosen not to tell her friends because she was convinced that they would start asking for money. She is back in Bolivia with her sons, her grandchild, and her four dogs and is currently thinking about setting up a new pharmacy like the one she had before migrating.

My dear friend Juliana went back to Brazil in 2013, to her elderly mother and her partner. The house she was building with the money she earned in London was still under construction. When she arrived in Brazil she was busy dealing with the final arrangements of the place that would cement her future. The house was finished in 2014. Juliana tells me in her emails that she is thrilled to be back, to be with her mother, partner, and family. Although she says that she misses London and wants to visit, she is proud to be able to enjoy the fruits of her hard work.

Mariana left London and returned to Brazil at the beginning of 2012. She told me that her return made her feel like she had gone back to who she really was, because she moved back to her mother's house and started a postgraduate course that kept her busy, motivated, and, as she says, using her brain. At the time of her departure, her relationship with her husband was on shaky ground and they did not know whether it would survive the distance. However, after talking and agreeing that they wanted to be together, he moved permanently to Brazil in August 2012. They decided to stay in Brazil, and in June 2013 she gave birth to a beautiful baby boy. As she told me, her dream had come true. However, last year, after having problems with her husband because he insisted on returning to Italy, they decided to separate and got divorced. She told me how hard it was to separate after everything they went through, but her work as a sales manager and her son keep her busy and fulfilled. In the end, after many twists and turns, she found the love she was looking for and, more important, achieved the dream of constructing her own family.

Like Mariana, Sabrina returned to Brazil in December 2011, back to her son and her family. She was thrilled to be able to be a mother again but was feeling a bit out of place. Although she already had bought several flats, which included one for her mother and another for her aunt and her son, she wanted more money to buy a separate house, one she had fantasized about as the perfect home for her son and herself. After deliberating for a few months, Sabrina decided to return to London in July 2012. The plan was to stay for one year and earn the rest of the money she needed to secure her future. She set up a flat and worked again with Giselle until October 2013, when she left for the second time. This time I had the chance to meet her mother. As I had done before, I helped to conceal Sabrina's London life from the people close to her. Having saved the money she wanted, she returned to her country in luxurious fashion by taking a cruise with her mother all the way to Brazil. She promised me that this time she would remain in Brazil with her son, and she felt she was ready to stay and construct a family life again.

Although Sabrina was ready, she eventually decided she did not want to be in Brazil, but in London. For the third time, she returned to London at the beginning of 2015, but this time she brought her son, after paying for a counterfeit marriage that would provide her with a visa. She did not want to risk being deported while living in London with her son. Sabrina now shares a flat with Giselle, where they live together with her son, and she has a separate flat where they work every day. She hides her work from her son and hopes he will not find out, but if he does she says she would explain that her work has given him the life that he has. Her life in London has changed dramatically because she is not only a sex worker but also a mother. Her new plan is to save as much as she can in two years and then retire. She believes that she is now too old for the business.

Amelia went back to Venezuela after growing tired of the humiliation associated with being a domestic worker. She returned to her flat in Caracas and started working in sales, but after a few months she had to go back to Spain because her mother passed away. Her mother's death unearthed a series of financial problems and expenses that she was unable to solve. With debts accumulating, Amelia decided to return to London in March 2013 and work, once again, as a live-in domestic worker. She remained in London until she saved enough money to settle her debts and swore that she would never be a domestic worker again. Amelia lives now in the south of Spain, working on and off as an entrepreneur trying to sell properties to rich foreigners. She does not make much money but tells me that she lives a good and tranquil life.

For women like Jovanna, going home did not involve achieving the future she had wanted for herself and her daughter. By the end of my fieldwork Jovanna's cancer was back and had already metastasized. Although she remained hopeful about healing, the doctors in the United Kingdom told her there was nothing they could do to stop it. She then decided to return to Bolivia and find an alternative treatment, which unfortunately did not help, but did give her the chance to see her father and siblings. After a month in Bolivia she came back to London because she wanted to guarantee that, even in her absence, her daughter would be able to stay in London and have the opportunities she had hoped for. During our last days together, Jovanna's concerns about her daughter's future occupied her mind. She tried unsuccessfully to find someone who might adopt her daughter. In the end, she accepted that the best thing for Sisely was to return to Bolivia and live among her family. Jovanna, Sisely, and Vilma went back to Bolivia in January 2013. Jovanna spent the last months of her life among her loved ones and died on April 16, 2013.

Still Hoping

Among those who remain in London, life has taken different routes. Monica and Vanessa left sex work for personal and very different reasons. Monica began a new relationship with a client who eventually asked her to move in with him. Her plan of setting up a massage therapist clinic with her sister never materialized, but her dream of having a family did. She became pregnant and lived with her partner for a while before, as she said, he got tired of the baby. Although she receives economic help from the father, the money is not enough for her to support her child and the lifestyle she had before leaving sex work. With the help of her sister, who babysits the child, Monica has gone back to sex work part-time, just to ensure she has enough money to give her son a good life.

Vanessa stopped receiving help from Mark at the end of 2012 and was abandoned by her husband Giorgio. For a while she continued seeing clients, but she grew tired of performing the emotional labor required by the job. She was not meeting any interesting men and the bills were expensive. She moved out of the flat, got a job at a coffee shop, and became the nanny of two children for a German couple in London. The jobs kept her busy, but she could not help thinking about her future in which, to renew her visa, she would have to prove that she has been in a relationship with her husband. Unfortunately, I have lost contact with her.

Those who remained in their original occupations are still struggling with the daily hassles. Amanda and Angelica continued in sex work. In 2013, while working in a flat with two other girls, Amanda was violently attacked by a group of men who entered the flat. She did not report the assault to the police because she was too scared of being prosecuted for managing a brothel. She continued working for a while but took more precautions by not working at night and working only for clients they already knew. But things changed for her when she fell in love with a client and got married in 2015. Of all the women I met, Amanda was the most adamant about separating herself from her work and clients because she did not believe that real intimacy could emerge from sex work. Although she loved her client, she was conflicted by the idea of marrying someone who was leaving his wife to be with her. As a way to resolve the conflict, she went back to Brazil for a while to put some distance between them. But she was in love and after much deliberation she returned to London, married the man, and left sex work for good.

Eva, Felipa, and Cristina are still in London working as domestic workers. Eva also became a Mary Kay saleswoman and wants to set up her own business. Her daughter is now at university, something in which Eva takes immense pride and which makes her venture to London worthwhile. Felipa now spends more time doing care work within her own family: she became an aunt in 2012. She takes care of the baby girl three times a week to help her brother and sister-in-law while they work. Cristina is no longer working as a live-in domestic worker. Instead she works in several houses all over London. In February 2012 she went back to Ecuador to fulfill a dream she had cherished for several years, to have plastic surgery. She had not managed to save enough money to pay for the operation, so she borrowed from her brother. After the surgery, she came back to London feeling like a "new woman" and ready to find a new romantic partner. After having to deal with the death of three of her brothers and getting her son out of jail for selling drugs, Cristina is now in love with an Ecuadorian man who lives in Sweden and is a friend of her family. In 2015 she got a 18 thousand pounds loan to start the construction of the ecohotel in Ecuador. She is slowly paying the loan by working as a freelance nanny and domestic worker in London. She is hopeful that in a few years she is going to be able to go back to Ecuador and live the life she dreams of.

*

The stories that I have presented show how women reoriented their futures through hope. Regardless of the difficult lives that they might have had in London and of new difficulties that appeared on their return home, women continued hoping that, at some point in the future, they would achieve the lives they imagined before migration. The temporal dimension of hope placed women between the present and the immediate future. On the one hand, hope sometimes appeared as "a positive resignation" (Crapanzano 2003, 6) in the present, but was transformed into an active desire for the future. These desires were articulated toward ideas of stability and happiness that turned out to be difficult to achieve. Nonetheless, the ability to keep hoping remained a central aspect that shaped women's lives. The hope for the future kept them motivated even though every day they found themselves exploited, morally challenged, and facing constant dissatisfaction. Hope protects the possibility of being able to reconstruct their fractured identities and personhood. They often found this process populated by contradictions, by holes and cracks that were difficult to fill, yet they remained hopeful that they would be able to solve the dilemma of fixing those parts of their inner selves that they felt were incomplete. It is the often-contradictory intertwinement of hope with ambitions, failures, successes, and disappointments—an interrelation comprising discourses, material investments, and imaginative processes—that gave significance and substance to the economy of their dreams.

NOTES

....

Introduction

1. Within the racial politics of Latin America, the category *indigenous* is systematically devalued in society (Twine 1997; Wade 2001; Telles 2004). Pejorative expressions like *mejorar la raza* (bettering the race) refer to marrying lighter and to the possibility of moving up in society.

2. The literature on care has made two general distinctions on the notion of care: care as an activity of taking care and mere caring about. Nel Noddings (1984) pays close attention to feelings, needs, and desires for those cared for as central to caring for someone. Joan Tronto sees care as an activity that includes "everything we do to maintain, continue and repair our 'world' so that we can live in it as well as possible" (1994, 103). Following Virginia Held (2006), I understand care as both a practice and a value. Held notes, "As a practice, it shows us how to respond to needs and why we should" (42). As value, "caring persons and caring attitudes should be valued, and we can organize many evaluations of how persons are interrelated around a constellation of moral considerations associated with care or its absence" (42).

3. Following Weedon, this dislocation could be explained as "the conscious and unconscious thoughts and emotions of the individual, her sense of self, and her ways of understanding her relations to the world" (1996, 32).

4. See Beneria and Feldman (1992) Harrison (2013) and Hochschild (1997).

5. For domestic work see Adams and Dickey (2000), Bujra (2000), Gill (1994), and Hansen (1986). For sex work see Moon (1997) and Muecke (1992).

6. For instance, in a study from 2012, the Institute for Public Policy Research in the United Kingdom showed that just over one in ten women (13 percent) say their husbands do more housework than they do, and only 3 percent of married women do fewer than three hours a week of housework, with half doing thirteen hours or more.

7. Discussions on migrant sex workers have focused on issues around trafficking and its consequences. While I do not deny the relevance of the topic, particularly when referring to the international sex trade, there is another story to tell. That is the story of those women migrants who choose to enter sex work. Laura Agustín's book *Sex at the Margins: Migration, Labour Markets and the Rescue Industry* (2007) and Rhacel Salazar Parreñas's *Illicit Flirtations: Labor, Migration and Sex Trafficking in Tokyo* (2011) provide a critical commentary on the labeling and stereotyping of the "trafficked" migrant sex worker by focusing on women's agency and choices.

8. See Brennan (2004) for an ethnographic account of the complexities that originate when sex work is used to find romance and love.

9. However, in 1979 the situation changed as the work permit scheme for unskilled workers was sharply reduced in scope, and the United Kingdom introduced the first tourist and working visa requirements for Colombians (McIlwaine, Cock, and Linneker 2010).

10. Their estimates are calculated using the core dataset of the 2011 Census combined with second-generation figures, the number of people who arrived between 2012 and 2013 (including those with National Insurance numbers [Social Security numbers in the United States]), the number of people with European Union passports, and information on the number of irregular migrants between 2012 and 2013. Based on 2011 census figures alone, Latin Americans are the eighth largest non–UK born population in London (83,000), including 31,000 Brazilians, followed by 19,000 Colombians, 7,171 Ecuadorians, 3,822 Venezuelans, 3,301 Peruvians, 2,694 Bolivians, and 164 Hondurans, among other nationalities. In total, 60 percent of Latin Americans in the United Kingdom live in London, most of whom are women (53 percent).

11. In 2017, the percentage female among all migrants was highest in Europe (52.0 percent) (http://www.un.org/en/development/desa/population/migration/publications/migrationreport/docs/MigrationReport2017.pdf).

12. From 2000 to 2008, Spain's population grew from 40 million to 45 million and from 1999 until 2007 the Spanish economy created more than one-third of all employment generated in the Eurozone (Mansanet Ripoll and Padilla 2010).

13. In 2017 unemployment hovered around 18.75 percent, followed by a collateral crisis on employment benefits (http://www.ine.es/infografias/tasasepa/desktop/tasas.html?t=0&lang=es, accessed April 27, 2017).

14. For similar explanations of secondary migration from Europe, see Evans et al. (2005), McIlwaine (2007), Sveinsson (2007), and Pellegrino (2004).

15. In terms of documentation, McIlwaine and Bunge (2016) report that 31 percent of Latin Americans have a British passport, with a further 22 percent holding a European Union passport. Ecuadorians are the most likely to have a British passport in London (53 percent), followed by Colombians (51 percent); only 14 percent of Brazilians have British passports (McIlwaine and Bunge 2016, 43).

16. This is not surprising given the fact that the UK's economy is more reliant on the service sector than that of any other G7 country; the service sector has driven the economic recovery since the downturn in 2008. See https://visual.ons.gov.uk/five-facts-about-the-uk-service-sector, accessed January 2018.

17. The emergent literature on Latin Americans in London includes a variety of research interests, such as employment and working conditions (Datta et al. 2007; May et al. 2007), legality and documentation (McIlwaine 2009, 2015), transnational practices and social spaces (Juan Cock 2011; Sheringham 2011; Brightwell 2012), migration trends, and the relevance of gender and class within migration (Horst, Pereira, and Sheringham 2015; McIlwaine 2010).

18. The migration of middle-class people has been explored by Constable (1997a, 1997b), Lindquist (2009), Parreñas (2001, 2011), and Maia (2012), among others.

19. See French ([1966] 2013), Garcia-Bryce (2004), and Parker (1998).

20. The return of the middle-class actor, as Hopenhayn (2010) calls it, was a result of the economic growth in the first half of the 1990s that allowed for the reemergence of the middle class.

21. Yet, historically speaking, the definitions of the middle class have been changing according to the national context, notions of race and ethnicity, and occupation (see de la Cadena [2000] and Parker [1998] for Peru and Telles [2004] and Andrews [1991] for Brazil).

22. McIlwaine and Bunge (2016) found that half of Latin Americans in England and Wales (although not in London) define their ethnicity as *white other.* This needs further explanation because the census does not include a categorization specifically for them; nonetheless, it is quite revealing that of the categories in the census, including *other ethnic group*, most Latin Americans choose *white other.*

23. This term, although quite common in Latin America, is highly ambiguous in London because people tend to use it to refer to black people. They use it to avoid the term *negro*, which has racist connotations.

24. For discussions on race and racism in Latin America, see Telles (2004), Twine (1997), and Wade (2001, 2005).

25. From a Weberian point of view there are not only those in dominant positions and propertied groups, but also the petty bourgeoisie: workers with formal credentials (the middle class) and those who only have their labor power (the working class) (Breen 2005, 2–3).

26. The ethnographic work of Nicole Constable (1997a), Rhacel Salazar Parreñas (2001, 2005, 2011), Pierrette Hondagneu-Sotelo (2001), and Pei-Chia Lan (2006) explores the political economic of domestic work and the impact that it has on women's lives and families.

27. The work of Patty Kelly (2008), Denise Brennan (2004), and Sophie Day (2007) offers an in-depth study of the intimate lives of sex workers embedded in neoliberal economic models. See also Agustín (2003, 2007) and Maia (2012).

28. Their work is deeply influenced by earlier scholarship on the topic. Their analyses depart from the discussion of Nancy Folbre and Julie Nelson (2000) on the role of reproductive labor within capitalism. As feminist economists these scholars have tried to relocate markets as entities that operate within networks of social relationships (Nelson, 1999, 56). They have also been key in examining the connections between care and money. See also England and Folbre (1999a, 1999b, 2003), Himmelweit (1999, 2005), and Nelson and England (2002).

29. This relates to what Viviana Zelizer calls relational labor: "a way in which people establish multiple links between their economic transactions and intimate relations" (2012, 152). She argues that by observing relational labor we can learn how people often mix economic activity with intimacy.

30. I follow Robbins's understanding of values as "things that possess an ability to consistently (rationally) organize the elements of the culture" (2007, 299).

31. See Muehlebach (2012), Ticktin (2011), and Han (2012).

32. For studies on self-fashioning within neoliberalism, see Freeman (2000, 2014), Ong (2006, 2007), Rose (1990, 1992), and Hardt and Negri (2000).

33. Recent anthropological discussions on the study of morality and ethics have moved along two theoretical lines of inquiry, one following the classical Durkheimian–Kantian definition of moral reproduction (Robbins 2007, 2009, 2012) and the other taking a Foucauldian–Aristotelian approach to ethical subjectivities and freedom (Faubion 2011; Laidlaw 2002; Mahmood 2005; Zigon 2007, 2008, 2009). The first approach stresses the importance of locating moral actions within wider cultural constructs in which individuals

are situated in hierarchical value complexes from which to have to choose whenever they face a conflict. The second approach, although acknowledging morality as some sort of unconscious embodied disposition, places more importance on the role of freedom as an ontological condition of ethics.

34. The first generation of care theorists, Sara Ruddick (1989), Carol Gilligan (1982), and Nel Noddings (1984), wrote about how care was foundational to women and counterposed (in the case of Noddings) to the attitudes of men.

35. My understanding of an ethics of care stands in opposition to Carol Gilligan's [1982] (2003) approach that—although pioneering in the advancement of the theory—focuses on caring and feelings of responsibility toward others without considering the roles that culture and power play in the making of these choices. As many critics have pointed out, this is highly problematic because it can be used as another excuse to keep women in disadvantaged positions. Further criticisms have questioned the empirical grounds of this approach. For instance, when education and occupation were comparable, or when the same research was conducted in different geographic and cultural settings, the differences between women and men were unclear (Held 2006, 27).

36. According to Robbins, when people become aware of choosing between values, "they come to see their decision-making process as one engaged with moral issues" (2007, 300), therefore engaged in what I refer to as ethical thinking.

37. While this makes sense in terms of the politics and power relations regarding our own positions within our research projects, it also raises important questions related to the position that these sex workers/activists (white, middle class) had in contrast to the migrant women who came to the project. Unfortunately, I do not have space to expand on these issues here.

38. Although I initially thought their decision was unfair, after having worked with women in sex work I could understand their concerns. They were doing their jobs and were protecting women who are especially vulnerable to being analyzed in ways that can potentially intrude and affect them in negative ways.

Chapter 1

1. The gangs were composed of deportees—mostly young men—convicted of minor or serious offenses who arrived in Central America with no prospects other than their gang connections, which functioned as social networks and provided access to cash. See Arana (2005), Bruneau, Dammert, and Skinner (2011), Seelke (2011), and Stevens (2011).

2. http://siteresources.worldbank.org/INTPGI/Resources/342674-1092157888460/493860-1192739384563/10412-04_p067-089.pdf

3. Even though the instability in Venezuela dates back to 1983 with the devaluation of the *bolivar* in the face of a slump in oil prices and the eventual introduction of neoliberal restructuring programs that caused the standard of living to plummet for millions of Venezuelans, Chávez has been accused of polarizing the people in the country and creating further economic inequalities (Cannon 2008, 739–40).

4. By the time I met Amelia in November 2009, she was earning £1,000 per month and, according to her, was slowly paying off her debt.

5. Gustav Peebles notes that one of the crucial features of credit/debt is its ability to link the present to the past and the future (2010, 226).

6. Brazil experienced one of its most severe economic crises in 2002 as a result of unregulated market forces that widened the gap between the rich and the poor. Like the election of Morales in Bolivia, the election of Lula da Silva in 2002 created suspicion and resentment among the international community because of the threat that he might ditch the economic policies imposed by the World Bank and the International Monetary Fund.

7. This corroborates Maureen O'Dougherty's (2002) findings among middle-class people in Brazil.

8. For similar situations among migrant women, see Lan (2006) and her analysis of Indonesian domestic workers in Taiwan.

9. Considering a transnational approach to migration, we could argue that my informants connected people and places beyond national borders and maintained transnational connections that sustained their social roles at a distance, but not without conflict and not without experiencing personal ruptures (see Schiller, Basch, and Blanc-Szanton 1992; Gupta 1992; Gupta and Ferguson 1992, 1997).

10. Caroline Moser (2009) explained that the oppressive gender relations that women experience in Ecuador, particularly within the family or in marriage, are part of their reasons for migrating.

11. The law currently states, "You are not allowed to work in the UK if you are on a course at any level with an education provider that is not a UK higher education institution or a publicly funded further education college" (http://www.workpermit.com/news/2012-04-19/uk/uk-tier4-student-visa-work-rights.htm, accessed October 31, 2013).

Chapter 2

1. See Iskander (2007, 324) for similar experiences among migrants in France.

2. For similar discussions regarding settlement and class transformation, see the work of Roger Rouse (1992) among Mexican migrants in the United States.

3. The work of Boehm (2012), Dreby (2016), and Willen (2007) has been particularly interesting in offering a nuanced phenomenological approach to the embodiment of illegality, along with an analysis of the dispositions (physical, mental, and social) that migrants develop to cope with their new status (see also Khosravi 2007; Sigona 2012).

4. I will refer to illegal persons as undocumented persons to avoid criminal, pejorative, and stigmatizing connotations. Several studies have paid particular attention to the role of history and the state in the construction of the illegal migrant (i.e., Mexicans) in the United States (e.g., Boehm 2009; Chavez 2007, 2008; De Genova 2002, 2005). Likewise in Europe (Andersson 2014; A. Bloch and McKay 2016; Calavita 1998, 2005; Fassin 2001; Iskander 2007; Suárez-Navaz 2004), and others have examined the relationship between the state, the law, and corporations in their efforts to define migrants as a different kind of person in Europe.

5. According to the law in the United Kingdom, illegal migration consists of an alien subject who, because of his or her lack of proper documentation, is a potential criminal. The legal immigration framework of the United Kingdom loosely defines illegal migration as: those who enter the country illegally, or break immigration rules in the United Kingdom by working full-time having been allowed in to study, or by fail to leave at the end of their stay. The immigration act of 1971 has been modified in various occasions throughout the twentieth century. However, the changes in 2014 and 2016 reflect the hostile environment against migration within the United Kingdom. The Immigration Bill 2015-16 introduced by Theresa May, Home Office Secretary at the time, was promoted under the motto "[T]o tackle illegal immigration by making it harder to live and work illegally in the United Kingdom." (https://www.theguardian.com/politics/2013/oct/10/immigration-bill-theresa-may-hostile-environment).

The Bill restricts irregular migrants' access to residential tenancies, driving and bank accounts; imposes a £200 levy for as a contribution to the National Health Insurance; enables the Home Secretary to remove from the United Kingdom migrants who are appealing a refusal on human rights claim before the appeal has been determined; introduces an "immigration skills charge", payable by employers who sponsor non-EEA national workers, among other restrictions. On top of these, it creates new offences and establishes penalties for employers of illegal workers (already modified in 2012), to landlords and letting agents who let properties to migrants who do not have a valid immigration status, and gives landlords new powers to evict tenants who do not have a 'right to rent', introduces obligations to banks to carry out immigration status checks on account holders and give new power to search for and seize driving licences held by irregular migrants and a new offence of driving a vehicle when unlawfully in the United Kingdom. https://beta.parliament.uk/search?q=Bill+74+2015-16.

6. McIlwaine and Bunge (2016, 43) found that 72 percent of Latin Americans who previously lived in Spain arrived on a tourist visa. This data was based on a face-to-face questionnaire survey with 400 migrants in London.

7. Three-quarters of Bolivians entered as tourists or visitors. Almost one-third of Colombians entered with student visas, while Brazilians and Ecuadorians were the most likely to enter the United Kingdom with European Union passports (a quarter in each case). Brazilians and Bolivians were also the most likely to be irregular (38 and 36.5 percent, respectively), with Colombians being the least likely (6 percent). In turn, Peruvians and Colombians were most likely to hold British passports (38 and 37 percent), while European Union passport ownership was highest among Brazilians (31 percent) (McIlwaine 2015, 499). See also Raijman, Schammah-Gesser, and Kemp (2006, 145) for the experiences of undocumented Latina American women migrants in Israel overstaying tourist visas.

8. Until 2009, Bolivians, Venezuelans, Ecuadorians, and Peruvians were not required to possess a tourist visa to visit the United Kingdom and other countries in Europe, such as France (Spain was an exception).

9. See Agustín (2007) and Oso Casas (2003, 2010) for the use of survival strategies among women migrants in Europe.

10. Elephant and Castle is a Latin American enclave in London, even though it includes migrant groups from all over London. It is now a middle-class, mixed-race area of the city quite close to the Centre.

11. See Datta et al. (2007), McIlwaine (2007), and Rhus and Anderson (2008, 2010).

12. http://www.ukba.homeoffice.gov.uk/business-sponsors/preventing-illegal-working/penaltiesemployers/, accessed May 2013.

13. National Assistance Act (1948), section 21, duty of local authorities to provide accommodation (http://www.legislation.gov.uk/ukpga/Geo6/11-12/29/section/21).

14. Immigration rules at the time allowed the dependents of the possessor of a student visa to work full-time.

15. I found many cases in which Latin American migrants managed, despite the odds, to maintain their previous occupations, such as dental practitioners, hairdressers, and masseuses. Such occupations were easily practiced in the domestic environment, hidden from the authorities and the public gaze.

16. See Hum Cam Thai (2008, 127) for similar middle-class conflicts and notions of masculinity among Vietnamese migrants in the United States.

17. It is an offence for a person to keep, or to manage, or to act or assist in the management of, a brothel to which people resort for practices involving prostitution. This offence is explained in section 33A (inserted in 2003) of the Sexual Offences Act of 1956. The premises that are frequented by men for intercourse with only one woman are not considered a brothel, and this is also related to whether she is a tenant. Section 33A: "Keeping a brothel used for prostitution. (1) It is an offence for a person to keep, or to manage, or act or assist in the management of, a brothel to which people resort for practices involving prostitution (whether or not also for other practices)." http://www .legislation.gov.uk/ukpga/Eliz2/4-5/69/section/33A

18. By the time they were working at this flat Amanda had married a Portuguese friend as a gateway to legality.

19. For analysis of the effects of illegality and immigration see Coutin (2005a, 2005b).

20. South London (especially Lambeth and Southwark) holds the highest number of Latin American people in London (McIlwaine and Bunge 2016).

21. These narratives of anxiety were similar to those found by Willen (2007) in Israel and Talavera, Núñez and Heyman (2010) in the United States among undocumented migrants.

22. Until 2011, their visas had allowed them to work up to twenty hours a week.

23. The recent work by James and Killick (2012) shows how migrants who were clients of a law center in South London used their accumulated years and experiences to construct their legal cases.

24. Many migrants came to the United Kingdom via Ireland because it was easier for them to obtain a visa to enter Ireland and then travel by ferry to the United Kingdom.

25. See Sigona and Hughes (2012) for similar cases in the United Kingdom.

26. Indefinite Leave to Remain is granted for ten years; however, when people have an ILR for one year, they are automatically entitled to apply for citizenship that involves other sets of conditions, including passing a Life in the UK test and an English test.

Chapter 3

1. The study of domestic work in other regions of the world has questioned whether the occupation is a manifestation of different forms of oppression that maintain the status quo of dominant groups. For Latin America and the Caribbean, Elsa Chaney and Mary Garcia Castro (1991) have developed an extraordinary overview and a comparative account of the situation of female household workers in the Americas.

2. See Dill (1988, 2015), Hondagneu-Sotelo (2002), Katzman (1978), Rollins (1985), and Romero (1992).

3. See Lan (2003, 2006), Constable (1997a, 1997b), Parreñas (2001), Moukarbel (2009, 2010), Lan (2003), Jureidini and Moukarbel (2004), Yeoh, Huang, and Gonzalez (1999), and Yeoh and Huang (2010).

4. See Andall (1992, 2017), Anderson (2000, 2001, 2003, 2012), Anderson and Shutes (2017) Campani (1993), Lutz (2002, 2008, 2010), and Ozyegin and Hondagneu-Sotelo (2008).

5. The same can be argued for the rest of Latin America; see Francois (2008) for a historical review on relevant literature in the region.

6. Graham, Skidmore, Helg, and Knight (1995) suggest that since the mid-nineteenth century, relations between house servants and patrons in Brazil have always been ambiguous and glutted with profound tensions as they were "personal and proximate, perhaps long-lasting, but never ones between equals" (Graham et al. 1995, 107).

7. Interestingly, Goldstein notes that even when domestic workers are white poor women, they are associated with the black skin color of slavery and its associations with unpleasant and dirty work (2003, 73).

8. Barker and Feiner (2009) analyze the relationship that exists between affect, race, and class. They explain that this type of paid work has become more and more common and it is done by people who have little status in society because of their race, class, or immigrant status.

9. See Anderson (2000) for a discussion of placement agencies in Europe.

10. Abigail Bakan and Daiva Stasiulis (1995, 309) have explained that stereotyping is endemic to the matching process that defines the parameters of placement agencies.

11. For similar experiences regarding hierarchy between employers and employees, see Lan (2006, 203), Parreñas (2001, 165), Constable (1997a, 100–101), and Moukarbel (2009, 337).

12. This would indeed apply to other forms of care work, such as nursing, elder care, teaching, and providing therapy or psychological support.

13. See Bakker (2007), Harris (1981), Laslett and Brenner (1989), and Moore (1998).

14. These notions prevail and are reflected not only in the ongoing international struggle for the recognition of rights of domestic workers around the world, but also in the legislation on domestic work in the United Kingdom, which affords only very limited labor rights and forms of protection to domestic workers. In the United Kingdom domestic workers are excluded from national minimum wage regulations if their employer can show that they are treated as part of the family. However, the legislation does not provide a

definition, nor does it outline the implications, rights, or obligations of such an ambiguous and contested term; the term appears to be deliberately used as a way to exclude domestic workers from protection under the Working Time Regulations of 1999, in particular the maximum lawful weekly limit of forty-eight hours, which does not apply to domestic workers. They are also not given the same entitlements to rest periods as other workers and can be made to work night shifts. The legislation demonstrates the conservative stance and view that English law takes on domestic work; it only reinforces ideologies regarding the perception of the occupation as reproductive labor and therefore intrinsically female. In addition to this labor legislation, according to immigration rules a domestic work visa exists for migrant women coming to work in private or diplomatic households. Previously the visa could be renewed for up to five years and the domestic worker could switch employers. However, since April 2012, the visa is limited to six months and no change of employer is allowed.

15. For the use of kinship idioms by employers, see Bakan and Stasiulis (1997), Jacklyn Cock (1980), and Constable (1997a).

Chapter 4

1. When I refer to sex work I include various forms of erotic labor that include strip dancing, prostitution, and escorts.

2. See Pateman (1988), MacKinnon (1989), Barry (1996), Dworkin (1997), Farley (2003), and Farley et al. (1998).

3. See Pheterson (1990), Bell (1994), Chapkis (1997), Doezema and Kempadoo (1998), and Agustín (2003, 2007).

4. Overall there are two broad positions in research on sex work, the antiprostitution and the pro-sex work stances. The first sees prostitution as violence against women and the second considers the occupation legitimate work but acknowledges that its illegal status does violate civil and workers' rights and the integrity of sex workers (see Vanwesenbeeck 2001, 243).

5. See also Chapkis (2000) and O'Connell Davidson (1995, 1998).

6. Kempadoo describes how in Cartagena and the Dominican Republic, the humiliations, abuse, and hunger experienced as domestic workers were reasons for the women to "prefer" sex work (2001, 46; 2004). Lahbabi and Rodriguez (2004) explain how migrant women in Spain switched from domestic work to sex work for economic reasons and issues related to their lack of documents.

7. None of them worked in street-based sex work because of its criminalized implications (in the United Kingdom it is illegal to loiter on the street), the

stigma around it, and the insecurity that it represented for women who were undocumented.

8. Women's recollections of some swing parties, especially at the beginning of their careers in sex work, expose sexual exploitation, violence, and high levels of insecurity. Out of respect for my informants' traumatic experiences I do not talk about them but feel obliged to point out the insecurity and violence that women in sex work experience because of the lack of proper regulations and laws to protect them.

9. In Brazil's popular culture, ample female hips, buttocks, and thighs have been the aesthetic ideal, while relatively smaller breasts were admired (Kulick 1998). "Plastic surgery specifically references this tradition. Surgeons praise the beautiful effects of racial mixture on the female body, echoing older nationalist celebrations of 'miscegenation.' And ads promote techniques to achieve a 'Brazilian *bunda*' ('bottom'), or use samba song lyrics to advertise the slender, 'pestle waist' as a national ideal" (Edmonds 2009, 30).

10. Denise Ferreira Da Silva talks about how the tole of black and mulatta women in relation to their sexuality was an important component of the *mestizaje* (miscegenation) in Brazil.

11. According to Suzana Maia, "the racial category *morena* can be understood as an attempt to articulate the tensions in the shifting identity of middle-class Brazilian women, having as references both local and global racial configurations" (2012, 49). See also Pinho (2009).

12. While I was contacting women online I received an email from a woman from Mozambique who advertised herself as Brazilian. When I talked to her, she explained to me that the moment she "became Brazilian" on the sex website, the number of clients radically increased.

13. From this moment, I remained vigilant at all times. I started hiding a knife under the cushion of my chair to protect us from a possible attacker.

14. The separation between the working and the real person has been widely analyzed within the literature on sex work (Bernstein 2007a, 2007b; Brennan 2004; Chapkis 1997; Day 2007; Kelly 2008).

15. Some argue that sex workers create pragmatic, symbolic, and psychological defense mechanisms to manage the tensions of selling sex (Day 2007; Phoenix 2000; Warr and Pyett 1999). O'Neill (2001) describes how the objective of "separating the body from the self" results in an "exceptional control of the inner world."

16. See Brewis and Linstead (2000a, 224).

17. Fortunately, her work identity remained secret and my incompetence and ignorance did not affect her social relations and life in London.

18. Sex workers engage in emotional labor for male clients, not only through physical relief but also, like beauty therapists, through pampering, frivolity, and empathy. Doezema and Kempadoo (1998), Chapkis (1997), Brewis and Linstead (2000a, 2000b, 2000c), and Sanders (2004, 2005a, 2005b) have also argued that when women engage in sexual or erotic activities in prostitution, it should be understood as selling a form of emotional labor.

19. Prince (1986) has discussed how women working for brothels in Nevada describe the wide range of emotional services that they offer to their clients, while Day (2007) explains how prostitutes in London develop long-term relationships with some of their clients.

20. Becoming independent prostitutes involved significant financial and personal investments because women had to pay for their rent and bills and fund their own publicity, which included a professional portfolio of photographs for the internet for different advertisements, a monthly payment for the publication of their photos, and the placing of contact information on websites that promoted independent escorts. Despite the costs, working independently was highly remunerated.

21. When Sabrina left in December 2011, she sold her contact list (£1,500) to Giselle and recommended Giselle's services to her regular clients. Sabrina's contact list included more than six hundred clients (in addition to those clients she had only worked with once). Before she left, I organized the list and sent text messages to her most cherished clients, thanking them for their preference and their help in fulfilling Sabrina's dreams.

Chapter 5

1. For anthropological literature on the gift, see Gudeman (2001), Strathern (1988), Sykes (2005), Weiner (1992), and Yan (1996).

2. He also states that "our ideology of the 'pure' gift is most likely to develop in state societies with an advanced division of labour and a significant commercial sector" (Parry 1986, 467).

3. This expression was said in English; women did not use referent in Spanish.

4. Zelizer explains that caring relationships that involve trust qualify as intimate: "they entrust at least one of the parties with information about, or attention to, another party that is not widely available that would be damaging if offered to third parties" (2009, 162).

5. At some point in my relationship with the two of them, Giorgio asked me whether Vanessa and I were having an affair. This assumption not only surprised me, but also allowed me to see how far his insecurity and jealousy stretched. He was suspicious of everyone in Vanessa's life. I assured him that besides being heterosexual, we were just friends.

6. For discussions on secondhand gifts in domestic work, see Anderson (2000, 2003), Bakan and Stasiulis (1997), Dill (2015), Radcliffe (1999), and Romero (1992). As Mary Romero notes, "this practice of giving old clothes within a work setting is unique to domestic settings. It is almost inconceivable that the same woman would consider offering her old linen jacket to her secretary" (1992, 109).

7. It took me a while to understand the logic of these transactions and, because I had very little contact with employers of domestic workers (as well as with most clients of sex workers), my views on these exchanges derived from those of my informants and reflect their perceptions of the objects received.

8. For those like Strathern (1992) and Weiner (1992), who emphasize the inalienable features of the gifts, the distinction between gifts and commodities remains essential.

9. Arjun Appadurai (1986) emphasizes the need for a historical perspective to avoid making sharp distinctions between gifts and other forms of exchange. Going beyond the dichotomy between gift and commodity allows us to understand the dynamics of how things circulate over time (1986, 11–13). See also Carrier (1990, 1991), Gregory (1982), Miller (1995a, 1995b), Parry (1986), Sahlins (1972), and Myers (2001) for discussions on the gift–commodity debate.

Chapter 6

1. This normality, as Kristina Fehérváry explains in postsocialist contexts, is equated with the market capitalism and the bourgeois middle classes of Europe (2002, 374).

2. In most cases their landlords had converted the lounge into an extra room to maximize profit.

3. See Ramphele (1993) for extreme notions of home.

4. Daniel Miller has provided important theoretical insights into and ethnographic examples of the role that material culture has in the space of home in regard to providing a sense of comfort and how things represent and reflect the social world in the private domain (Miller 2001, 2008).

5. For studies on middle-class people's experiences and notions of normality, see Fehérváry (2002, 2011), Berdahl (1999), and Patico (2008).

6. Taste, for Bourdieu, is a reflection of the interrelation between his three dimensions of social life: the economic, the cultural, and the educational. It is "the propensity and capacity to appropriate (materially or symbolically) a given class of classified, classifying objects or practices, is the generative formula of life-style, a unitary set of distinctive preferences which express the

same expressive intention in the specific logic of each of the symbolic sub-spaces, furniture, clothing, language or body hexis" (Bourdieu 1984, 173).

7. For approaches to consumption as status seeking, see Campbell (1994), McCracken (1990), Heyman (1994), and Wilks (1989). For approach to consumption as an expression of a lifestyle, see Featherstone (1990) and Shields (1992).

8. In Marxist terms, false consciousness is the result of ideological control of which the proletariat is unaware. According to Boudreaux, the term is used as a label for people's systematic failure to adequately understand and respond to social reality in full. It exists when the degree of misunderstanding is so great that people mistake social arrangements that really harm them as being social arrangements that benefit them (Boudreaux and Crampton 2003, 2).

9. In her analysis of Turkish women migrants in Germany, Ruba Salih explains that through shopping women confer a higher status to their families back in Turkey (Salih, 2003). See also O'Dougherty (2002) and Freeman (2014).

10. For similar strategies regarding the making of home in working spaces among live-in domestic workers, see Geraldine Pratt (1997), who worked with Philippine migrants in Vancouver.

11. The expenses were covered between Camila's father, Ricardo, a Colombian man who had been living in the United Kingdom for many years and held British citizenship, and Pedro.

REFERENCES CITED

....

Abrego, Leisy. 2009. "Economic Well-Being in Salvadoran Transnational
    Families: How Gender Affects Remittance Practices." *Journal of Marriage
    and Family* 71 (4): 1070–85.

Abrego, Leisy J., and Cecilia Menjívar. 2011. "Immigrant Latina Mothers as
    Targets of Legal Violence." *International Journal of Sociology of the Family*
    37 (1): 9–26.

Adams, Kathleen M., and Sara Dickey. 2000. *Home and Hegemony: Domestic
    Service and Identity Politics in South and Southeast Asia.* Ann Arbor:
    University of Michigan Press.

Agustín, Laura M. 2003. "A Migrant World of Services." *Social Politics: International
    Studies in Gender, State & Society* 10, no. 3 (September 21): 377–96.

———. 2007. *Sex at the Margins: Migration, Labour Markets and the Rescue
    Industry.* London: Zed Books.

Andall, Jacqueline. 1992. "Women Migrant Workers in Italy." In "A Continent in
    Transition: Issues for Women in Europe in the 1990s," special issue.
    Women's Studies International Forum 15 (1): 41–48.

———. 2017. *Gender, Migration and Domestic Service: The Politics of Black
    Women in Italy.* London: Routledge.

Anderson, Bridget. 2000. *Doing the Dirty Work? The Global Politics of Domestic
    Labour.* New York: Zed Books.

———. 2003. Just Another Job? "The Commodification of Domestic Labor." In
    Global Women: Nannies, Maids and Sex Workers in the New Economy,
    edited by Barbara Ehrenreich and Arlie R. Hochschild. New York:
    Metropolitan Books.

———. 2012. "¿Quién Los Necesita? Trabajo de Cuidados, Migración y Política Pública." *Cuadernos de Relaciones Laborales* 30 (1): 45–61.

Anderson, Bridget, and Isabel Shutes. 2017. *Migration and Care Labour.* Houndmills, UK: Palgrave Macmillan.

Andersson, Ruben. 2014. *Illegality, Inc.: Clandestine Migration and the Business of Bordering Europe.* Oakland: University of California Press.

Andrews, George Reid. 1991. *Blacks & Whites in São Paulo, Brazil, 1888–1988.* Madison: University of Wisconsin Press.

Appadurai, Arjun. 1986. *The Social Life of Things: Commodities in Cultural Perspective.* Cambridge: Cambridge University Press.

Arana, Ana. 2005. "How the Street Gangs Took Central America." *Foreign Affairs* 84 (3): 98–110.

Bakan, Abigail Bess, and Daiva Kristina Stasiulis. 1995. "Making the Match: Domestic Placement Agencies and the Racialization of Women's Household Work." *Signs: Journal of Women in Culture and Society* 20 (2): 303–35.

———. 1997. *Not One of the Family: Foreign Domestic Workers in Canada.* Toronto: University of Toronto Press.

Bakker, Isabella. 2007. "Social Reproduction and the Constitution of a Gendered Political Economy." *New Political Economy* 12 (4): 541–56.

Barker, Drucilla K. 2012. "Querying the Paradox of Caring Labor." *Rethinking Marxism* 24 (4): 574–91.

Barker, Drucilla, and Susan F. Feiner. 2009. *Liberating Economics: Feminist Perspectives on Families, Work, and Globalization.* Ann Arbor: University of Michigan Press.

Barry, Kathleen. 1996. *The Prostitution of Sexuality.* New York: New York University Press.

Bastia, Tanja, and Siobhan McGrath. 2011. "Temporality, Migration and Unfree Labour: Migrant Garment Workers." Manchester Papers in Political Economy. Working paper no. 6. Manchester: University of Manchester, July.

Bell, Shannon. 1994. *Reading, Writing, and Rewriting the Prostitute Body.* Bloomington: Indiana University Press.

Beneria, Lourdes, and Shelley Feldman. 1992. "Unequal Burden: Economic Crises, Persistent Poverty, and Women's Work." http://agris.fao.org/agris-search/search.do?recordID=XF2016023084.

Berdahl, Daphne. 1999. "'(N)Ostalgie' for the Present: Memory, Longing, and East German Things." *Ethnos* 64 (2): 192–211.

Bernstein, Elizabeth. 2007a. *Temporarily Yours: Intimacy, Authenticity, and the Commerce of Sex.* Chicago: University of Chicago Press.

———. 2007b "Sex Work for the Middle Classes." *Sexualities* 10 (4): 473–88.

———. 2010. "Bounded Authenticity and the Commerce of Sex." In *Intimate Labors: Cultures, Technologies, and the Politics of Care*, edited by Eileen

Boris and Rhacel Salazar Parreñas. Stanford, CA: Stanford University Press.

Bloch, Alice, and Sonia McKay. 2016. *Living on the Margins: Undocumented Migrants in a Global City*. Bristol: Policy Press.

Bloch, Maurice, and Jonathan Parry. 1989. *Money and the Morality of Exchange*. Cambridge: Cambridge University Press.

Boehm, Deborah A. 2009. "'¿Quien Sabe?': Deportation and Temporality among Transnational Mexicans." *Urban Anthropology and Studies of Cultural Systems and World Economic Development* 38 (2/3/4): 345–74.

———. 2012. *Intimate Migrations: Gender, Family, and Illegality among Transnational Mexicans*. New York: New York University Press.

Boris, Eileen, and Rhacel Salazar Parreñas. 2010. *Intimate Labors: Cultures, Technologies, and the Politics of Care*. Stanford, CA: Stanford University Press.

Boudreaux, Donald J., and Eric Crampton. 2003. "Truth and Consequences: Some Economics of False Consciousness." *Independent Review* 8 (1): 27–46.

Bourdieu, Pierre. 1977. *Outline of a Theory of Practice*. Cambridge: Cambridge University Press.

———. 1984. *Distinction: A Social Critique of the Judgement of Taste*. New York: Routledge & Kegan Paul.

———. 1994. "Structure, Habitus, Power. Basis for a Theory of Symbolic Power." In *Culture/Power/History: A Reader in Contemporary Social Theory*, edited by Nicholas B. Dirks, Geoff Eley, and Sherry. B. Ortner. Princeton, NJ: Princeton University Press.

Breen, Richard. 2005. "Foundations of a Neo-Weberian Class Analysis." In *Approaches to Class Analysis*, edited by E. Olin Wright. New York: Cambridge University Press.

Brennan, Denise. 2004. *What's Love Got to Do with It?: Transnational Desires and Sex Tourism in the Dominican Republic*. Durham, NC: Duke University Press.

Brewis, Joanna, and Stephen Linstead. 2000a. *Sex, Work and Sex Work: Eroticizing Organization*. London: Routledge.

———. 2000b. "'The Worst Thing Is the Screwing' (1): Consumption and the Management of Identity in Sex Work." *Gender, Work & Organization* 7 (2): 84–97.

———. 2000c. "'The Worst Thing Is the Screwing' (2): Context and Career in Sex Work." *Gender, Work & Organization* 7 (3): 168–80.

Brightwell, Maria das Graças. 2012. "A Taste of Home?: Food, Identity and Belonging among Brazilians in London." PhD diss., Royal Holloway, University of London.

Brown, Wendy. 2003. "Neo-Liberalism and the End of Liberal Democracy." *Theory & Event* 7 (1).

Bruneau, Thomas C., Lucía Dammert, and Elizabeth Skinner. 2011. *Maras: Gang Violence and Security in Central America*. Austin, TX: University of Texas Press.

Bujra, Janet, M. 2000. *Serving Class: Masculinity and the Feminisation of Domestic Service in Tanzania*. International African Library 24. Edinburgh: Edinburgh University Press for the International African Institute.

Cabezas, Amalia L. 2009. *Economies of Desire: Sex and Tourism in Cuba and the Dominican Republic*. Philadelphia: Temple University Press.

Calavita, Kitty. 1998. "Immigration, Law, and Marginalization in a Global Economy: Notes from Spain." *Law and Society Review* 32 (3): 529–566.

———. 2005. *Immigrants at the Margins: Law, Race, and Exclusion in Southern Europe*. Cambridge: Cambridge University Press.

Campani, Giovanna. 1993. "Labour Markets and Family Networks: Filipino Women in Italy." In *Bridging States and Markets*, edited by Rudolph Hedwig and Mirjana Morokvsic. Berlin: Sigma.

Campbell, Colin. 1994. "Capitalism, Consumption and the Problem of Motives: Some Issues in the Understanding of Conduct as Illustrated by an Examination of the Treatment of Motive and Meaning in the Words of Weber and Veblen." In *Consumption and Identity. Studies in Anthropology and History*, edited by Jonathan Friedman. Vol. 15 of *Studies in Anthropology and History*. Chur, Switzerland: Harwood Academic.

Cannon, Barry. 2008. "Class/Race Polarisation in Venezuela and the Electoral Success of Hugo Chávez: A Break with the Past or the Song Remains the Same?" *Third World Quarterly* 29 (4): 731–48.

Carrier, James. 1990. "Gifts in a World of Commodities: The Ideology of the Perfect Gift in American Society." *Social Analysis* 29 (1): 19–37.

———. 1991. "Gifts, Commodities and Social Relations: A Maussian View of Exchange." *Sociological Forum* 6, no. 1 (March): 119–36.

———. 1995. *Gifts and commodities: exchange and Western capitalism since 1700*. London: Routledge.

Carrier-Moisan, Marie-Eve. 2018. "'I Have to Feel Something': Gringo Love in the Sexual Economy of Tourism in Natal, Brazil." *The Journal of Latin American and Caribbean Anthropology* 23 (1): 131–51.

Carsten, Janet. 2004. *After Kinship*. New York: Cambridge University Press.

Chaney, Elsa, and Mary Garcia Castro, eds. 1991. *Muchachas No More: Household Workers in Latin America and the Caribbean*. Philadelphia: Temple University Press.

Chant, Sylvia H., and Nikki Craske. 2003. *Gender in Latin America*. New Brunswick, NJ: Rutgers University Press.

Chapkis, Wendy. 1997. *Live Sex Acts: Women Performing Erotic Labor*. London: Routledge.

———. 2000. "Power and Control in the Commercial Sex Trade." In *Sex for Sale: Prostitution, Pornography, and the Sex Industry*, edited by Ronald John Weitzer. New York: Routledge.

Chavez, Leo R. 2007. "The Condition of Illegality." *International Migration* 45 (3): 192–96.

———. 2008. *The Latino Threat: Constructing Immigrants, Citizens, and the Nation*, 2nd ed. Stanford, CA: Stanford University Press.

Cock, Jacklyn. 1980. *Maids and Madams: A Study in the Politics of Exploitation*. Johannesburg: Ravan Press.

Cock, Juan. 2011. "The 'Latin American Shopping Centre': Commercial Spaces, Transnational Practices and Ethnicity amongst Colombian Migrants in London." In *Cross-Border Migration among Latin Americans: European Perspectives and Beyond*, edited by Cathy McIlwaine. New York: Palgrave Macmillan.

Cockburn, Tom. 2005. "Children and the Feminist Ethic of Care." *Childhood: A Global Journal of Child Research* 12 (1): 71–89.

Collins, Jane L., and Victoria Mayer. 2010. *Both Hands Tied: Welfare Reform and the Race to the Bottom in the Low-Wage Labor Market*. Chicago: University of Chicago Press.

Constable, Nicole. 1997a. *Maid to Order in Hong Kong: Stories of Filipina Workers*. Ithaca, NY: Cornell University Press.

———. 1997b. "Sexuality and Discipline among Filipina Domestic Workers in Hong Kong." *American Ethnologist* 24 (3): 539–58.

———. 2003. *Romance on a Global Stage: Pen Pals, Virtual Ethnography, and "Mail Order" Marriages*. Berkeley: University of California Press.

———. 2009. "The Commodification of Intimacy: Marriage, Sex, and Reproductive Labor." *Annual Review of Anthropology* 38 (1): 49–64.

Coutin, Susan Bibler. 2000. *Legalizing Moves: Salvadoran Immigrants' Struggle for U.S. Residency*. Ann Arbor: University of Michigan Press.

———. 2005a. "Being en Route." *American Anthropologist* 107 (2): 195–206.

———. 2005b. "Contesting Criminality: Illegal Immigration and the Spatialization of Legality." *Theoretical Criminology* 9, no. 1 (February 1): 5–33.

Crapanzano, Vincent. 2003. "Reflections on Hope as a Category of Social and Psychological Analysis." *Cultural Anthropology* 18 (1): 3–32.

Cresswell, Tim. 2005. *Place: A Short Introduction*. Malden, MA: Blackwell.

Datta, Kavita, Cathy McIlwaine, Yara Evans, Joanna Herbert, John May, and Jane Wills. 2007. "From Coping Strategies to Tactics: London's Low Paid Economy and Migrant Labour." *British Journal of Industrial Relations* 45 (2): 404–32.

Day, Sophie. 2007. *On the Game*. London: Pluto Press.

De Certeau, Michel. (1984) 2000. *The Practice of Everyday Life*. Berkeley: University of California Press.

De Genova, Nicolas. P. 2002. "Migrant 'Illegality' and Deportability in Everyday Life." *Annual Review of Anthropology* 31 (January 1): 419–447.

———. 2004. "The Legal Production of Mexican/Migrant 'Illegality.'" *Latino Studies* 2, no. 2 (July): 160–85.

———. 2005. *Working the Boundaries: Race, Space, and "Illegality" in Mexican Chicago.* Durham, NC: Duke University Press.

De la Cadena, Marisol. 2000. *Indigenous Mestizos: The Politics of Race and Culture in Cuzco, Peru, 1919–1991.* Durham, NC: Duke University Press.

de Lauretis, Teresa, ed. 1986. *Feminist Studies/Cultural Studies.* Bloomington: Indiana University Press.

Derrida, Jacques. 1992. *Given Time 1: Counterfeit Money.* Chicago: Chicago University Press.

Di Leonardo, Micaela. 2008. "Introduction." In *New Landscapes of Inequality: Neoliberalism and the Erosion of Democracy in America,* edited by Jane L. Collins, Brett Williams, and Micaela di Leonardo. Santa Fe, NM: SAR Press.

Dill, Bonnie T. 1988. "Making Your Job Good Yourself: Domestic Service and the Construction of Personal Dignity." In *Women and the Politics of Empowerment,* edited by Sandra Morgen and Ann Bookman, 33–52. Philadelphia: Temple University Press.

———. 2015. *Across the Boundaries of Race & Class: An Exploration of Work & Family among Black Female Domestic Servants.* London: Routledge.

Doezema, Jo, and Kamala Kempadoo. 1998. *Global Sex Workers: Rights, Resistance and Redefinition.* New York: Routledge.

Douglas, Mary, and Baron C. Isherwood. (1978) 1980. *The World of Goods: Towards an Anthropology of Consumption.* New York: Penguin.

Dreby, Joanna. 2016. *Everyday Illegal.* Berkeley: University California Press.

Durkheim, Emile. (1906) 1974. "The Determination of Moral Facts." In *Sociology and Philosophy,* translated by D. F. Pocock. London: Routledge.

Dworkin, Andrea. 1997. *Life and Death: Unapologetic Writings on the Continuing War against Women.* New York: Free Press.

Edmonds, Alexander. 2009. "Beauty, Health and Risk in Brazilian Plastic Surgery." *Medische antropologie* 21 (1): 21.

Ehrenreich, Barbara, and Arlie Russell Hochschild, eds. 2002. *Global Woman: Nannies, Maids, and Sex Workers in the New Economy.* New York: Metropolitan Books.

England, Paula, and Nancy Folbre. 1999a. "The Cost of Caring." *The Annals of the American Academy of Political and Social Science* 561, no. 1 (January 1): 39–51.

———. 1999b. "Who Should Pay for the Kids?" *The Annals of the American Academy of Political and Social Science* 563 (1): 194–207.

———. 2003. "Contracting for Care." In *Feminist Economics Today: Beyond Economic Man,* edited by Marianne A. Ferber and Julie A. Nelson. Chicago: University of Chicago Press.

Escrivá, Angeles. 2003. *Peruvian Families between Peru and Spain*. Instituto de Estudios Sociales de Andalucía (IESA-CSIC). Paper prepared for delivery at the 2003 meeting of the Latin American Studies Association Dallas, Texas, March 27-29, 2003. http://lasa.international.pitt.edu/lasa2003/escrivaangeles.pdf

Evans, Yara, Joanna Herbert, Kavita Datta, John May, Cathy McIlwaine, and Jane Wills. 2005. *Making the City Work: Low Paid Employment in London*. London: Queen Mary, University of London.

Farley, Melissa. 2003. *Prostitution, Trafficking and Traumatic Stress*. New York: Psychology Press.

Farley, Melissa, Isin Baral, Merab Kiremire, and Ufuk Sezgin. 1998. "Prostitution in Five Countries: Violence and Post-Traumatic Stress Disorder." *Feminism & Psychology* 8 (4): 405–26.

Fassin, Didier. 2001. "The Biopolitics of Otherness: Undocumented Foreigners and Racial Discrimination in French Public Debate." *Anthropology Today* 17 (1): 3–7.

Faubion D. James. 2011. *An Anthropology of Ethics*. New York: Cambridge University Press.

Featherstone, Mike. 1990. *Consumer Culture and Postmodernism. Theory, Culture and Society*. London: Sage.

Fehérváry, Krisztina. 2002. "American Kitchens, Luxury Bathrooms, and the Search for a 'Normal' Life in Postsocialist Hungary." *Ethnos* 67 (3): 369–400.

———. 2011. "The Postsocialist Middle Classes and the New 'Family House' in Hungary." In *The Global Middle Classes: Theorizing through Ethnography*, edited by Rachel Heiman, Carla Freeman, and Mark Liechty. Santa Fe, NM: SAR Press.

FLACSO-Ecuador and UNFPA. 2008. *Ecuador: la migración internacional en cifras*. Quito: FLACSO Sede Ecuador and UNFPA.

Francois, Marie Eileen. 2008. "The Products of Consumption: Housework in Latin American Political Economies and Cultures." *History Compass* 6 (1): 207–42.

Fraser, Nancy. 2016. "Contradictions of Capital and Care." *New Left Review* II (100): 99–117.

Freeman, Carla. 2000. *High Tech and High Heels in the Global Economy: Women, Work, and Pink-Collar Identities in the Caribbean*. Durham, NC: Duke University Press.

———. 2012. "Neoliberal Respectability: Entrepreneurial Marriage, Affective Labor, and a New Caribbean Middle Class" In *The Global Middle Classes: Theorizing through Ethnography* edited by Rachel Heiman, Carla Freeman and Mark Liechty. School for Advanced Research Advanced Seminar Series. Santa Fe, N.M.: SAR Press.

———. 2014. *Entrepreneurial Selves: Neoliberal Respectability and the Making of a Caribbean Middle Class*. Durham, NC: Duke University Press.

French, E. William. (1966) 2013. "Moralizing the Masses." In *Latin America's Middle Class: Unsettled Debates and New Histories*, edited by David S. Parker and Louise E. Walker. Plymouth, UK: Lexington Books.

Folbre, Nancy, and Julie A. Nelson. 2000. "For Love or Money—or Both?" *Journal of Economic Perspectives* 14 (4): 123–40.

Foucault, Michel. 1988. *Technologies of the Self: A Seminar with Michel Foucault*. London: Tavistock.

García, Vera, and Julio Miguel. 2013. *Crisis económica y pautas de estructuración social de las clases medias en el Ecuador*. Quito, Ecuador: Pontificia Universidad Católica del Ecuador.

García-Bryce, Iñigo L. 2004. *Crafting the Republic: Lima's Artisans and Nation Building in Peru, 1821–1879*. Albuquerque: University of New Mexico Press.

Gill, Lesley. 1994. *Precarious Dependencies: Gender, Class, and Domestic Service in Bolivia*. New York: Columbia University Press.

Gilligan, Carol. (1982) 2003. *In a Different Voice: Psychological Theory and Women's Development*. Cambridge, MA: Harvard University Press.

Gilroy, Paul. 1987. *There Ain't No Black in the Union Jack: The Cultural Politics of Race and Nation*. London: Hutchinson.

Godelier, M. 1999. *The Enigma of the Gift*. Cambridge: Polity Press.

Goffman, Erving. 1968. *Stigma: Notes on the Management of Spoiled Identity*. Harmondsworth, UK: Penguin.

Goldberg, Theo. 2009. *The Threat of Race: Reflections on Racial Neoliberalism*. Malden, MA: Wiley–Blackwell.

Goldstein, Donna M. 2003. *Laughter out of Place: Race, Class, Violence, and Sexuality in a Rio Shantytown*. Berkeley: University of California Press.

Gouldner, Alvin W. 1960. "The Norm of Reciprocity: A Preliminary Statement." *American Sociological Review* 25 (2): 161–78.

Graeber, David. 2001. *Toward an Anthropological Theory of Value. The False Coin of Our Dreams*. New York: Palgrave.

———. David. 2012. *Debt: The First 5000 Years*. New York: Melville House.

Graham, Richard, Thomas E. Skidmore, Aline Helg, and Alan Knight. 1995. *The Idea of Race in Latin America, 1870–1940*. Austin: University of Texas Press.

Gregory, Chris. A. 1982. *Gifts and Commodities*. London: Academic Press.

Gudeman, Stephen. 2001. *The Anthropology of Economy: Community, Market, and Culture*. Cambridge: Wiley.

Gupta, Akhil. 1992. "The Song of the Nonaligned World: Transnational Identities and the Reinscription of Space in Late Capitalism." *Cultural Anthropology* 7 (1): 63–79.

Gupta, Akhil, and James Ferguson. 1992. "Beyond 'Culture': Space, Identity, and the Politics of Difference." *Cultural Anthropology* 7 (1): 6–23.

———. 1997. *Culture, Power, Place: Explorations in Critical Anthropology.* Durham, NC: Duke University Press.

Hagan, Jacqueline Maria. 1994. *Deciding to Be Legal: A Maya Community in Houston.* Philadelphia: Temple University Press.

Han, Clara. 2012. *Life in Debt: Times of Care and Violence in Neoliberal Chile.* Berkeley: University of California Press.

Hansen, Karen Tranberg. 1986. "Domestic Service in Zambia." *Journal of Southern African Studies* 13 (1): 57–81.

Hardt, Michael, and Antonio Negri. 2000. *Empire.* Cambridge, MA: Harvard University Press.

Harris, Olivia. 1981. "Households as Natural Units." In *Of Marriage and the Market: Women's Subordination in International Perspective,* edited by Kate Young, Carol Wolkowitz, and Roslyn McCullagh. London: CSe Books.

Harrison, Graham. 2013. *Neoliberal Africa: The Impact of Global Social Engineering.* London: Zed Books.

Held, Virginia. 2006. *The Ethics of Care: Personal, Political, and Global.* Oxford: Oxford University Press.

Heidegger, Martin. 1972. *On Time and Being.* Chicago: University of Chicago Press.

Heiman, Rachel. 2009. "'At Risk' for Becoming Neoliberal Subjects: Rethinking the 'Normal' Middle-Class Family." In *Childhood, Youth, and Social Work in Transformation: Implications for Policy and Practice,* edited by Lynn M. Nybell, Jeffrey J. Shook, and Janet L. Finn. New York: Columbia University Press.

Heiman, Rachel, Carla Freeman, and Mark Liechty. 2012. *The Global Middle Classes: Theorizing through Ethnography.* Santa Fe, NM: SAR Press.

Herzfeld, Michael. 2015. "Anthropology and the Inchoate Intimacies of Power." *American Ethnologist* 42 (1): 18–32.

Heyman, Josiah. 1994. "The Organizational Logic of Capitalist Consumption on the Mexico–United States Border." *Research in Economic Anthropology* 15: 175–238.

Himmelweit, Susan. 1999. "Caring Labor." *The Annals of the American Academy of Political and Social Science* 561 (1): 27–38.

———. 2005. "Caring." *Public Policy Research* 12 (3): 168–73.

Hochschild, Arlie Russell. 1997. *The Time Bind: When Work Becomes Home and Home Becomes Work.* New York: Metropolitan Books.

———. 2003. (1983) *The Managed Heart. Commercialization of the Human Feeling.* Berkeley: University of California Press.

Hondagneu-Sotelo, Pierrette. 1994. *Gendered Transitions: Mexican Experiences of Immigration.* Berkeley: University of California Press.

———. 2001. *Doméstica: Immigrant Workers Cleaning and Caring in the Shadows of Affluence.* Berkeley: University of California Press.

———. 2002. "Blowups and Other Unhappy Endings." In *Global Woman. Nannies, Maids and Sex Workers in the New Economy*, edited by Barbara Ehrenreich and Arlie Russell Hochschild. New York: Metropolitan Books.

Hopenhayn, Martin. 2010. "Como ha cambiado la clase media en America Latina? Elementos para el debate." In *Clases medias y gobernabilidad en América Latina*, edited by Ludolfo Parmio. Madrid: Editorial Pablo Iglesias.

Horst, C., S. Pereira, and O. Sheringham. 2015. "A Matter of Class? The Impact of Social Distinctions on the Migration of Brazilians to Norway, Portugal and the UK." In *Beyond Networks: Feedback in International Migration*, edited by O. Bakewell, M. L. Fonseca, G. Engberson, and C. Horst. Basingstoke, UK: Palgrave Macmillan.

Huang Shirlena and Joaquin Gonzalez. 1999. "Migrant Female Domestic Workers: Debating the Economic, Social and Political Impacts in Singapore." *The International Migration Review* 33 (1): 114–36.

Humphrey, Caroline, and Stephen Hugh-Jones. 1992. *Barter, Exchange and Value: An Anthropological Approach*. Cambridge: Cambridge University Press.

Immigration Act of 1971. http://www.legislation.gov.uk/ukpga/1971/77/contents.

Immigration, Asylum and Nationality Act of 2006. http://www.legislation.gov.uk/ukpga/2006/13/contents.

Immigration Bill 2015-16. https://beta.parliament.uk/search?q=Bill+74+2015-16.

Institute for Public Policy Research. 2012. *Eight out of ten married women do more housework than their husbands*. https://www.ippr.org/news-and-media/press-releases/eight-out-of-ten-married-women-do-more-housework-than-their-husbands.

Iskander, Natasha. 2007. "Informal Work and Protest: Undocumented Immigrant Activism in France, 1996–2000." *British Journal of Industrial Relations* 45 (2): 309–34.

James, Deborah. 2015. *Money from Nothing: Indebtedness and Aspiration in South Africa*. Stanford, CA: Stanford University Press.

James, Deborah, and Evan Killick. 2012. "Empathy and Expertise: Case Workers and Immigration/Asylum Applicants in London." *Law & Social Inquiry* 37 (2): 430–55.

Jureidini, Ray, and Nayla Moukarbel. 2004. "Female Sri Lankan Domestic Workers in Lebanon: A Case of 'Contract Slavery'?" *Journal of Ethnic and Migration Studies* 30 (4): 581–607.

Katzman, David. 1978. *Seven Days a Week: Women and Domestic Service in Industrialising America*. New York: Oxford University Press.

Kelly, Patty. 2008. *Lydia's Open Door. Inside Mexico's Most Modern Brothel*. Berkeley: University of California Press.

Kempadoo, Kamala. 2001. "Freelancers, Temporary Wives, and Beach-Boys: Researching Sex Work in the Caribbean." *Feminist Review* 67 (1): 39–62.

————. 2004. *Sexing the Caribbean: Gender, Race, and Sexual Labor.* New York: Psychology Press.

Khosravi, Shahram. 2007. "The 'Illegal' Traveller: An Auto-Ethnography of Borders." *Social Anthropology* 15 (3): 321–34.

Kulick, Don. 1998. *Travesti: Sex, Gender, and Culture among Brazilian Transgendered Prostitutes.* Chicago: University of Chicago Press.

Lahbabi, Fátima, and Pilar Rodriguez. 2004. *Migrantes y trabajadoras del sexo.* Leon: Del Blanco Editores.

Laidlaw, James. 2000. "A Free Gift Makes No Friends." *The Journal of the Royal Anthropological Institute* 6, no. 4 (December 1): 617–34.

————. 2002. "For an Anthropology of Ethics and Freedom." *The Journal of the Royal Anthropological Institute* 8, no. 2 (June 1): 311–32.

Lambek, Michael, ed. 2010. *Ordinary Ethics: Anthropology, Language, and Action.* New York: Fordham University Press.

————. 2013. "The Continuous and Discontinuous Person: Two Dimensions of Ethical Life." *Journal of the Royal Anthropological Institute* 19 (4): 837–58.

Lan, Pei-Chia. 2003. "Negotiating Social Boundaries and Private Zones: The Micropolitics of Employing Migrant Domestic Workers." *Social Problems* 50 (4): 525–49.

————. 2006. *Global Cinderellas: Migrant Domestics and Newly Rich Employers in Taiwan.* Durham, NC: Duke University Press.

Laslett, Barbara, and Johanna Brenner. 1989. "Gender and Social Reproduction: Historical Perspectives." *Annual Review of Sociology* 15 (1): 381–404.

Lefebvre, Henri. 2014. *Critique of Everyday Life: The Three-Volume Text,* translated by John Moore. London: Verso.

Lehtonen, Turo-Kimmo. 1999. "Any Room for Aesthetics?: Shopping Practices of Heavily Indebted Consumers." *Journal of Material Culture* 4 (3): 243–62.

Liechty, Mark. 2003. *Suitably Modern: Making Middle-Class Culture in a New Consumer Society.* Princeton, NJ: Princeton University Press.

Lindquist, Johan. 2009. *The Anxieties of Mobility Migration and Tourism in the Indonesian Borderlands.* Honolulu: University of Hawai'i Press.

Link, Bruce G., and Jo C. Phelan. 2001. "Conceptualizing Stigma." *Annual Review of Sociology* 27 (January 1): 363–85.

López de Lera, Diego, and Laura Oso Casas. 2007. "La inmigración latinoamericana en España. Tendencias y estado de la cuestion." In *Nuevas Migraciones latinoamericanas a Europa. Balances y Desafíos,* edited by Isabel Yepez del Castillo and Gioconda Herrera. Quito, Ecuador: FLACSO.

Lovell, Peggy A. 2000. "Race, Gender and Regional Labor Market Inequalities in Brazil." *Review of Social Economy* 58 (3): 277–93.

Lutz, Helma. 2002. "At Your Service Madam! The Globalization of Domestic Service." *Feminist Review,* no. 70, 89–104.

————, ed. 2008. *Migration and Domestic Work: A European Perspective on a Global Theme*. Farnham, UK: Ashgate.

————. 2010. "Gender in the Migratory Process." *Journal of Ethnic and Migration Studies* 36 (10): 1647–63.

MacCormack, Geoffrey. 1976. "Reciprocity." *Man* 11 (1): 89–103.

MacKinnon, Catharine A. 1989. *Toward a Feminist Theory of the State*. Cambridge, MA: Harvard University Press.

Mahmood, Saba. 2005. *Feminist Theory, Agency, and the Liberatory Subject. On Shifting Ground: Muslim Women in the Global Era*. New York: Feminist Press.

Maia, Suzana. 2012. *Transnational Desires: Brazilian Erotic Dancers in New York*. Nashville, TN: Vanderbilt University Press.

Malinowski, Bronislaw. 1922. *Argonauts of the Pacific*. New York: Holt, Rinehart and Winston.

————. (1926) 1962. Crime and custom in savage society. Paterson, New Jersey: Adams & Co.

Mansanet Ripoll, Erika, and Beatriz Padilla. 2010. "La inmigración brasileña en Portugal y España: ¿sistema migratorio ibérico?" *OBETS. Revista de Ciencias Sociales* 5 (1): 49–86.

Martin, Biddy, and Chandra T. Mohanty. 1997. "Feminist Politics: What's Home Got to Do with It?" In *Feminisms: An Anthology of Literary Theory and Criticism*, edited by Robyn R. Warhol and Diane Price Herndl. New Brunswick, NJ: Rutgers University Press.

Mauss, Marcel. (1950) 1990. *The Gift: The Form and Reason for Exchange in Archaic Societies*. New York: W. W. Norton.

May, John, Jane Wills, Kavita Datta, Yara Evans, Joanna Herbert and Cathy McIlwaine. 2007. "Keeping London working: global cities, the British state and London's migrant division of labour", *Transactions of the Institute of British Geographers*, 32 (2):151-167.

McCoy, Jennifer L., and David J. Myers. 2006. *The Unraveling of Representative Democracy in Venezuela*. Baltimore: Johns Hopkins University Press.

McCracken, Grant David. 1990. *Culture and Consumption: New Approaches to the Symbolic Character of Consumer Goods and Activities*. Bloomington: Indiana University Press.

McIlwaine, Cathy. 2007. *Living in Latin London: How Latin American Migrants Survive in the City*. London, Queen Mary, University of London.

————. 2009. Legal Latins? "Webs of (Ir)regularity among Latin American Migrants in London. Identity, Citizenship and Migration Centre." Working paper no. 4. University of Nottingham.

————. 2010. "Migrant Machismos: Exploring Gender Ideologies and Practices among Latin American Migrants in London from a Multi-scalar Perspective." *Gender, Place and Culture* 17 (3): 281–300.

———. 2015. "Legal Latins: Creating Webs and Practices of Immigration Status among Latin American Migrants in London." *Journal of Ethnic & Migration Studies* 41 (3): 493–511.

McIlwaine, Cathy, and Diego Bunge. 2016. *Towards Visibility: the Latin American Community in London.* London: Trust for London. https://www.kcl.ac.uk/sspp/departments/geography/people/academic/mcilwaine/reports/Towards-Visibility-full-report.pdf

McIlwaine, Cathy, Juan Camillo Cock, and Brian Linneker. 2010. *No Longer Invisible: The Latin American Community in London.* London: Queen Mary, University of London.

Menjívar, Cecilia. 2000. *Fragmented Ties: Salvadoran Immigrant Networks in America.* Berkeley: University of California Press.

———. 2006. "Liminal Legality: Salvadoran and Guatemalan Immigrants' Lives in the United States." *American Journal of Sociology* 111 (4): 999–1037.

Miller, Daniel. 1995a. *Acknowledging Consumption.* London: Routledge.

———. 1995b. "Consumption and Commodities." *Annual Review of Anthropology* 24 (11): 141–61.

———, ed. 1998. *Shopping, Place and Identity.* London: Routledge.

———. 2001. *Home Possessions. Material Culture behind Closed Doors.* Oxford: Berg.

———. 2008. *The Comfort of Things.* Cambridge: Polity Press.

Mills, Mary Beth. 1997. "Contesting the Margins of Modernity: Women, Migration and Consumption in Thailand." *American Ethnologist* 24 (1): 37–61.

Molyneux, Maxine. 2002. "Gender and the Silences of Social Capital: Lessons from Latin America." *Development and Change* 33 (2): 167–88.

Moon, Katharine H. S. 1997. *Sex among Allies: Military Prostitution in U.S.-Korea Relations.* New York: Columbia University Press.

Moser, Caroline. 2009. *Ordinary Families: Extraordinary Lives: Getting out of poverty in Guayaquil, Ecuador 1978–2004.* Washington, D.C: Brookings Institution Press.

Moukarbel, Nayla. 2009. "Not Allowed to Love? Sri Lankan Maids in Lebanon." *Mobilities* 4 (3): 329–47.

———. 2010. *Sri Lankan Housemaids in Lebanon: A Case of "Symbolic Violence" and "Everyday Forms of Resistance."* Amsterdam: Amsterdam University Press.

Muecke, Margorie A. 1992. "Mother Sold Food, Daughter Sells Her Body: The Cultural Continuity of Prostitution." *Social Science & Medicine* 35 (7): 891–901.

Muehlebach, Andrea. 2012. *The Moral Neoliberal: Welfare and Citizenship in Italy.* Chicago: University of Chicago Press.

Myers, Fred R., ed. 2001. *The Empire of Things: Regimes of Value and Material Culture.* Santa Fe, NM: SAR Press.

Nelson, Julie A. 1999. "Of Markets and Martyrs: Is It OK to Pay Well for Care?" *Feminist Economics* 5 (3): 43–59.

Nelson, Julie A., and Paula England. 2002. "Feminist Philosophies of Love and Work." *Hypatia* 17 (2): 1–18.

Noddings, Nel. 1984. *Caring: A Feminine Approach to Ethics and Moral Education*. Berkeley: University of California Press.

O'Connell Davidson, Julia. 1995. "The Anatomy of 'Free Choice' Prostitution." *Gender, Work & Organization* 2 (1): 1–10.

———. 1998. *Prostitution, Power and Freedom*. London: Polity Press.

O'Dougherty, Maureen. 2002. *Consumption Intensified: The Politics of Middle-Class Daily Life in Brazil*. Durham, NC: Duke University Press.

O'Neill, Maggie. 2001. *Prostitution and Feminism: Towards a Politics of Feeling*. London: Polity Press.

Olin Wright, Erik. 1997. *Class Counts: Comparative Studies in Class Analysis*. Cambridge: Cambridge University Press.

Ong, Aihwa. 2006. *Neoliberalism as Exception: Mutations in Citizenship and Sovereignty*. Durham, NC: Duke University Press.

———. 2007. "Neoliberalism as a Mobile Technology." *Transactions of the Institute of British Geographers* 32 (1): 3–8.

Ortner, Sherry B. 1995. "Resistance and the Problem of Ethnographic Refusal." *Comparative Studies in Society and History* 37 (1): 173–93.

Oso Casas, Laura. 2003. *Estrategias Migratorias de Las Mujeres Ecuatorianas y Colombianas en Situación Irregular: Servicio Doméstico y Prostitución en Galicia, Madrid y Pamplona*. Madrid: Facultad de Socioloxia, Universidade Da Coruña.

———. 2010. "Money, Sex, Love and the Family: Economic and Affective Strategies of Latin American Sex Workers in Spain." *Journal of Ethnic and Migration Studies* 36 (1): 47–65.

Ozyegin, Gul, and Pierrette Hondagneu-Sotelo. 2008. "Domestic Work, Migration and the New Gender Order in Contemporary Europe." In *Migration and Domestic Work: A European Perspective on a Global Theme*, edited by Helma Lutz, 195–202. Aldershot, UK: Ashgate.

Padilla, Beatriz. 2007. "Estado del arte de las investigaciones sobre los brasileños y brasileñas en Portugal." In *Nuevas Migraciones latinoamericanas a Europa. Balances y Desafíos*, edited by Isabel Yepez del Castillo and Gioconda Herrera. Quito: Ecuador: FLACSO.

Parker, David Stuart. 1998. *The Idea of the Middle Class: White-Collar Workers and Peruvian Society, 1900–1950*. University Park, PA: Penn State University Press.

Parker, David Stuart, and Louise E. Walker. 2013. *Latin America's Middle Class: Unsettled Debates and New Histories*. Lanham, MD: Lexington Books.

Parreñas, Rhacel Salazar. 2001. *Servants of Globalization: Women, Migration and Domestic Work*. Stanford, CA: Stanford University Press:

———. 2005. *Children of Global Migration: Transnational Families and Gendered Woes*. Stanford, CA: Stanford University Press.

———. 2011. *Illicit Flirtations: Labor, Migration, and Sex Trafficking in Tokyo*. Stanford, CA: Stanford University Press.

Parry, Jonathan. 1986. "The Gift, the Indian Gift, and the 'Indian Gift.'" *Man* 21 (3): 453–73.

Pateman, Carole. 1988. *The Sexual Contract*. Cambridge: Polity Press.

Patico, Jennifer. 2008. *Consumption and Social Change in a Post-Soviet Middle Class*. Stanford, CA: Stanford University Press.

Peebles, Gustav. 2010. "The Anthropology of Credit and Debt." *Annual Review of Anthropology* 39 (1): 225–40.

Pellegrino, Adella. 2004. *Migration from Latin America to Europe: Trends and Policy Challenges*. Geneva: Institute of Medicine.

Pheterson, Gail. 1990. "The Category 'Prostitute' in Scientific Inquiry." *The Journal of Sex Research* 27, no. 3 (August 1): 397–407.

Phoenix, Joanna. 2000. "Prostitute Identities." *British Journal of Criminology* 40 (1): 37–55.

Pinho, Patrica de Santana. 2009. "White but Not Quite: Tones and Overtones of Whiteness in Brazil." *Small Axe* 13 (2): 39–56.

Portes, Alejandro, and Kelly Hoffman. 2003. "Latin American Class Structures: Their Composition and Change during the Neoliberal Era." *Latin American Research Review* 38 (1): 41–82.

Pratt, Geraldine. 1997. "Stereotypes and Ambivalence: The Construction of Domestic Workers in Vancouver, British Columbia." *Gender, Place and Culture* 4 (2): 159–77.

Prince, Diana A. 1986. "A Psychological Study of Prostitutes in California and Nevada." PhD diss., United States International University, San Diego, CA.

Radcliffe, Sarah. 1999. "Race and Domestic Service: Migration and Identity in Ecuador." In *Gender, Migration, and Domestic Service*, edited by Janet Henshall Momsen, 83–97. London: Routledge.

Raijman Rebeca, Sivina Schammah-Gesser, and Adriana Kemp. 2006. "International Migration, Domestic Work and Care Work: Undocumented Latina Migrants in Israel." In *Global Dimensions of Gender and Carework*, edited by Mary Zimmerman, Jacquelyn S. Litt, and Christine E. Bose. Stanford, CA: Stanford University Press.

Ramphele, Mamphela. 1993. *A Bed Called Home: Life in the Migrant Labour Hostels of Cape Town*. Cape Town, South Africa: New Africa Books.

Rhus, Martin, and Anderson Bridget. 2008. "The Origin and Functions of Illegality in Migrant Labour Markets: An Analysis of Migrants, Employers and the State in the UK." Working paper no. 30a. Centre on Migration, Policy and Society, University of Oxford.

———, eds. 2010. *Who Needs Migrant Workers? Labour Shortages, Immigration and Public Policy*. Oxford: Oxford University Press.

Robbins, Joel. 2007. "Between Reproduction and Freedom: Morality, Value, and Radical Cultural Change." *Ethnos* 72 (3): 293–314.

———. 2009. "Value, Structure, and the Range of Possibilities: A Response to Zigon." *Ethnos* 74 (2): 277–85.

———. 2012. "On Becoming Ethical Subjects: Freedom, Constraint, and the Anthropology of Morality." *Anthropology of this Century* 5 (October).

Robinson, Fiona. 2013. "Global Care Ethics: Beyond Distribution, beyond Justice." *Journal of Global Ethics* 9 (2), 131–43.

Rollins, Judith. 1985. *Between Women: Domestics and Their Employers.* Philadelphia: Temple University Press.

Romero, Mary. 1992. *Maid in the U.S.A. Perspectives on Gender.* New York: Routledge.

Rose, Nikolas. 1990. *Governing the Soul: The Shaping of the Private Self.* New York: Taylor & Francis.

———. 1992. "Governing the Enterprising Self." In *The Values of the Enterprise Culture: The Moral Debate*, edited by Paul Hellas and Paul Morris, 141–64. London: Routledge.

———. 1992. "Making Sense of Settlement: Class Transformation, Cultural Struggle, and Transnationalism among Mexican Migrants in the United States." *Annals of the New York Academy of Sciences* 645 (1): 25–52.

Ruddick, Sara. 1989. *Maternal Thinking.* Boston: Beacon Press.

Salih, Ruba. 2003. *Gender in Transnationalism. Home, Longing and Belonging among Moroccan Migrant Women.* London: Routledge.

Sahlins, Marshall.D. 1972. "The Original Affluent Society." In *Stone Age Economics*, 1–39. London: Tavistock.

———. 1976. *Culture and Practical Reason.* Chicago: University of Chicago Press.

Sanders, Teela. 2004. "Controllable Laughter: Managing Sex Work through Humour." *Sociology* 38 (2): 273–91.

———. 2005a. *Sex Work.* Abingdon, Oxon: Routledge.

———. 2005b. "'It's Just Acting': Sex Workers' Strategies for Capitalizing on Sexuality." *Gender, Work & Organization* 12 (4): 319–42.

Sassen, Saskia. 1999. *Guests and Aliens.* New York: New Press.

Schielke, Samuli. 2012. "Living in the Future Tense: Aspiring for World and Class in Provincial Egypt." In *The Global Middle Classes: Theorizing through Ethnography*, edited by Rachel Heinman, Carla Freeman, and Mark Liechty. Santa Fe, NM: SAR Press.

Schiller, Nina Glick, Linda Basch, and Cristina Blanc-Szanton. 1992. "Towards a Definition of Transnationalism." *Annals of the New York Academy of Sciences* 645 (1): ix–xiv.

Seelke, Clare Ribando. 2011. "Gangs in Central America." *Current Politics and Economics of South and Central America* 4 (1): 67–96.

Sexual Offences Act of 1956. http://www.legislation.gov.uk/ukpga/Eliz2/4-5/69/contents.

Sheringham, Olivia. 2011. "Creating 'Alternative Geographies': Religion and Brazilian Migrants in London and 'Back Home.'" In *Cross-Border Migration among Latin Americans: European Perspectives and Beyond*, edited by Cathy McIlwaine. New York: Palgrave Macmillan.

Shields, Rob. 1992. *Lifestyle Shopping: The Subject of Consumption*. London: Routledge.

Sigona, Nando. 2012. "'I Have Too Much Baggage': The Impacts of Legal Status on the Social Worlds of Irregular Migrants." *Social Anthropology* 20 (1): 50–65.

——— and Hughes, Vanessa. 2012. "No Way Out, No Way In. Irregular Migrant Children and Families in the UK." Research Report. Oxford: Compas Oxford.

Skeggs, Beverley. 1997. *Formations of Class & Gender: Becoming Respectable*. London: Sage.

Sleeboom-Faulkner, Margaret. 2014. "The Twenty-First-Century Gift and the Co-circulation of Things." *Anthropological Forum* 24 (4): 323–37.

Stevens, Dudley. 2011. "Central America Besieged: Cartels and Maras Country Threat Analysis." *Small Wars & Insurgencies* 22 (5): 890–913.

Stewart, Kathleen. 1988. "Nostalgia—a Polemic." *Cultural Anthropology* 3 (3): 227–41.

Strathern, M. 1988. *The Gender of the Gift: Problems with Women and Problems with Society in Melanesia*. Berkeley: University of California Press.

———. 1992. "Qualified value: the perspective of gift exchange." *In Barter, exchange and value: an anthropological approach*, edited by Caroline Humphrey and Stephen Hugh-Jones. Cambridge: Cambridge University Press.

Suárez-Navaz, Liliana. 2004. *Rebordering the Mediterranean: Boundaries and Citizenship in Southern Europe*. New York: Berghahn Books.

Sveinsson, Kjartan. P. 2007. *Bolivians in London. Challenges and Achievements of a London Community*. West Sussex, UK: Runnymede Trust.

Sykes, Karen. M. 2005. *Arguing with Anthropology: An Introduction to Critical Theories of the Gift*. London: Routledge.

Talavera, Victor, Guillermina Gina Núñez-Michiri and Josiah Heyman, 2010. "Deportation in the U.S-Mexico Borderlands: Anticipation, Experience and Memory." In *The Deportation Regime: Sovereignty, Space, and the Freedom of Movement* edited by Nicholas De Genova and Nathalie Peutz. Chicago: Duke University Press.

Telles, Edward Eric. 2004. *Race in Another America: The Significance of Skin Color in Brazil*. Princeton, NJ: Princeton University Press.

Telles, Edward, and Tianna Paschel. 2014. "Who Is Black, White, or Mixed Race? How Skin Color, Status, and Nation Shape Racial Classification in Latin America." *American Journal of Sociology* 120 (3): 864–907.

Thai, Hung Cam. 2008. *For Better or for Worse: Vietnamese International Marriages in the New Global Economy*. New Brunswick, NJ: Rutgers University Press.

Ticktin, Miriam I. 2011. *Casualties of Care: Immigration and the Politics of Humanitarianism in France*. Berkeley: University of California Press.

Trinh, T. Minh-Ha. 1989. *Woman, Native, Other: Writing Postcoloniality and Feminism*. Bloomington: Indiana University Press.

Tronto Joan. 1994. *Moral Boundaries: A Political Argument for an Ethic of Care*. London: Rutledge.

———. 2001. "Who Cares? Public and Private Caring and the Rethinking of Citizenship." In *Women and Welfare: Theory and Practice in the United States and Europe*, edited by Nancy Hirschmann and Ulrike Liebert, 65–83. New Brunswick, NJ: Rutgers University Press.

Tuan, Yan. 1977. *Space and Place: The Perspective of Experience*. London: Edward Arnold.

Twine, France Winddance. 1997. "Mapping the Terrain of Brazilian Racism." *Race & Class* 38 (3): 49–61.

Vanwesenbeeck, Ine. 2001. "Another Decade of Social Scientific Work on Sex Work: A Review of Research 1990–2000." *Annual Review of Sex Research* 12 (1): 242–89.

Wade, Peter. 2001. "Racial Identity and Nationalism: A Theoretical View from Latin America." *Ethnic & Racial Studies* 24 (5): 845–65.

———. 2005. "Rethinking Mestizaje: Ideology and Lived Experience." *Journal of Latin American Studies* 37 (2): 239–57.

———. 2008. "Race in Latin America". In *A Companion to Latin American Anthropology*, edited by Deborah Poole. Malden, MA: Blackwell. pp. 175–192.

———. 2010. "The Presence and Absence of Race." *Patterns of Prejudice* 44 (1): 43–60.

Walker, U. Margaret. 1998. *Moral Understandings: A Feminist Study in Ethics*. London: Routledge.

Warnock, Mary. 1970. *Existentialism*. New York: Oxford University Press.

Warr, Deborah J., and Priscilla M. Pyett. 1999. "Difficult Relations: Sex Work, Love and Intimacy." *Sociology of Health & Illness* 21 (3): 290–309.

Weedon, Chris. 1996. *Feminist Practice and Poststructuralist Theory*, 2nd ed. Cambridge, MA: Wiley–Blackwell.

Weiner, Anette B. 1992. *Inalienable Possessions: The Paradox of Keeping while Giving*. Berkeley: University of California Press.

Weitzer, Ronald. 2009. "Sociology of Sex Work." *Annual Review of Sociology* 35 (1): 213–34.

Wilks, Richard. 1989. "Houses as Consumer Goods: Social Processes and Allocation Decisions." In *The Social Economy of Consumption*, edited by Henry J. Ruiz and Benjamin S. Orlove, 6. Lanham, MD: University Press of America.

Willen, Sarah S. 2007. "Toward a Critical Phenomenology of 'Illegality': State Power, Criminalization, and Abjectivity among Undocumented Migrant Workers in Tel Aviv, Israel." *International Migration* 45, no. 3 (July 19): 8–38.

Williams, Brett. 2004. *Debt for Sale: A Social History of the Credit Trap.* Philadelphia: University of Pennsylvania Press.

Williams, Fiona. 2011. "Towards a Transnational Analysis of the Political Economy of Care." In *Feminist Ethics and Social Policy: Towards a New Global Political Economy of Care*, edited by Rianne Mahon and Fiona Robinson. Vancouver: UBC Press.

Working Time Regulations Act of 1999. http://www.legislation.gov.uk/uksi/1999/3372/contents/made.

Yan, Yunxiang. 1996. *The Flow of Gifts: Reciprocity and Social Networks in a Chinese Village.* Stanford, CA: Stanford University Press.

———. 2005. "The Gift and the Gift Economy." In *A Handbook of Economic Anthropology*, edited by J. Carrier. Cheltenham, UK: Edward Elgar.

Yeoh, Brenda S. A., and Shirlena Huang. 2010. "Transnational Domestic Workers and the Negotiation of Mobility and Work Practices in Singapore's Home-Spaces." *Mobilities* 5 (2): 219–36.

Zelizer, Viviana A. 2009. *The Purchase of Intimacy.* Princeton, NJ: Princeton University Press.

———. 2011. *Economic Lives: How Culture Shapes the Economy.* New Princeton, NJ: Princeton University Press.

———. 2012. "How I Became a Relational Economic Sociologist and What Does That Mean?" *Politics & Society* 40 (2): 145–74.

Zheng, Tiantian. 2009. *Red Lights: The Lives of Sex Workers in Postsocialist China.* Minneapolis: University of Minnesota Press.

Zigon, Jarrett. 2007. "Moral Breakdown and the Ethical Demand: A Theoretical Framework for an Anthropology of Moralities." *Anthropological Theory* 7, no. 2 (June 1): 131–50.

———. 2008. *Morality: An Anthropological Perspective.* Oxford: Berg.

———. 2009. "Within a Range of Possibilities: Morality and Ethics in Social Life." *Ethnos* 74 (2): 251–76.

INDEX